Never

Never a D ...ment

By
Keith Hearn

ISBN-13: 978-1511744904
ISBN-10: 1511744901

**Artwork designed and created by
Dan Bee Illustration in association with ApexCreate.**

http://www.danbeeillustration.co.uk
https://apexcreate.com

i

Contents

Acknowledgements

I would like to thank everyone I know for their support.

I wish to thank my brothers for showing me that anything can be achieved if I put my mind to it and that nothing is impossible.

To my children Sara-Ann and Paul.

My sincerest thanks to Sandra my sister-in-law who has proof read many chapters.

To my brother Garry for helping me with the technical stage of the book, and for Faye for a much needed hand.

Candy Close for putting up with me and distracting her at work.

Paul Blackwell for reading the book.

Brian Terry for interfering with his club "work"

Gus and Nikki – for the sound advice

Early Days

Ben Thompson

Michael Culhane – for investing 100 pence and having faith

Nick Culhane – for inspiring me to finish

Steve Branch - for recently final proof reading the book

Jacquie Broadbank - for the encouragement to write my stories down and have them published.

Carol Keightley - for putting up with me going on and on and correcting my grammar

Pam Reid – for proof reading the book and providing a valid overview

Andy   - For reading the book with an eye on the story line.

Maxine Netherwood – For volunteering to proof read the book for the final time.

Zoey C – for inspiring me to follow my dreams.

Life is what we make of it
We only have one go
Make it the best

Keith Hearn

INTRODUCTION

This is a true story of my life and events that have help shape it in adulthood.

During my childhood my parents were continually on the move, due to my father's line of work. We travelled to Europe mainly West Germany as it was known then, and South Arabia.

I hope that you will enjoy reading my story it is full of interesting recollections which will make reading the book an enjoyable experience.

These are the memories and anecdotes of the son of a serving soldier who spent part of my childhood in conflict zones and eventually led me to join the Military.

This is not an historical or possibly accurate book, it is written solely from my memories and experiences which took place in my life and greatly influenced me. There will be many who will have their own point of view.

I wish to say thank you to my parents for showing me. Including my brothers Michael and Garry. Nothing in life is impossible.

My parents had a pivotal bearing on my life and still do but to a lesser degree; I enjoyed my childhood albeit it was slightly unusual.

I hope that you find my story interesting and an enjoyable read.

Chapter 1 - Early Days

First of all let me introduce myself. My name is Keith Hearn I was born in Liverpool in "Smithdown Road Hospital", or Sefton General Hospital in Toxteth depending on how posh you are. The hospital is no longer standing it has been replaced by a supermarket. Penny Lane (the same one as in the Beatles song) is on a junction with Smithdown Road, the area is listed in the Doomsday book.

The doctors and nurses that helped deliver me referred to me as the "D-Day Baby." I was born on the sixth of June although I must add that I was not born in 1944! The reference is due to the historic date of 6th June 1944, when the allies invaded Europe to ultimately overthrow the NAZI occupation. Many of the doctors and nurses in the hospital had served in the Armed Forces during the Second World War. The sixth of June was a date that they would ever forget! My mum did not realise the significance of the date until my father explained the significance to her. To this day I still remind her of the significance.

My parents at the time were living at my father's parent's house, which was on the corner of Fernhill Street and Northhill Street, Toxteth. It was a four floor Victorian house it was one of the larger houses in the street. It did not have a garden, only a paved courtyard including an outside toilet; the front of the house formed part of a furniture shop.
We were not as poor as others in the area; my mum's family on the other hand were extremely poor.

Early Days

My father was called up towards the end of National Service; it was a period of compulsory conscription into the Armed Forces following the war. After his National Service training he was given an opportunity to join the Regular Army. He told me that he jumped at the chance since his civilian job at the time was as a motor mechanic; I have seen the garage where he worked, the garage is still there, it is now a KWIK-FIT centre on Smithdown Road.

He once told me that due to being newly married and with a baby, life would be very difficult. Finding a house and a well-paid job to support a young family was going to be tough. My mum was very hot headed and had many a falling out with my gran, mainly over myself and my two brothers. After my dad had finished his basic training and joined his first regiment overseas. He was a Regular Soldier and not a conscript, he was earning more money and could afford so much more. My mum's sister, Anne, would babysit me, while my mum went off to work. My mum had a confectionary job in the city centre, which again brought more money into the household.

At times during my early childhood was spent living at my Grandparents' house in Toxteth. My Gran was the one who wore the trousers in the family, or so she liked to think that she did. There was no front door to the house. Only large double doors at the side opened onto a small courtyard. I did not realise it at the time, but most of the houses were slums. They had been built during the Victorian period, and had suffered considerable bomb damage during the Second World War. These derelict buildings were to be our playground. My dad told me that his cousin "Buster" was killed in a bombed out house during the war; he was playing with an unexploded bomb when it suddenly went off.

Never a Dull Moment

The housing around the docks area, where we lived, was much older and dilapidated than some other areas of Liverpool.

One afternoon I was walking towards the docks, the houses in this area were built on a slope. I passed some very old houses which were extremely dilapidated. As a child I would not take any notice of houses unless they were burnt out or falling down. These particular houses had steep steps leading from the road side to the front door. At one particular house I saw an old lady at the top of the stairs and she was beckoning me to come over. As I approached her, she asked if I could help her fill her kettle up with water, and she explained that she could not turn the tap on in her kitchen. The house was very Dickensian looking; her kitchen was so old fashioned compared to my Gran's. I filled the kettle up. There was no oven and I struggled with the kettle, it was so heavy. I had to hold it with both hands, it was almost touching the floor. I managed to carry it into the living room. A large fire was burning in the grate within which sat a metal contraption, serving as an oven. It looked ancient, straight out of a Charles Dickens novel. I placed the kettle on the top of a round metal stand in the fire. She thanked me and tried to give me some pennies; I declined the offer and promptly left to carry on with my adventure in the docks. When I arrived at the dock road I was very disappointed to find the docks were enclosed within a large brick wall. Numerous old warehouses ran the full length of the dock road. I could see vehicles entering and leaving and lots of Dockers were coming and going through an entrance some distance away. I realised that I would not be able to gain entry into the docks and headed back to my Gran's house feeling very disappointed.

Early Days

Most of the children in the area would make their own fun, and taking the idea of fun to another level by jumping onto the rear of the dustbin Lorries as they passed. The Lorries were not as hi tech as they are today and they were very basic. However they crushed waste in much the same way as they do today. Sometimes on bin day the lorry would travel at speed, taking the rubbish to the council tip. It was well known that some children would jump onto the step just as the Lorries slowed down. Occasionally a child would fall in and be crushed. On other occasions the lorry would suddenly break and they would fall into the path of an oncoming vehicle. As a youngster I knew that the games my friends played were far too risky, even for me.

I can still remember the smells, and the smoke pouring out of the chimneys due to the many open fires in the houses. The smoke would swirl around the streets. At times the smoke would not disperse, hemmed in by the fog rolling in from the River Mersey. Smog would cover the streets. It seemed especially bad in winter and on hot summer days.

My cousins lived in and around our grandparents' house. We were always in and out of one another's houses, except our gran's house; we all knew not to mess around in her house. My brothers and I slept in the attic, and it was very cramped. Sometimes we would sleep in the same bed with our cousins. My grandfather had his workshop in another part of the attic. He would not let my brothers Michael and Garry into the workshop since Garry was too young and Michael was always touching things and breaking them. I was the chosen one, because I was allegedly more sensible! I was also interested in what he made and how things worked, and the stories behind the objects he was making. He made warships and aeroplanes from scratch. I never saw the models working, but I know that he had put engines in them and they worked. I often asked him what he did in the war, initially he would not respond to my questions. Eventually he told me that he was on guard in Palestine when he was attacked. His assailant had a knife, resulting in a deep damaging cut from his shoulder all the way down to his lower arm. He managed to sound the alarm and was admitted to hospital to get patched up. He continued to suffer with pain in his arm and shoulder for the rest of his life.

My grandfather was small in stature and very quiet. My Gran on the other hand was tall and broad and, as I mentioned, she liked to think that she wore the trousers. Outside of the house there was an old gas lamp, at the same time every day she and her friends would stand near the lamp. She wore a hat that looked like a tea cosy and she would stand chatting with her arms folded just like the character, the comedian Les Dawson portrayed. My brothers and I would walk up the street towards our Gran's house. We could see a shape in the distance and knew it was her standing waiting for us to return from school.

My brothers and I attended St Silas Primary School in Toxteth. On the first day of the school term, during the school assembly, some of the teachers gave speeches, after which the headmaster stood up and read out the names of new arrivals. When it came to our names being read out we stood up and answered "here sir" and sat down. He stopped reading out the rest of the names and asked if we were related to Patricia and Robert Hearn. I answered, "Yes, sir, they are my cousins." He responded, "I hope that you do not cheat like they did whilst they attended this school," there was a deathly silence in the assembly. He had not

finished with us, he asked, "What Hearn branch of the family are you related to?"
Obviously we were not used to calling our dad by his Christian name so I meekly replied, "Ron Hearn." He said, "Ah, I see, so you are related to Ronald, the clever one in the family." I am not sure if my introduction to St Silas' was good or bad!

As I have mentioned previously my dad's first overseas posting after completing his training was to Germany. My mum and I soon joined him there. The style of living was British. I never heard them talking in German except for rare snippets of German words like 'I love you' and how to order beer and chips in German. They would buy the bulk of their food at the NAAFI, Navy, Army and Air Force Institutes, supermarket.

At a very early age I was fascinated by fire, it seemed to have a hypnotic control over me, it held such a huge fascination for me. One of my first recollections of playing with fire was when I crept down stairs into the cellar, my mum was attending to the boiler.
The boiler was fuelled by coal, and she was emptying the red hot coal ash and throwing the ashes into a metal bucket. I must have startled her as she dropped the red hot ash onto my left foot. To this day I can still recall a lump of coal burning into the top of my foot. I would show the scar off as a sort of trophy. During this period my brother Michael was born in a British Military Hospital, BMH. I do not recall too much during this period of my life. What I do remember I was very jealous of my brother and it continued for a very long time. During this time in Germany my dad had another move within the country and my younger brother Garry was born. I was nearly four by this time. I remember travelling with my dad and Michael to the hospital, and Garry was born in the same British Military Hospital

6

Never a Dull Moment

Iserlohn, the same hospital that Michael was born in. During the Second World War the hospital was built to house a panzer (Tank) Regiment. While my mum was in hospital with Garry we came to visit, and Michael my dad and I were in the grounds of the hospital. Around the hospital there were ornamental ponds full of fish. My dad was outside chain smoking, Michael was eighteen months old, and my dad was not really keeping a close eye on the pair of us. I think that he was worried about my mum and Garry, or how he was going to continue coping with Michael and I whilst she was in hospital. As I have mentioned we were outside and I ended up in one of the ponds, soaked through, and Michael was running around like someone possessed, which for him is normal. I cannot remember going to the ward to see our mum and Garry. The memories from that day, I recently recounted to my sister in law Faye many decades later when Garry was very ill and admitted to hospital to have a cancerous growth removed.

My fascination for fire struck once again, and I had learnt nothing from my previous brush with hot coals. I had observed that my mum kept candles on a shelf, together with a box of matches. We slept in one room with Garry in a cot; as a child it looked like a large bedroom. For whatever reason I thought that it would be a good idea to go downstairs. I pulled a chair up to the shelf where the matches and candles were and helped myself to the candles were and matches. I had watched mum lighting the cooker and I had an idea of what to do. I placed the candles on the window sill in the bedroom, I lit them and the flames set fire to the curtains. I still have a very vivid picture in my mind of the flames shooting up the curtains and burning the wooden pelmets. Michael was shouting, he looked terrified, Garry was wide awake. I can see him in my mind standing up in his cot crying his eyes out Michael was scared and shouting, it was pure bedlam, I can see the scene now. Mum attempted to open the bedroom door I had locked it from the inside and the keys for every door in the house at the time were always in the locks. She was telling me to turn the key so that she could get into the bedroom. I didn't seem to hear her as I was mesmerized by the flames and stood transfixed. I heard the fire engines, the sirens and blue lights and men with German voices appeared at the bedroom windows and put the flames out; there was some damage to the room. My mum was in a state of shock, she was obviously worried about her three boys. After the event my mum and dad stopped putting the keys into the doors. Whenever they moved house they would place all the keys in a drawer until they moved again. I will never forget dad coming home that evening. I was lying face down on my stomach in bed. I felt the covers on the bed being pulled off and my pyjama bottoms being pulled down. He smacked me so hard I cried, it really hurt. He was fuming, he was shouting at me for setting fire to the bedroom. He said that I could have killed everyone. I was five and I knew that I had done wrong, but I did not understand why all of his anger was directed towards me. I sobbed alone in bed not understanding why there was so much anger. As an adult I know why my father was so angry, as a child it was the fact that no one explained to me what I had done wrong; it is not an excuse. I did not understand the consequences of my actions.

This was something that I came across more and more as I grew up, it did cause some issues between myself and my father. Do not get me wrong, I loved my father and he loved me, but our personalities and ideas clashed. Thankfully we reconciled during the period leading up to his death many years later, we finally made our peace with one another.

In 1965 the film "The Sound of Music" was all the rage in the cinemas. It was the 'must see' film. My Gran thought it would be a good idea for the whole family to go and watch it. This included the extended family less the men folk, I think it was the pub that they had in mind. It was going to be a family outing with everyone dressed in their Sunday best. My Gran thought that it was a good idea for us to go as a treat before we travelled to Aden. My brothers and I knew that we had no choice but to go and watch it. It was not a film for young boys there was no war or fighting. Instead we decided to go to Princess Park with some of our friends and play out. Garry and I thought we should go home, thinking that the adults must have left for the cinema. How wrong we were! As we entered the house we were pounced on by my Gran and frog marched to the bathroom. While this was occurring she shouted to my mum, "Can you see where Michael is, Margaret?" My mum could not find him. He was still in the park. Meanwhile we were scrubbed "red raw" to within an inch of our lives and dressed in clean clothes. As we were frog marched to a bus stop on Park Avenue, Michael appeared further down the avenue. Gran said to my mum, "Marg, get the bus into town, I will bring Michael with me." Michael was moaning as he was marched off by the scruff of his neck back to the house, Garry and I thought that it was so funny. Anyway, we eventually sat down to watch the film, we were bored stupid.

My Gran would sometimes take us on a Saturday afternoon into Liverpool city centre to spend our pocket money and for her to get some shopping. Most occasions my mum would come along to make sure that we were not too unruly. On this one occasion our mum did not accompany us, she kept telling my Gran that we could be a handful and was she feeling up to taking us. Gran said that she would be fine, although mum was not so keen for us to go. Gran took us to a tea shop she bought three warm sausage rolls. I cannot eat hot sausage rolls, they make my stomach turn; just the smell of them makes me feel sick. Michael and Garry told her that I did not like hot sausage rolls and she scoffed at them.

I tried to explain to her, but to no avail, and I refused to eat it. I said, "Can I please have a cold one Gran?" She reluctantly gave in and got me a cold one and muttered something to herself about me liking cold sausage rolls. There was another occasion at dinner when I asked for hot jelly. Well, that just tipped her over the top, and she called my dad into the kitchen and told him that all three of us were spoilt rotten. He agreed with her!!

In and around the area during the 1960's there were many houses with black curtains drawn. My Gran explained that the black curtains were closed as some of the women living there were still in mourning for loved ones killed during both world wars. How true that was I do not know, but as a child you do not question what an adult tells you, especially if it is your Gran.

I know that one of my Gran's sisters had lost a loved one in the Second World War; she remained a spinster.

During one of our trips into the city centre we were walking past the Adelphi Hotel. Our Gran said, "You know that you have made it when you can afford to stay at the Adelphi." It still remains an up market hotel in Liverpool.

My Gran worked as a cleaner at one of the buildings in Liverpool, and on one occasion we met Mr Dixie Dean for some reason my gran knew him. He was a famous footballer who had played for Everton FC. Dixie still holds the record for the most goals scored in a season. Garry and I are both Liverpool supporters and Michael supports Everton. One afternoon we went with my Gran to meet Mr Dean at her place of work, and she introduced the three of us to him. She said, "Mr Dean, these are the grandchildren that I have mentioned to you." He looked at all three of us and said, "Fine looking boys, Mrs Hearn." With a notebook and pencil in hand he asked, "Would you like an autograph?" Garry and I said, "No thank you." Mr Dean replied "Ah, two reds in the family I see". (Meaning that we supported Liverpool). Michael said, "Yes please," and Mr Dean signed three sheets of paper. He gave one for Michael from Dixie Dean with the date, and the other two for Garry and I. This takes me onto the subject of Liverpool and Everton. Most of our family were Liverpool supporters, but the odd one was a "blue" Everton supporter, Michael. It was the same in most families, the majority blue and the one red supporter or vice versa. It was the same with the houses; some were painted red and white or blue and white.

We would play football in the street which consisted of back to back housing, very similar to those shown in the TV series Coronation Street. My Gran was always looking out onto the street to ensure that we weren't causing mischief. Regularly the football would break a parlour window, the occupants of the houses would know who to contact it would be our Gran!

We were always in the nearby, Princess Park and Sefton Park trying to stay out of trouble! We would play in the parks for hours, sometimes not coming home for lunch. The Parks were the lungs of smoky foggy Liverpool. A fishing lake provided recreation for some. For us it was somewhere to run and splash much to the anger of the recreational anglers. I was in a fish and chip shop one day with my Gran when one of the men who was at the pond fishing entered the chip shop. He seemed to know my

Gran and said, "Hello Mrs Hearn." He asked, "Who is this with you?" My Gran told him who I was and he said to me, "I am sure that I have seen you somewhere before." I quickly responded, "I do not think so." Out of earshot Gran whispered, "You don't want to get on the wrong side of the likes of him, Keith, he is a very nasty man." I gulped, and nothing more was said. I am not sure if she was trying to scare me off so that I would keep out of trouble. If she was it did not work.

My grandparents' neighbour had two sons who were forever getting into trouble, and not just with the Police. Friday and Saturday nights women would bang on their front door. Often shouting abuse at the sons, on one occasion a woman threw a brick through the living room window. It was suspected that the brothers would steal the penny bubble gum machines; and smash the machines open to get at the pennies and dump the bubble gum in the dirty stinking entries (alleyways) between the backs of the houses. I remember the distinct smell of urine and dog muck in those darkened areas. My Mum and Gran would tell us to keep out of them because they harboured all sorts of diseases. But the lure of bubble gum proved too much.

During my lifetime I have never been one to conform, even when I later joined the Army. It felt like I did not conform, I like to think that I have always retained my individualism and uniqueness.

I realised at an early age that our mum was slightly different to other mums, not in a bad way; she has some very peculiar habits and ideas which have rubbed off onto all three of us. I distinctly remember a particular ordinary day, let's just say it started off as an ordinary day. The three of us and our mum were in a large park at the zoo in Dortmund, (West) Germany. I can remember a large gated entrance; this is why I think that it was Dortmund Zoo. I was on a scooter, Michael was able to walk, he had reigns attached to him; he was after all the mischievous one. Garry was in his pram. I was merrily riding around on my scooter weaving in and out of the flower beds. As I rode back to where I had last seen my mum, she had vanished. I wasn't surprised, as mum always meandered in her own world and still does. I rode around the park for what seemed to me like ages and I was starting to panic. I went back to the zoo entrance, thinking that she may have realised that she was one son short. It was the logical spot but she was not there. Even at the age of five I found that I was trying to be analytical. I was stopped by a park warden who took me into an office; he spoke to me in German. He realised straight away that I was English and called the Police. Someone who could speak English announced on the public address system in English and German that there was a lost little boy at the warden's office. I was asked what my mother's name was, and I said 'mummy and Michael and Garry'. I think I may have confused the police, I think that they may have thought that one of my brothers was in fact my dad. My mum eventually responded and came to pick me up. I heard words I would hear often thereafter, "Do not tell your father what has happened". I also realised all was not right in our little world.

Mum must have really worried about our education. As she had never been taught the everyday life skills as a child, how was she going to pass those skills onto her own children? Even at a very early age we knew that she could not read or write.
One area of our education was reading and nursery rhymes. My mum would read some sections of a book and make up the words that she could not read with tra, ala a la. I know that my dad was

trying to help her to read and write. We all realised that our mum did not know all of the words to the nursery rhymes or any of the stories in children's books. It became even more apparent as we began to learn to read and write. As we became older we knew more words than our mum and at the bus stops we could work out the twenty four hour clock timings for her.

I never felt hampered or embarrassed by my mum's lack of education, far from it, she was my mum and she thought the world of her "three boys". We are all self-taught, and determined to succeed. As a child I loved reading comics, and especially the Commando comics. I would read them over and over again. The content was not academic, but the comics did enhance my reading capability and subsequently made me hungry for more information. Life can be such a struggle without an education.

It did seem like my dad was forever on the move. On one of our "in-between" moves we once again stayed at my Grandparent's house in Liverpool. It was a shorter period, waiting for our dad's posting to Blackdown Deepcut, Surrey. He travelled to Blackdown first and we followed later, travelling by train, which was not such a good idea. We knew that this was a recipe for disaster, travelling with our mum without dad. We thought it was great, just another adventure and doubted it would go smoothly. My mum said that all we had to do was to get the train at Lime Street railway station in Liverpool and get off at Brookwood station in surrey. Even as children we knew anything that our mum said, would be the complete opposite. As it turned out to be! We travelled through the night. The ticket collector instructed our mum that we had to change at Birmingham. We meanwhile had no interest in such details. Running around the train and messing around was far more interesting. A lot of our fellow travellers complained because we had woken them up. Luckily the ticket collector came into the carriage and told my mum that she needed to change at the next station, which was Birmingham. We changed and got a connecting train that would stop at Brookwood, but unfortunately Brookwood was not the last stop, as we were about to discover. The train ploughed on through the night. My brothers and I we were worn out and fell asleep. As the train passed various stations we wrote the names of the stations down on a piece of paper and handed them to her. We informed her that Brookwood was not the last stop. If we missed it we would arrive in another town. My dad was due to meet us at the station and take us to our new house. In the early hours of the morning our mum woke us up. She said that we had arrived at our destination. How wrong could she be? We had arrived at the last stop, it was not our stop. We had gone past Brookwood, and we arrived in Portsmouth. It was impossible for mum to contact our dad. In the end it was all sorted and we stayed in Portsmouth and went back up the line the next morning and finally arrived at Brookwood Station.

Living in Deepcut was like being in a huge play area. There were vast expanses of land that stretched from the Blackdown Training area over the Surrey heath. In the front of the house was an outdoor swimming pool. In the summer months swimming competitions were held it was during this time that I had the chance to swim for Surrey County. Many hours were spent enjoying ourselves in the pool.

The primary School we attended was the Blackdown Primary school which was a short walk away from the house; the only memory I have from the time at this school was a teacher called Mr Brown; he stood out because he only had one arm. Whenever he spoke about the loss of his arm, he would recount a story about being a fighter pilot. During the Second World War he was shot down during the battle of Britain. He said that when he opened the cockpit to bail out the cockpit closed shut on his arm. The plane plunged towards the ground and he went in the opposite direction. His parachute opened and the force ripped his arm out of its socket. I doubt if that was a true story, but once again at that age you will believe anything.

We were always outside come rain, sun and snow the outside had a great attraction for us and our mum would always encourage the three of us to play outside. We would spend hours playing in the ruins of the abandoned Barracks, Minden Barracks, it is now The Princess Royal Barracks. At the time the Barracks were made of wood nature was reclaiming it back. There was a large statue of a soldier near the old parade square. It reminded me of the soldiers who were depicted in the film "Zulu". This statue looked like it was modelled on a soldier from the Boer war in South Africa he was wearing a Khaki patterned uniform wearing a pith helmet and rifle. He looked forlorn standing on his own within the decaying barracks. There were some old assault courses still standing on the site and they were a magnet for children. The only part of the assault course that we could not scale was the six foot assault course wall, of course we did try. Part of the course had stagnated water in the pits. Within the pools of water there were newts, we would try to catch them and place them on the grass and they would soon find their way back to the ponds. The old sports pitches had long since reverted back to nature and we would watch English civil war re-enactments, it looked amazing watching these people enacting out various civil war skirmishes. There was smoke from muskets being fired and from cannons; we would spend hours watching the enactments.

Never a Dull Moment

Around Camberley and Cobham there was a tank range. During the weekends the training area was quiet, being children we walked for miles through woods and inhospitable training areas.
We discovered an old tank with many holes in the armour plate. Thinking it had been abandoned by the Army we managed to gain access and messed around inside. When we got home our dad asked us about our day, we told him of the tank. The colour in his face drained away. He told us not to go near the area again the tank was used as a target on a live firing range, obviously not on this particular day?

During the same period we would visit the Pirbright Military Ranges. We would cross close to the top of the ranges where the targets and butts were housed. Waited until the soldiers moved forward we would scamper and pick up as much discarded bullet brass as possible. Sometimes there would be live ammunition amongst the spent ammunition. This would be taken home and hidden.

We began to collect Action Man figures, which was a doll for boys and we would buy military uniforms for the figures. My brothers had a military vehicle for their Action Man. We would dig bunkers into banks and make sand bags for the bunkers and place Action man figures into the bunkers it was then that the fun would begin. Over a period of time we would steal our mum's hair spray and use it as a flame thrower. We would also snap the tops off the live ammunition to extract the gun powder. We would pour the gun powder liberally on the bunkers and set fire to the gun powder and watch them burn and melt our figures. On some occasions we managed to obtain petrol. Mixing the gunpowder and petrol created an atmospheric, and somewhat dangerous, children's theatre of war. It is a different world now children are huddled around game consoles and televisions rather than setting fire to themselves.

One particular build up to bonfire night we watched and waited as soldiers piled empty boxes, pianos and all sorts of combustible material onto the growing pyre. On bonfire night we could see the bonfire glowing in the dark, the flames growing higher and higher. For me it was like a mystical being. The heat was tremendous and the fire-works were in full swing. All of a sudden a terrific explosion out-did all the others. It came from within the bonfire and I heard my dad and others say that it sounded just like bullets going off. Another huge explosion occurred and someone crumpled to the ground screaming. In light of our previous escapades with ammunition, my friends and I looked at one another and smartly disappeared! Behind us people gathered around and first aid was given to the stricken individual. The bonfire was abandoned, the police and ambulance turned up, and the fire was gradually dampened down. I have to make clear that we had not placed any ammunition into the bonfire, it was subsequently found that someone had not checked an empty wooden ammunition box. Later on that night my dad asked if we knew anything about kids running about on Pirbright ranges, obvious we denied any knowledge, he looked unconvinced.

On another occasion I was headed to the local outdoor swimming pool. However on arrival I was met by a sign informing the public that the pool would be closed until further notice. Returning home our mum asked me why the long face. I told her about the pool being closed and she headed next door to see if our neighbour was aware. She returned and told me that I would be unable to swim for some time. A little girl had managed to get into the pool area when it was closed. She could not swim and unfortunately had fallen into the pool and drowned.

Our brushes with danger continued when a friend had managed to get hold of an adult size bow and arrow. Many a time my brothers and some of our friends were seen on the main sports pitch seemingly running around aimlessly. In fact what we were doing we were using ourselves as moving human targets. From one end of the sports fields our friend would shoot an arrow into the sky to see if he could hit anyone. We would seek to dodge the missile! If he had hit someone they could have been killed.

It was whilst I was living at Blackdown that I attended my first secondary school in Chobham. I really enjoyed the school it was such a shame that it had to close within a year of me starting. I really liked the school. I travelled from Blackdown in a school bus I never once missed a day at the school. It was at this school that I saw someone throwing a javelin and piercing someone's plimsoll with the javelin burying itself in the unfortunate person's foot. After the school was closed I had to attend a secondary school in Frimley Green, I was not very keen on this school and I didn't seem to settle. It was at this school that one of my school reports commented on my poor hand writing. My dad took it upon himself to correct my handwriting. I had to sit with him every Saturday and Sunday afternoon for a few weeks and copy his handwriting. I naturally rebelled and it ended up a battle of wills between the pair of us. In the end my dad gave up he was not happy with me because I had defied him, he took it as an affront to his authority. The school in Frimely was a very strict school especially when it came to homework. I was struggling and my mum could not comprehend the homework and would say she would ask my dad if he could help. The majority of the time she would inform me that my dad was "too tired", and so I would end up not handing in my homework. At school I would report sick prior to any lesson for which I should have produced the homework. I struggled and to compensate I would feign sickness. I did enjoy the maths lessons more so because of the maths teacher he was a rugby player who taught maths. It soon got around the school that he had broken his collar bone and could not teach. One particular maths lesson we all knew that he was still injured. He turned up to teach, our faces must have been a picture. He had each of us writing maths answers on the blackboard while he looked on. One sunny afternoon I watched from the classroom as two horses were running around in the tennis courts being chased by two teenagers. They were Romany gypsies and had lost control of the horses it was quite comical to watch. Much better than any lesson!

During another United Kingdom posting we moved to Colchester once again we enjoyed our time. We were constantly in the woods behind the house. Deep in the woods there were hunt kennels, as children we would visit the hounds, and it was in Colchester that I saw a hunt in progress. I was wandering the countryside and spotted the hunt in the distance; people were on horses and there were hounds closing in on the fox as it scampered across the fields. At the same time there was a craze for collecting American Civil War trading cards. We were forever buying bubble gum and collecting the cards. Some of the scenes depicted were quite gruesome I do not think that they would be sold to children today. During the summer holidays our mum would take all of us fruit picking. It was paid work and earned her a few extra pennies. We would move from farm to farm, and some weeks it would be apple picking and others strawberry picking. It was very hard work, it was outside and my mum enjoyed it, she was forever out in the sun. Other times she would take us walking for miles, although she never knew where she was taking us; our sustenance was packets of spangles, a type of hard boiled fruit sweet.

In Colchester I attended one of those old fashioned schools which had an entrance for girls and a separate one for boys. The playground was also segregated by a low wall in the middle of the playground, although the classrooms were mixed. It was at this school that I was informed by the music teacher that I could not sing and that I was tone deaf. I noticed that things were not quite right when I started singing in the front row of the choir. I gradually progressed, I think. I was moved from the front row to the middle and then eventually the back row. It was during one of the choir sessions that the music teacher told me that I would not be singing with the rest of the class anymore. She informed me, 'I was tone deaf'! I was taken out of the music lessons, and I thought, 'Ah, this is good, no more music, I can do whatever I want'. How wrong I was. Instead of music lessons I had to go to another classroom and listen to Peter and the Wolf and other short stories and later I would have to write about the story. I would sit and daydream, looking out of the classroom window, and watch what was happening outside. I knew once the story had finished I would be asked to write about it. I must have written such drivel; I never took anything in. I invented my own stories instead of listening. This may have been the start of me switching off at school. It was a crying shame as I would have liked to have done well at school, but my interest was killed off at an early age. One thing that has remained with me is the love of writing and storytelling.

An event stands out in my mind; I had my right knee sliced open. There was a park very close to the house, my brothers and I had a gang. The ground in the park was made up of a lot of pebbles and sharp flint stones which can slice the skin open like a knife. The stones were used to throw at other gangs. This particular day we thought that we could confront a group of older children. A varying amount of verbal abuse went on and some punching and kicking, this quickly escalated into throwing stones at one another. As I bent down to pick up more stones. As I looked up I realised I was alone and surrounded by the rival gang members. I was grabbed by two of the older boys, each held an arm and swung me around, they let go of me I landed on top of the sharp flints. I picked myself up and realised that there was blood running down my right leg. The boys who had grabbed me looked down and realised what they had done. My brothers came back and said "look at your knee, there is a big hole in it". Looking down blood was pouring from a large hole in my knee. I could see the ragged pieces of skin where the knee had been ripped open. It was at this point that the pain kicked in. It was excruciatingly painful; I was wearing black plimsolls, known as pumps, the right one was completely covered in blood. Running towards our house my right pump was making a squelching noise as though it was full of water. Bubbles of blood escaped from the pump. Someone said that I was leaving a trail of blood down the road, when I looked behind me there was blood on the road and the imprint of my pump. The fun really started when I got home. My dad was at work so it was left to my mum to patch me up. Florence Nightingale she isn't. Even as children we knew what to expect from her. I tried to tell her the gravity of the situation even my brothers were telling her, but it fell on deaf ears. She told me to go through to the kitchen, where she lifted me into the kitchen sink. We all knew what was going to happen next, and whatever she was going to do I knew it would hurt ... meanwhile the blood was still gushing from the cut. As soon as I saw the tea towel in her hand I knew what was going to happen next. She poured neat Antiseptic Ointment, TCP, onto the tea towel and applied it directly onto my knee, the pain shot through my body. She kept the tea towel on my knee for quite a while. Tears were rolling down my cheeks as I tried to tear myself away. There was no getting away from her firm grip. My mum thought that disinfectant was the cure for everything, including kitchen floors and bodies, she swore by it. She had no comprehension of what she was doing. She was never unkind or cruel it was her way; she doted on all three of us. All three of us were shouting at her. Her hands were covered in blood and the tea towel was also full of blood. "Don't be a baby it was only a drop of disinfectant" she said. The sink was covered in blood. Everyone was shouting it was absolute pandemonium. She decided at this point to put the plug into the sink. I was still standing in the sink with both pumps soaked with blood while the sink started to fill with blood. It was chaos in the kitchen - my brothers and I had more sense than my mum. Just then there was a knock at the door and one of my brothers answered it. I was still smarting from the disinfectant in my cut. It was our next door neighbour. My brother had told him what had happened; he was becoming concerned about the noise coming from the house. He took one look at my mum and said, "What the hell you are doing?" She said, "Oh, it's ok, just kids messing around, Keith will be fine". He lifted me out of the sink with the thick congealed blood sticking to my shoes. At that precise moment my dad came home. He was livid seeing what mum was doing to me. She said, "It's OK, Ron, it has only just happened". All three of us explained to him what had happened, and he soon got the true picture, needless to say he was not surprised. I was eventually taken to hospital to have twenty two stitches inserted into my knee.

Early Days

On one of my dad's various moves we ended up in a town called Osnabruck in West Germany, and once again we followed him. In the town there were no facilities for a British secondary school. I therefore had to attend a boarding school Windsor Boy's school, in a German town called Hamm. Hamm was sixty four miles away, an hour's drive away. It was a daunting prospect and I initially thought that I had done something wrong. Mostly we travelled to school by coach. Although once we travelled by train, which was an exciting change. The school was housed in an old Second World War Wehrmacht Artillery Camp, and the barracks were originally built in 1936. The Regiment fought at Stalingrad, Russia, in 1943. After the war ended the British renamed the barracks Brixton Camp and it became home to German and Austrian Prisoners of War. In 1948 it housed the Polish 61st Tank Transporter Unit. In 1953 it opened as a mixed boarding school and in 1960 became Windsor Boys School. By 1983 the School had closed. I initially attended the school on my own, later my brother Michael joined me; he was in the same dorm house as me. Attending boarding school was an experience, but they were not necessarily fond memories. The house that my brother and I were in was called Sandringham House. We were both boarders, like most children at the school. We lived in a dorm on the very top floor of our block. There was a house master who lived at the end of the corridor in a flat with his wife and family. I cannot remember seeing too much of them during my time at the school. We had German matrons, one of whom was a German Jew. I only mention her religion as there is relevance further on in the chapter. She had been liberated from a concentration camp after the war. I did not enquire why being a Jew was relevant. However she mentioned it frequently as though it was a badge of honour. I did not comprehend what it meant apart from the history books; it is only now as an adult that I wished I had asked her for more details. She worked for the British after her release. Each evening we would shower, change into our pyjamas and trot down to matron's office. She would inspect our hair, ears, neck and finger nails. Anyone she thought had not washed or showered would be sent them back to the washrooms. The incentive, a cake or bun, did the trick. The gymnasium was housed in the old German Army workshop, and it was very large indeed. In front of the Gym was a large tarmac area which, thinking about it, must have been the parade square. In the winter, if you let your mind wander, one could imagine the area busy with German troops and vehicles. The woodwork class was in large offices attached to the left of the Gymnasium. The woodwork teacher at the time had worked in a borstal school, a school for delinquent boys. He told us if we stepped out of line he would come down on us like a tonne of bricks. He implied that he was hard and knew all of the tricks that school children pull, and no one at the borstal ever got one over on him.

Sport was such an important element of the school curriculum. Each day we played some form of sport, in the summer we played after school. I remember playing softball most summer evenings. Someone threw the softball bat behind them after hitting the ball, the bat smashed into someone's face he had stood too close behind him as he hit the ball. It was not a pretty sight.

War related rumours abounded. Allegedly there were tunnels running from the chapel and under the sports fields and parade square. Furthermore, German tanks had been buried beneath the parade square! I have mentioned sports at the school because I was a very good swimmer. During one parents' day there was a swimming marathon and I was chosen to take part. The parents sat in plastic chairs pool side; the skies were grey and overcast. It was such a cold day when we dived into the open air swimming pool; it was so cold that my head felt as though someone had hit it with a sledge hammer. I remember the skies getting darker and darker as we swam and there were bolts of lightning and terrific claps of thunder. At the turn-around at the end and swimming up a lane I noticed the parents and school dignitaries had left. The other swimmers had obviously noticed this as well and began to slow down or stop altogether. It was then that we realised the Physical Education teacher, PE teacher, dressed in his white cricket jumper, he was hollering. 'Get swimming you lazy bunch of good for nothings, your parents haven't come all this way for you to stop. Keep swimming'. He reminded me much later on in life, when I was in the Army, he must have been ex-military. The school had horticultural lessons. I found the lessons quite boring until a new teacher started. To a thirteen year old he looked old, although I think that he may have come straight out of teacher training college. The lessons were still boring, but this particular summer we were outside tending to the various vegetables and fruit, someone was playing music. It was coming from one of the classroom windows we could see the old wooden style school speakers on the window ledge. The teacher was playing Jimi Hendrix's music; it was blasting out over the gardens. He was playing songs like Hey Joe, Purple Haze and The Wind Cries Mary. Many years later I had goose bumps when I was watching the Hollywood film Apocalypse Now, some of the sound track had Jimi Hendrix's music playing; it did remind me of my horticultural lessons and listening to his music. It was in the September of the same year, 1970 that Hendrix died.

In this year there were quite a few civil aircraft hijackings by the Popular Front for the Liberation of Palestine, PFLP. The aircraft were diverted to Dawson's Field in Jordan; the airfield was a former British Royal Air Force base. The matron that I have previously mentioned had the German TV News on in her room and was talking to one of the other Matrons; I heard the German words 'des juden'. The terrorists had segregated fifty six Jewish hostages and we could see that she was very upset. Eventually all of the hostages were released. For me personally the troubles of Northern Ireland had not entered my life yet, but would do fairly soon. Most weekends we would visit the local German Town of Hamm. It is not a large town; it does have one of the largest railway hubs in Germany. It was one of the greatest marshalling yards in Europe. During the Second World War allied air raids destroyed nearly sixty percent of the old city. We had permission to visit Windsor Girls School. I can only remember a handful of times visiting the Girls School, which was a few miles away. One of my visits to the school was to the dentist, he extracted a wisdom tooth.

Much of the time we were left to our own devices during the trips into the town. There was a shop that sold Chinese fireworks and boys being boys we were able to purchase them. They were very small fireworks attached together by string. I think that the Chinese lit them on the string and threw them in the air; because the fireworks were stuck together it had a huge fire cracker affect. We would stuff the individual firecrackers down frog's throats sometimes they would explode inside the frogs. The majority of the time we threw them at one another. At school assembly the headmaster or head of form would lecture us on the hazards of fireworks.

This brings me onto the school assembly hall, which doubled up as a cinema. One particular year we had to attend, there was no arguing - the whole school had to attend the screening of Jungle

Book. Michael. He had to sit near the back of the hall just under the balcony where the sixth form were seated. At the end of the film someone pointed out to Michael that the back of his blazer was covered in spit; the sixth formers were spitting onto the first form from the balcony. Needless to say he was unimpressed and still gripes about it today.

I remember one night in the dorm someone decided to have a séance in the room that I shared with three others. It was pitch black and someone had an Ouija board, which is meant to enable those using it to summon the spirit world. Using a plastic beaker it suddenly moved when someone screamed 'there she is, look at the window there's a face of a woman'. Well I nearly shit myself; I was all over the place. I could not see or hear anything but it certainly spooked me. Some boys suggested they had seen Eva Braun's face in the window. Extremely uncomfortable, I had a very disturbed sleep that night I slept under my blankets. In the morning it appeared the séance was common knowledge and we were summoned to the headmaster. We received such a severe telling off, and naturally the Ouija board was confiscated. I did not sleep comfortably in that room and was eventually moved to another room. Later the matron explained that we should never meddle in the occult, but it went right over my head. She then explained that Eva Braun was Adolf Hitler's mistress and later his wife. Moreover, to stay away from anything linked with Adolf Hitler, as anything associated with him was pure evil. I left with everyone else none the wiser, I did not dare ask anyone what she was talking about. It was only in later life that I understood what she was trying to tell us, especially what she meant about Hitler; as I have previously mentioned our matron had spent time in a concentration camp for being a Jew in Hitler's Germany. Later on

28

in my journey through life I would get to visit the mass graves at Bergen-Belsen concentration camp.

My brother Michael was always getting himself into mischief and scrapes and I can clearly remember some of his friends from his 'end' of the corridor; it makes it sound like a form of ghetto. Someone from his room told me that Michael was being beaten up in his room. I entered the room and someone in the fifth year was thumping Michael. I picked up the nearest weighty item. It was a table tennis bat. I threw it so hard at the other boy just as he raised his fist to hit Michael again. The bat hit him on the hand and it must have done some damage as he screamed and the school medical staff had to have a look at his damaged hand. Michael would find himself involved in fights on many an occasion thereafter.

During this time my brother Garry was living at home in Osnabruck with my parents he was not of boarding school age, which Michael and I resented a little.

During one of my half term breaks my parents thought that I was mature enough to baby sit for my brothers whilst my parents attended an evening function. Reluctantly, and against my dad's better judgement, he agreed since I was at secondary school I could baby sit; let us just say that their decision was a recipe for disaster. Michael was eleven and Garry was nine, I bossed them around something chronic. They moaned like hell at me, but I laid down the ground rules about when they should go to bed. Well, it was just like the natural selection process. Michael was eleven and nearly as old as me therefore he felt he was entitled to the same bedtime. Garry's face was looking glummer and glummer as he realised what was coming. Michael and I rounded on Garry and told him that he was going to bed first. In the flat my dad had a Philips music cabinet and the latest music. I had a few vinyl singles which I played, the one record that sticks in my mind was the Kinks 'Lola'. Being the type of children we were we soon found the booze, my parents had tried to hide from us, and it was stashed under the sink. I became the cocktail maker; my parents had every spirit under the sun, and this included Garry sampling the various concoctions. I remember the Kinks record Lola blasting away the more we drank the more we played the record. I was absolutely hammered. I did not hear my parents returning the music was blasting out from the music centre. I was starting to feel sick even more so when I saw my dad's face. He was furious. My mum was OK about the whole situation, mind you I could not see straight at the time due to, too much booze. She went into Michael and Garry's room to check if they were asleep, but by this time my dad had found them drunk on the settee. I was rarely trusted to babysit again.

It was in the same flat, for my birthday I received an electronics kit, I set about making a radio. I did not want to build the one in the instruction manual. I wanted to make a real one, a much bigger and one that worked. I used a cardboard box and inserted some components from the kit. I found an old electrical lead with a plug on the end, spliced the cable and connected it to some pieces of metal in the box. I put the plug into the power socket then touched some metal in the box. A bolt of light and a loud bang sent me flying across the room and I crumpled against the opposite wall. I may have been knocked out; I certainly knew that I was electrocuted. My mum came into the bedroom and there was a burning smell and smoke coming out of the box. I knew that I must have blown a fuse. I was frazzled, but managed to check the fuses and change the blown one. Had dad discovered that mum had let me change fuses he would have blown his top. She knew this and said, "Don't tell your father that I blew a fuse or that you have changed the fuse." I said, "Don't worry, mum, I won't," and I thought 'phew that was close'. I felt rough for a couple of days! I would also steal my mum's hair spray and put the cans under my bed. She would go out to the shops and buy more, instead of asking any of us boys if we had been taking them. I used them as flame throwers on my brothers and friends outside. I did not only attack my brothers and friends, I would kill ants with my home made flame throwers.

I have written down some conclusions from this chapter and how my childhood impacted on me.

My childhood was a very carefree world and my brothers and I wanted for nothing. My mother's lack of education did not seem to hinder me as a youngster. It was only in later life that I believe that all three of us realised that our education at home had a lot to be desired. For me it was when I started primary school, the school system expected children to be at a certain level of education. I soon felt that I was not even at the basic level expected by the school; I struggled to catch up and felt that I was lagging behind in the most basic of subjects. The rest of my school life was negatively impacted by being 'shown up' so early in my schooling. It has not stopped me from having an insatiable thirst for knowledge and to learn.

The following chapter is another phase of my upbringing which I deemed required a chapter all of its own.

Early Days

Chapter 2 – End of Empire – Aden South Arabia

This chapter documents a period of my life when I was living during the demise of the British Empire. At the time I had no idea that Aden was part of the British Empire. As a child, I was living in a very hot country with my parents and my brothers, and I was acutely aware that there was a war raging around me. The conflict would become a normal everyday world for me. Aden was a hot, smelly and stifling. It was the capital of South Arabia the majority of the city was built inside an extinct volcano. The city has seventy five square miles of desert and waterfront. The Arab population lived in shanty towns made of flimsy huts made from packing cases and tea chests.

Today, Aden is part of the Yemeni state. It is situated on the southern tip of Yemen. The Red sea joins the Gulf of Aden and the Gulf of Aden joins the Arabian Sea.

My story is not an historic account of Britain or of its foreign policies in South Arabia at the time. This is an account through the eyes of a child. The place holds many memories for me. There will be others who have served or lived in Aden at the same time, and their memories will be totally different to mine.

My father was posted to Aden in August 1965. My mum was adamant that she and the "kids", as she referred to us and still does, would join my father. It was going to be a completely different play-ground for the next couple of years. It was a completely different environment and culture to that of the United Kingdom. It was a bit of a culture shock to say the least.

The first physical thing that I noticed getting off the plane at Royal Air Force (RAF) Khormaksar was the sudden rush of heat as the aircraft doors opened; it felt as though the oxygen in my lungs was being sucked from me. The temperature was nearly always over ninety degrees Fahrenheit during the day. My dad was at the airport to meet us. There were military buses waiting to take those who had just arrived to their married quarters or billets, as there were military personnel arriving on their own without their families. I noticed that there were armed soldiers in land rovers escorting the busses. This will become significant further on in this chapter. My dad had arrived in a Landrover to take us to where we were to live. His driver was an Arab soldier, and my dad spoke to him in Arabic and the driver spoke to my dad in English. My dad said that he was learning Arabic and the driver was learning to speak English, well English with a scouse accent. I noticed a Navy Army Air Force Institute (NAAFI) shop and a cinema. We travelled through many Arab shanty houses in the Crata district it looked like it was a very busy built up area. It reminded me of the films of Arab countries in the middle ages. We drove onto the Ma'alla Straight - people had named the area as the murder mile because it was a mile long dual carriageway. With flats and shops either side of the road. It had a more sinister nick name of 'murder mile'. The land rover pulled up near some flats and my dad told us to get out; we had arrived at our flat.

The sun was so strong for a few seconds it blinded me and I ended up with black dots in my eyes. As a child you learn quickly, I never did that again, looking directly into the bright sunlight. Many decades later, I had a cancerous growth cut away from my face, the surgeon told me that it had been growing under my skin for decades; he thought that it was attributed to my time in Aden.

Never a Dull Moment

Our flat was behind the main Ma'alla Road. From our flat my mum could see into the back of the flats in front. She could see the Arab families who lived in them. Underneath the flat there were shops, and under our flat there was a soft drinks shop, it also sold alcohol. My dad would buy his beer from the shop.

It was a time in my life when the majority of my day was spent outside due to the heat. As a family we would spend most of our time at the beach or playing outside. The flats were made of concrete slabs and the outsides were painted white, to reflect the sun, like most of the buildings in South Arabia. The front of our flat had metal shutters over the doorway; the shutters were secured and closed at night.

The balcony overlooked the Ma'alla Wharf and the Aden Telephone exchange. In the bay is an island, called Slave Island, and when we were living in Aden people made Dhows and repaired them on the Island. A dhow is an Arab boat made of wood with a large sail. The story regarding slave Island in South Arabia's history the Queen of Sheba would bring slaves into Aden. The slaves came from nearby Africa. The slaves were offloaded onto Slave Island, hence the island's name. As children we were told not to go near the Island, as with all children, the adventurous side of our inquisitive minds kicked in and we wanted to investigate the island. Whenever we had the chance we would go to the docks area and would try to get over to slave island, we never did get to the Island. The Arab dhows used by the local fisherman would tie up in the docks at Ma'alla; I and some neighbours' children were allowed on board one of the dhows the skipper took a great risk. Not knowing it at the time we were also taking an even greater risk. We wandered around the dhow and the fishermen on board seemed a little nervous,

35

suddenly they started laughing and talking to us in Arabic, and ruffling our hair. We were very dark-skinned, with very blonde-haired, this was due to the sun and swimming in the sea every day the sea and the sun bleached our hair. The Dhow did not sail anywhere and the fishermen let us take a look around the ship then let us off the dhow we all waved goodbye. It was many years later my mother informed me that this was unusual. It was too dangerous for children to be playing out on their own. There were strict rules on children they could only play outside when escorted by an adult at all times. My mum forgets that she let the three of us run around freely without any adult supervision.

Most British families could have an 'arma' (a local housemaid) allocated to the house/flat, who was a lady who would tidy the house and help with the house work. They were mainly from Somalia; they would make a bed up at night and sleep on the veranda outside, my mum refused to have one. I think that it was because of my mum's background. She would have thought that it was a form of slave labour and she wanted to bring up her own family on her own. My mum was also acutely aware that my younger brother Michael had threatened our neighbour's arma with a kitchen knife. He would push the fruit out of the arms of the laundry man who would supplement his living by selling fruit. My mum was furious with Michael as it was the man's living that he was destroying. Michael had a very explosive temper. I did hear that in Aden a British teenager had killed an arma. He was convicted in Aden of her murder and was incarcerated in an Arab prison. He later served the remainder of his sentence in Britain.

My father was a Sergeant and was seconded to the 2nd Battalion Federal Regular Army (FRA). It was a locally raised Army he was a British Military Advisor. For months at a time he was engaged in keeping the rebels in the North of South Arabia at bay. He was based at a British Army Base "up country" in South Arabia. We would not see him for months he would come back to Ma'alla and be on Rest & Recuperation (R&R). It was not all R&R as he was armed all the time and aware of the volatile situation in Aden. Everyone was classed as a potential terrorist target. During my dad's R&R in Ma'alla he would volunteer to go on patrol. Which gave someone who 'looked after the families', a break as they ensured all the service families were safe. He did this during his time off; he felt that he owed it to them, even though he was based in the RADFAN, it was an area called Dhala where the British forces were fighting Marxist terrorists and guerrillas.

During the periods that my dad was away fighting in the Radfan, we remained in Aden and carried on with a normal family life. I cannot ever remember feeling scared of the violence. I think that it was because we were doing something all of the time, we did not have time to ponder about the situation. We heard gunshots and bombs going off at all hours of the day and it became the norm.

I only felt scared once when a man tried to throw me off a roof. The roofs of the flats had a small wall running around the edge. I was with some friends playing on the roof, all of a sudden a man ran onto the roof. He grabbed hold of me. I was very wiry and was quite strong for my age and he could not get hold of me properly. He was trying to pick me up and throw me over the wall. He must have known that he needed to do it quickly as my friends had called a 'Snow drop'. This was the nick name for The Royal Air Force, RAF police, the policeman could hear me shouting.

The man soon got me over the wall, I managed to stay on the ledge, the policeman fired a shot into the air the man immediately released me. He was taken away and another RAF Policeman came to see if I was alright.

We knew that we were living in a very violent part of the world. My mother never gave any inkling to us nor did she show any fear during the time that we lived in Aden. At times I would stare up to the night sky and think of relatives in England who were living in a very safe part of the world and tucked up in bed. Here I was in a dangerous part of the world living within a defunct volcano. These were very interesting times. I somehow knew that I was going to have an interesting life ahead of me.

Aden during the time was still a British protectorate. The British Government of the day informed the people of Britain and Aden that by 1968 Aden would gain its independence. There was a political void and various Adenies political parties and one would take over power when Britain left the protectorate. The announcement encouraged more violence and terrorist incidents. Britain had a commitment to protect the population of South Arabia until the handover of power to the people of Aden.

This is was the political situation that we had arrived in, and the one that we lived through. My mother had no idea of the history or the political situation. My dad explained about the ancient history of South Arabia; it formed the Kingdom of Saba, or Sheba, which had been ruled by the Queen of Sheba. The country was on the incense route, and the Myrrh and Frankincense trees still grow in the country. During the days of the British Empire, when steam ships ploughed the sea routes of the empire, Aden became an important 'coal bunker',

Never a Dull Moment

Refuelling ships passing through via the Suez Canal or coming back from India or the Middle East.

We all attended school at a place called Steamer Point. The school was Chappel Hill Junior School; we travelled to school daily on the Military School Busses. The school buses had an armed escort. Which consisted of heavily armed Army land rovers and armed guards. The Regiment who carried out this task when we were there was the 1st Battalion the Cameron (Scottish Rifles).
The young soldiers would tell us to sit down in their broad Scottish accents; we would tell them that we did not understand what they were saying, which would pee them off, and they would shout "ye cheeky wee Sassenachs". Once the vehicles moved off in convoy we would not play them up, as we knew that they had a very serious job to fulfil. We did not need telling, we could see how on edge they were and we could see that they were concentrating on the surrounding area; they only had our interests and safety in mind.

One morning while we travelled to school we saw another British school bus pulled over on the side of the road. It had been ripped apart by what looked like a grenade and had bullet holes sprayed across the body work. The Land rover that had been escorting the bus was strewn across the road; it was also covered in bullet holes. Lying around the bus were dead terrorists. The soldiers on our bus were shouting at not to look out of the windows. It was too late some of us had already looked at the scene outside.
I can remember a girl and a boy crossing the road to catch a school bus. They were deliberately ran over by an Arab who drove his car straight at them. He drove away without stopping, the soldiers started to shoot at the car.

Those who have been exposed to this environment take it in their stride and, after their first encounter, they somehow get used to it.

At school, my teacher would check that everyone had a packed lunch and a drink. Most children had fruit and vegetables in their packed lunch. My brothers and I most days had sausage sandwiches with my mum's finger marks imprinted into the bread. My mum still squeezes the bread and leaves her finger imprints on the bread. The flasks that contained our drinks were made of plastic I can still smell the plastic in the heat; the heat would warm the juice very quickly.

The school uniform consisted of sandals, white socks, shorts, short sleeve white shirt and a cap. The school badge was a camel motif.

This was the most clothing that we ever got to wear when we were out in Aden, the remainder of the time we wore swimming trunks and flip flops. School started at 08:30 am and finished at midday, the school was situated on the top of a hill called Chapel Hill. Birds of prey would glide on the warm thermals. I would struggle with my homework; I made up excuses about not completing my work. I did not wish to embarrass myself nor my brothers by admitting that our mum could not help with the homework because it was beyond her abilities.

The heat was unbearably hot, at certain times of the day it would sting the throat. The volcano within which the city was built had filled up in places with sand. The flat faced onto the old Aden port of Ma'alla, where the sea had broken into the lip of the volcano and created a natural harbour.

Never a Dull Moment

I have many small scars around my ankles due to wearing flip flops, where the rough glass had cut into the foot and ankle. It was quite painful at the time and could become infected very quickly unless you had a mother who swore by TCP, which is a mild antiseptic, and disinfectant.

After school, we travelled by military bus from Ma'alla back towards steamer point, to the lido and beach area. It was contained inside a huge British Army base called Fort Morbarik. As I have already pointed out, we were always under armed escort; travelling without the military buses and protection was highly dangerous.

There were many instances when my mum would miss the military bus. This mishap never deterred her in any shape or form. We would catch the civilian bus to the beach.
We were very brown, it was obvious we were British, we had white hair; the sea had bleached our hair turning it white. The locals would say in English 'the blonde ones', my brother Michael would not let the women touch his hair. Most of the men would stare at us. I remember my mum telling the Arab women 'do not worry, just touch it'. We were also referred to by most Arabs as 'cheekos'. An Arab policeman was stood gawping, and possibly thinking what is she doing queuing up for a civilian bus. As we got on board the bus the driver also looked gob smacked the three of us knew a little Arabic, we always seemed to get to where we needed to get to.

My mum told me that a lot of the Arabs who lived in and around the area where we lived, knew that she was bringing up three children on her own, while our dad was away. They knew that my dad was serving away, she said that they did know her and

41

that they did keep an eye out. In later life I wonder if these people were relatives of those Arab soldiers serving in the Federal Regular Army to which my dad was seconded to. Did they keep an eye out for us? We shall never know?

The civilian bus would take us through the Arab quarter and then onto the long route to where the Military camp was. Every time we travelled on the civilian bus we would get off at the bus stop outside of the camp. The soldiers on guard would stand staring at us. It was because we were getting off a civilian bus, as though it was a normal everyday thing to do. My mum would flash her cardboard identity card and be waved on. My mum has informed me that she was never reported by the guard. She never had to explain why we were travelling on a civilian bus and travelling around the Arab quarter.

Living in Ma'alla, we got used to the shootings at night, sometimes we would be woken by the sound of a large explosion going off; mainly hand grenades, in and around the flats on the Ma'alla Road. On one occasion when we arrived back from the beach, we found that the stairs to our flat had been blown up; one of the soldiers had noticed a large thermos flask on the stairs and had kicked it, as he kicked it the device exploded and his back was covered in shrapnel. At school the military would brief the children regarding the different types of Improvised Explosive Devices; IEDs, we would get regular updates, since the terrorists were forever changing their modus operandi. The terrorists would place bombs in the latest toys and leave them lying around, and some children had lost hands and eyes from picking the toys up. Soft drinks cans and footballs were a favourite of the terrorists.

Never a Dull Moment

My mum would on occasions shop in the Arab Market place in the Ma'alla district. It was an open air market with stalls selling fruit and veg that looked like they were sweltering in the shade; it was eighty degrees in the shade. In fact they were wilting. In the heat of Aden food did not stay fresh for very long. Obviously, being British in an Arab Market we stood out a mile. It was the same market during the night where the terrorists would snipe at the Army patrols. It was the same area that the Arab snipers would fire from and attempt to shoot at the Military Married Quarter housing on the Ma'alla mile. I remember a very tall and broad Arab telling me in English to 'persuade your mum to get out of the market area'. I was to learn many years later by my father that the Special Air Service Regiment, (SAS), in Aden had Fijians dressed as Arabs. Who knows, he could have been one of them?

The swimming area at the beach had a shark's net, which protected swimmers from the sharks and barracudas. I can remember standing on the beach; I could see the ship SS Canberra with its two distinct yellow funnels passing by. I asked my dad, "where was the ship going to?" He told me that, "It was coming back from Australia." I asked myself if anyone on board knew what was happening in Aden. SS Canberra was to turn up in my family's life again, this time as a troopship during the Falklands war in 1982.

The rocks around the beach were made up of volcanic rock, it was very sharp and would cut the skin just like a sharp knife; the volcanic rock had the appearance of brown glass.

My brothers and our friends would fish off the nearby rocks; it is where we caught the best fish. The hooks that we used were shaped just like grappling hooks, four hooks welded together. As

I placed some bait on the hook with a heavy lead weight. The heavier the better as I could cast further out to sea. As I cast the line over my shoulder I heard a scream. I looked over my shoulder, and the hooks had dug into another boy's back, the more I pulled on the line the deeper the hooks dug into his back. I cut the line and told him to get to the Medical Centre and to bring my hook back when they had cut it out of his back.

Running around and swimming, being out in the fresh air would make the three of us very hungry. One of our favourite treats was a plate of chips with tomato sauce mixed in with sand. My brothers and I would walk up and down the beach and collect the empty Pepsi and Fanta bottles, the soldiers had left behind, or they would let us have the empty bottles. We would take them back to the NAAFI at the Mermaid Club. The club was the bar complex that we would retrieve the money on the empty bottles. My younger brother, Garry, would have to stand on wooden steps at the bar's serving hatch. This helped him to be seen and it enabled him to hand in his bottles.

One particular day, Garry slipped off the steps and landed heavily on to the floor, the empty bottles that he had collected smashed and his hand was badly cut open. I was on the beach with our mum and I could see Garry running along the open air veranda that ran along the front of the mermaid club. He had his red swimming trunks on, from a distance it looked as though he was holding onto the bottom of his swimming trunks; I could see from a distance that his hand, was bright red. I told my mum what I had seen and she said that it could be just tomato sauce. Garry ran towards our mum. There were soldiers chasing after him, they had seen what had happened and they chased after Garry to make sure he was alright. His hand was pouring with blood, he had a serious cut, he was taken to the medical centre and had his hand stitched up. He had a large bandage around his hand for quite some time, the unsanitary conditions in Aden meant that a cut could soon become seriously infected; the heat is not the best environment for a wound to heal.

In the swimming pool area there was the obligatory fountain this particular one was made of copper. The off duty military personnel would have a few drinks and then climb the slippery copper fountain. They would attempt to dive from the top of it into the pool. Someone had climbed to the top and as he was stood on the top he slipped and cut himself very badly. There was blood everywhere. I could tell that it was serious because he was not moving, I could hear him moaning he was in a lot of pain. I saw him being carried away on a stretcher.

The only down side of visiting the beach was the off duty soldiers who would let their hair down, by getting drunk. I think that the mixture of families, children and drunken adults is not a good mix. When my dad would leave on his many trips "up country" he would tell me that I was the man of the house. I remember being on the beach when my dad was away, a drunken soldier came up to my mum and her friend. I told him to leave my mum alone. My mum assured me that everything was OK and that she could handle the situation. It was because my dad had told me that while he was away I was the man of the house I must have taken his words literally.

The money that we had collected from the empty bottles we would save up to buy Dinky and Corgi cars from the local toy shop in Ma'alla. There were times that the three of us, including our mum, would be coming back from the toy shops during a curfew. On one particular occasion we bumped into our dad. He had come looking for us during the curfew and he was not happy. He managed to get a flight from RADFAN to take some short notice R&R. He shouted at our mum, 'what the bloody hell do you think you are doing having the kids out during a curfew'. Our dad said that if our mum stayed out after curfew again, we would be on a flight back to the UK. We did it time and time again. My mum said that 'we should all stick together and not to tell dad if he ever asked if we had been out during any curfews'. As I look back now on events I can understand my dad's frustration at not knowing what we were up to. He could do nothing about our situation in Aden, with its own terrorist atrocities. My mum remains very much a maverick. I was told that some British children had a birthday party in one of the flats in Ma'alla, and the flat was blown up.

The following section has been a difficult to write about. One particular time, my dad came to stay during a period of R & R. I remember an argument between my parents. My mum seemed to draw me into my parent's arguments, which would set my dad off. I was like the trigger that would tilt him over the edge. He always carried a pistol, a particular argument was becoming very heated and dad had been drinking and my mum was shouting out for me to come to her. My parents were in their bedroom I opened the door to see my dad stood there with his pistol pointing towards my mum. He looked at me and put the pistol down by his side, my mum told me to leave. Eventually, a few hours later, they told me not to worry and that they only had a little argument. I had been mortified to see my dad with his pistol pointed at my mum. Once again another memory that has stayed with me I can remember it as though it was yesterday.

Never a Dull Moment

After school the heat outside was often a hundred degrees. Some parents kept their children indoors most of the time. Some of the families returned to the United Kingdom soon after arriving in Aden, never to return, rather than to stay in Aden a moment longer. For myself and brothers, our time was spent enjoying ourselves.

There was an occasion when we travelled to the beach by taxi. The taxi was climbing out of the volcano surrounding Aden, heading up and over the lip to drive into Steamer Point, when suddenly one the doors of the car flew open. I was in the back of the taxi and I was not wearing a seat belt, and I ended up hanging onto the open door; I could see the tarmac and the white lines of the road flashing past me. My mum was in the passenger seat; she was shouting to me to 'stop messing around and get back into the car'. Michael and Garry were shouting at the driver to stop the car, mum said to the taxi driver 'oh, don't worry, he will be OK'. It was pandemonium, one of my brothers told me later that the taxi driver looked petrified; his eyes were bulging out of their sockets. Michael managed to pull the door closed, and before he managed to get the door closed I was hanging half in and out of the taxi. We were all shouting, and the taxi driver was shouting in Arabic; it was utter chaos in the car. The only one who was not flustered was our mum; she thought that we were fooling around. The scene was set: a petrified taxi driving shouting in English and Arabic. My mum shouting at the three of us telling us to stop messing around. We were shouting at the driver to stop the car. Our mum was telling him not to worry – 'they are only playing around and to carry on driving or we will be late'......

Once the tide was out at the beach, the shark net and the large metal buoys that held the nets up in the sea would be resting on the sand. On the sea bed the coral was exposed. This particular occasion the tide was out within the pools of water there were stranded aquatic life. I was walking out onto the exposed sea bed with a friend we were wearing flip flops. He put a foot into one of the pools, and as he did so he suddenly yelled out in agony; he had stepped onto some coral which had a moray eel lurking inside. The eel had bitten through most of one of his big toes, blood was pouring out of what was left of his toe. We got back to the beach his mum took him to the medical centre. By now reading this book you may have formed an impression that this particular medical centre was kept very busy, you would be correct in your assumption. Weeks later, he showed off his big toe, or at least the gap where his missing big toe should have been, he was boasting about the loss of it. His toe had to be amputated. I can assure you that at the time he was in agony when the moray eel had bitten into his toe. I had never seen so much blood and ripped flesh.

As I have mentioned my mother is well known within the family as a sun goddess. All of the family including my father had gone to the beach as usual. For some reason my dad could only swim under the water. He could never swim on top of the water. Also, he was not a very strong swimmer. Something was wrong, and he said 'one of you boys will have to rescue your mum'. My mum had seemingly fallen asleep on a lilo. For the un-initiated a Lilo is best used in a swimming pool not the 'high seas'! The tide had taken her out to sea and was close to the shark net. Which was roughly half a mile from the beach. Garry was too young, and even though Michael was a strong swimmer he may have been too exhausted once he had reached mum. He may not have been able to swim back to the beach. My dad decided that I would be capable of swimming out and bring her back to the beach. The problem was trying to find her with so many swimmers and even more people using the same style and colour Lilo. We noticed in the distance a Lilo slipping over a gap in the shark net, the three of us looked at one another. I think that we were thinking the same thing, my dad suddenly shouted, 'bloody hell, I bet that's your mum'. He had a pair of binoculars he used for spotting the many ships passing the beach; I suspect that they were his military binoculars. He confirmed that it was our mum on the lilo. He said, "It looks as though she is still asleep. Right Keith, off you go." At this point my dad was becoming very worried; my mum was not a strong swimmer. After a mammoth swim I reached my mum. She had drifted a little bit further out to sea and was way past the shark net. Others on the beach began to realise that something was up. When I reached her, my mum was fast asleep I woke her up and told her that I needed to get her back to the beach. My mum at this point realised just how serious the situation was. I grabbed the rope and pulled my mum back to the beach. Once we were over the shark net I knew that we were into safer waters. I slowly got her safely back to the beach.

Whenever I saw an Arab man he seemed to be chewing on a piece of wood with lots of leaves. I found out that it was called 'khat' or 'qat', it is a narcotic plant. The men would chew lots of leaves and chew them into a ball and eventually spit it out. A horrible mixture would then be spat out onto the ground. The goats which were everywhere would eat it, they seemed to eat anything. At school, I remember the good times in Aden, and even though I was aware of what was happening around me. As for the adults, my mum, my dad and all of the soldiers and their families, it was obviously a very dangerous and stressful place to live in. More so when the British government of the day announced the withdrawal of Britain from South Arabia.

I saw lots of Arab children who were beggars, many of them had missing hands. Or they could not walk and had makeshift boards with wheels (similar to a skateboard) to enable them to move around the streets. Some of the children who could not walk would drag themselves along on some pieces of cardboard along the ground in the dirt and stinking water, and they were covered in filth of all descriptions. There were also lots of adults in the same condition. My dad told me that some had a form of local punishment metered out to them for stealing or other offences. He explained that some Arabs were not as fortunate enough to have access to medical facilities. Some of their injuries would have to go untreated, hence the many body deformities. They had to beg to stay alive. Most locals ignored them or would walk past them or spit on them, some threw money at the beggars; we would give them some of our 'bottle money'.

My dad managed to stay with us during the Christmas period. I remember one Christmas receiving metal press toys robots, planes, tanks and dinky toys and Airfix models, including the paints to paint the models. The tin plate toys needed batteries, which were included, and the various tin toys made such a racket the noise woke my dad and he stormed into the bedroom and snatched the batteries out of the toys, he took the batteries away with him. He was mad because we had got up early and were playing with our battery powered toys and the noise had woken him. It did not dampen our spirits and we got the paints out and painted the new dinky toys. We used the Airfix model paint to paint our brand new cars, he went ballistic with rage when he got up. My mum said, "I told you to leave them to play with the tin toys."

Never a Dull Moment

My dad never knew in advance when he would be able to take R&R. There was a time when he had to cancel a trip to Aden. The plane that he was meant to be on was blown up in mid-air. It was an Aden Airlines DC3 (Dakota).

We spent hours fishing from the rocks, and the sea was so clear that I could see the fish in the clear water. I would try to catch squid first and use it as bait. Above the rocks I could see the Governor's Residence, to me at that age it looked quite an imposing building. There was a very large pool of water, people were walking in front of the children as we walked towards the rocks to go fishing. Someone had just walked through a large puddle when a huge Manta Ray moved in the puddle and flapped its 'wings'. Lots of men came running out of the scuba club, they made sure that everyone was safe. They taped off the area so that no one could get hurt or attacked by the ray. The tide came in it swam out of the large puddle and out into sea.

Just outside of our flat there were lots of shacks made out of various wooden packing cases, more than likely taken from the docks in Ma'alla. We would play with an Arab boy he owned a donkey. We would pay him to have a ride on the donkey.

One morning traveling to school, driving into Steamer Point, there was a massive ship in port; it was taller than every port building. It was out of proportion with other surrounding structures, and it was an American Aircraft Carrier. It was either on its way or coming back from the Vietnam War.

In 1964, the then British Government informed the people of Southern Arabia that Britain would pull out of the Protectorate. As a family, we all left Aden on the 5 February 1967. The last

British soldier to leave Aden left on the 29 November 1967.
The country was falling into a spiral of violence and blood- letting between South Arabian factions. After living in Aden, as a family, we had some months living in Liverpool, and of course once again we had to attend St Silas Junior School in Toxteth.

Moving to Aden gave me an insight to other people and cultures living in such a far off land in a mystical land. For me it was a fascinating time of my life, for others an inhospitable violent land. I did not realise that it was the beginning of the end of the British Empire; I was too young to understand what was happening during the family's time in South Arabia.

Chapter 3 – The Seventies

During the 1970's as a family we were living in Bielefeld, West Germany. This was an historic time in West Germany's sporting history, 1972 was the year of the Olympic Games. The Olympics were held in Munich and it was the second time that the Olympics had been held in Germany. The only previous time was the infamous 1936 Games held in Berlin. The Olympics in 1972 were to be overshadowed by the "Munich Massacre" in the Olympic Village, it was the massacre of members of the Israeli Olympic Team.

As a teenager I was very interested in playing sports, mostly football. My brothers and I and were forever playing football and wearing sports clothing. My favourite football boots were Adidas Borussia Dortmund and my favourite trainers were Adidas Roma. This particular year during the summer holidays a group of friends gained access to a local German high school's football pitches. No one seemed to be around. There may have been a caretaker on site, we never saw one the caretaker may well have seen us and may have just turned a blind eye. We took a short cut across the school playground towards the football fields and thinking that it was quieter than usual. In fact it was eerily quiet. As we cut across the fields I noticed a bird of prey on a fence post. – The bird was ripping a field mouse to pieces - since that day I have been fascinated by birds of prey. On This particular day we were meant to be playing a football match against some German children. They never turned up, we had a kick about between ourselves it was silly not to miss such an opportunity to play football on such immaculate football pitches. During the walk home it was noticeable that there were hardly any cars and hardly any people around. When we arrived home my mum said that our dad had been watching the Olympics on the TV. As we entered the living room I remember the TV cameras were showing some flats in the Olympic village. The TV coverage was showing images of the infamous Black September Palestinian terrorist atrocity. Everyone must have been watching the news coverage and the unfolding events live on the TV.

I have mentioned the type of clothing that we wore at the time. My dad did not like the clothes we wore. He disliked the three of us wearing what he referred to as 'those scruffy looking jeans', and as for wearing trainers he could not stand us wearing them either. He did like the Ben Sherman shirts; he liked anything that had a collar. One afternoon there was smoke billowing from one of the back gardens, as we got closer to our house we could see our dad stuffing clothing into a dustbin and burning them. It was clear that it was our clothing that he was burning; jeans, T-shirts and football tops. He was burning our beloved Levi jeans. Inside the house my mum explained that our dad had lost his patience and decided to get rid of our clothes, once and for all. We were told by our dad that we were not allowed to wear jeans and T-shirts any more. Our mum said 'do not worry; I will give you some money to buy new clothes'. The following weekend we were out buying brand new jeans, T-shirts and trainers.

There was a lanky sixth former who travelled on the same school bus. He was very much the 'hippie' type, he always seemed to say 'yeah man', 'cool man' including other slang words. He was forever playing his single vinyl records on a plastic mobile record player, the single would slot between two pieces of plastic, like making a sandwich. He would hold it against his ear; he played music like Yes, Golden Earring and Bony M.

The school was in an old German barracks from the Second World War it was the base for a former Luftwaffe unit (equivalent to the Royal Air Force). The school was a mishmash of modern and old buildings; the maths block was housed in an old Nissen hut style of buildings. I was a prefect at the school and one of my duties as a prefect at lunch time was to make sure that no one smoked during the lunch break. There were only a few subjects at school that I enjoyed - geography, history, sports, technical drawing and metalwork. The school had a large area of sports fields, tennis courts and a running track. I remember the school football strip was the same as Borussia Dortmund's. It consisted of gold/yellow and black, of course I would wear my Adidas Dortmund boots I did look the part. My favourite position on the field was right back; I based myself on the legendary Tommy Smith of Liverpool.

I was selected for the school Rugby team. Enough said about this part of my sporting prowess.

At lunch time, if I was not smuggling people into class rooms for a sly smoke, I would play football. I remember one particular lunchtime. Many weeks before I had upset someone in the year above. As I walked back from the sports fields I was set upon by four other boys, including the boy that I had annoyed previously. I could see them on the path in front of me, shouting and hurling abuse. As I walked past them one of his friends jumped me, and then the rest joined in. One of them had me around the neck and the others were punching me around the head, one of them stuck the boot in. All of a sudden something very hard smashed into

55

my face, cutting my lip and smashing into my teeth. I could see half a building brick on the ground which I assumed was the object that was thrown at my face. As I was struggling to get free, the boy who had me around the neck tightened his grip and I blacked out. I came round on the path, my lips were tingly and my head was spinning. There was blood on the path and covering my football shirt. I went to the changing rooms and took a shower and changed for lessons. My lips were scratched and swollen. My teeth had a bit of discoloration – which was from the blood flowing into them, all in all I was lucky. I vowed to track down those who had done this to me and meted out my own justice.

At the time there were two books that were a great hit with the kids at school. The books were written by Richard Allen and published by New English Library. The title of the books were Skinhead and Suede Head, everyone at school was going mad over them. I had a copy of one and my brother Michael had the other. The first book Skinhead was about a character called Joe Hawkins and his gang of skinheads, it had mindless street violence and easy sex. The second book Suede head was continuation of the same theme. The books were well read.

The two woodwork and metalwork classrooms had large glass windows which looked out over the playground. My brother had woodwork lessons and I had metalwork lessons. On a lunch break I was in the playground there was a crowd of kids gathered around the woodwork class window, someone said 'can you see his thumb'. My brother was also stood in the crowd. He told me the woodwork teacher had been sanding a piece of wood on a lathe; the lathe was positioned close to the window. The teacher screamed out in agony; he had caught his thumb on the sander and it had sliced his thumb off or sanded most of it off. The blood had splashed over the glass window hence the crowd of onlookers.

My English literature lessons were easy and I was under the impression that I would sail through the English Literature exams. I did not read any of the set books. Whenever the class had homework which entailed reading a book I would read the back of the book to see what the book was about. I would flick through the salient points. I would never read the book from cover to cover, and it is a little ironic as in later life I am writing a book. I remember vividly having to go into a room with the English teacher to take the English Oral exam. My English teacher was such a laid back person; we would have music playing during lessons. I can remember one of the girls in the class playing music by the group The Sweet, the song was 'The Ballroom Blitz'.

The chemistry labs were just as bad, especially during the handling of the likes of sulphuric acid. Some of the class poured the concentrated acid onto the work tops. To see how long it would take to burn through. One of the girls had spilt some acid onto her leg. She was wearing tights the acid burnt through the material. Smoke came from her legs as the acid began to burn into the material she was screaming she was in agony. The teacher had to use the first aid ointment on her skin and got her some medical attention; she ended up with a very nasty scar.
During a chemistry theory lesson the teacher was concerned about pupils at the back of the class dozing off. Hidden between the radiators the teacher found mercury in test tubes; these were giving off poisonous fumes and the classroom was evacuated.

The Seventies

Before I leave my formal education reminisces, I would like to mention the school lunches, the dreaded school lunches. I was out for lunch with a good friend of mine many years later and we were talking about the food that we disliked and it reminded me of school lunchtimes. Once again, we had music piped into the dining hall. This particular lunch consisted of liver and onions. I dislike liver and as I sat picking at the mash potato and the liver, a popular song at the time was being piped into the hall. It was 'Mouldy old dough' by Lieutenant Pigeon, and every time I either hear or see the music or liver, it reminds me of this particular lunchtime.

I met my first girlfriend during this period. Her dad was a physical training instructor, and he was in charge of one of the local Army Regiments boxing team. He was also a boxer himself he certainly looked like one. You would not want to mess with him, or his daughter. Her dad owned a Ford Capri, which at the time was smart and cool, considering our dad had his Volkswagen Beetle. Her dad's car was his pride and joy, and groups of kids would look at it and admire it; he would come out of his house and chase them away. Each time he chased them away he would walk around the car to see if anyone had scratched the paint work. It was more than anyone's life was worth if anyone was to damage his beloved car.

Once I left school I worked at the same Army stores depot as my dad. It was a labouring job, offloading and loading military container trucks. The labourers consisted of people from all over Eastern Europe. Most of them were displaced people from the Second World War, and some of them were former German prisoners of war. A few had been incarcerated in various concentration camps. They would have had to be well over fifty years of age. They could speak and read English, unlike myself - who could not speak any of their native tongues. The trucks would drive into the bays and drop the containers off. The containers had various lettering on the sides, and a particular container had the letters 'BB', one of the men shouted unload 'Bridget Bardot'. Some of the men were laughing and were making the shape of a woman's body with their hands I did not know who they were referring to. It was only later when I asked my dad who Bridget Bardot was; he explained that she was a French actress and singer. I was still clueless; it was only later on in life I understood who she was. I asked some of the men why they were still living in Germany and why they had not gone home at the end of the war. Some of them told me that they could never go back whilst the Russians were occupying their countries.

Every Friday afternoon was "happy hour" on the military bases. This would have been a very good time for the Russians to have invaded West Germany. My dad would go off drinking with his mates until late at night. I remember one particular Friday, I had left work and as soon as I arrived home my mum said, "Come on, we are going to find your dad". She got a neighbour to give us a lift back to the barracks. Once we had arrived she headed for the WO's and Sgts Mess (which is like a club). I could see my dad's car in the car park. Once we were in the Mess mum demanded to know where 'her husband' was, everyone denied having seen him since he left work. She was not convinced or amused. After checking the public rooms, there was only the one room remained to be checked. It was the snooker room, my dad was in there and he was very drunk he was still wearing his uniform. When he saw her it was like a red rag to a bull and when he saw me, he shouted, "What the bloody hell are you doing here?" He took one look at me and shouted, "Get your bloody interfering mother out of here." An almighty public row subsequently ensued. The situation was not a new phenomenon to me I was used to it.

One day my dad had managed to get home drunk. He had been drinking most of day and he carried the motions on when he got home. Once again my parents started an almighty argument, as soon as the arguments started the three of us trotted off to our bedrooms. It was the norm for us. I hated the arguing and when we were upstairs we could hear them; it would go on for hours. The crux of the matter would always be about my dad's drinking, my mum would goad him and argue for the sake of arguing. I was always brought into the arguments. As a child this worried me as I did not want to take sides nor upset either of them. I think that this is where my sense of having to please people stems from. I wanted to please both of my parents, it was an impossible position to be in.

My father once again had been drinking in the house and once again my parents started arguing. My brothers and I were sent upstairs, and when my mum called me down I was bare footed.
It was the same old thing; swearing, arguing and shouting at one another. As I entered the room I did not notice a mug on the floor. My dad took a lunge at me – it was not to hit me, his sudden movement made me instinctively step back. My left foot stepped on top of the mug and the rim snapped. What was left of the mug had cut a large V shape into the sole of my foot, the cut was very deep. My dad realised what had happened but he had too much to drink to be able to help me. He shouted at my mum, and her first reaction was to try and cover the cut with plasters; the cut was far too deep and wide for plasters. He told my

mother not to be so bloody stupid and to wrap a towel around my foot. By this time the cut was stinging and my foot was bleeding profusely; shades of Colchester. She got a towel and wrapped my foot in it. To my horror she produced a bottle of disinfectant, I told her not to come anywhere near me with it. My dad was shouting at her not to be so bloody stupid. It was too late; she poured some of it directly into the wound. If I could have sworn I would have done. The pain was unbelievable; it brought tears to my eyes. Once again my dad got a neighbour to drive my mum and myself to the medical centre. I ended up with eight stitches in my foot.

One morning my mum opened the kitchen curtains. She shouted, "Boys, take a look outside and see if the silver car out the front is your dad's". We took a look outside, there was a silver car 'parked' I use the term loosely because the car was wrapped around a tree. We informed mum that there was indeed a silver VW beetle wrapped around a tree. The driver's door and the passenger's door were wide open; my dad it seems had driven home from work and managed to wrap the car around the tree. Some of our neighbours came out and pushed the car back into a parking bay. There was no damage to the tree, but there was considerable damage to the car. VW Beetles have the engine in the back of the car in a normal car it is where the boot is housed. A VW beetle has the boot in the front of the car. The tree had crumpled the front of the car; it does not bear thinking about if he had hit another car or killed someone. Needless to say, when my dad woke up my parents had yet another blazing row. It transpires that he could not remember driving back home the previous evening and had no idea how the car came to be wrapped around a tree.

The Seventies

At the ripe old age of sixteen I was smoking like a trooper. My dad did not approve, but he did not do anything about it. He did not want me to smoke indoors he thought that it would be disrespectful. On my 16th birthday he bought me two hundred JPS (John Player Specials) black. He knew that they were not my favourite cigarette. He may have bought them thinking that if I smoked them it would make me feel sick and possibly give up smoking. I smoked a couple of packets and sold a few. I had my jeans on and decided to go for a swim in a lake and the remaining packets of JPS were stuffed into my pocket. The wet cigarettes ruined my jeans they smelt of tobacco for a very long time. For my birthday I bought myself Black Sabbath's album 'Black Sabbath'.

My brothers and I are very competitive and were always trying to get one up on our dad. One summer's afternoon he set up badminton net and he took us on one by one. We were always trying to beat him but he was always cheating. After the tournament he sat down and complained to my mum of having chest pains. She advised him to get a doctor to check him out. He said he was fine and that he was only out of breath and started drinking his beers. There is a reason for mentioning this incident as it will become more apparent later on in this chapter. Unknown to my brothers and I this was my dad's first heart attack.

The next journey was one that helped me to understand how others treat one another. It would help me to develop an open mind and not to judge others.

My dad moved to Northern Ireland from Germany; at the time I had no intention of moving with my parents. At my age I thought that I knew everything about life and I wanted to find my own way in the world. I thought it would be a lifetime before I would leave home. I had so many plans and ideas and they did not feature moving with my parents. As I was sixteen my dad explained to me that as I was under eighteen and he was responsible for my parental control. He promised me that he would find work for me in Northern Ireland. I had no reason not to take him at his word. We arrived in Northern Ireland in 1973; we were housed in married quarters in Palace Barracks, just outside the small town of Holywood and about six miles outside of Belfast. After we arrived in Northern Ireland my dad never mentioned work again. He finally plucked up courage to tell me that he could not find me a job. This was Northern Ireland at the height of the troubles. He decided to tell me when he had a skin full of booze. He was tipsy, and I was devastated, and I felt trapped. I could not walk out. I found myself stuck on an Army camp with nowhere to go and with no work I was a very pissed off young man. I eventually found work with a small family building company which was based in a town near the coast. The company's work consisted of fixing small buildings and repairing Military Establishments. I had to stand outside of the camp gates to get a lift in the company van. The van had the company's logo painted on the side, if anyone was monitoring me they would have easily have known which company I was working for. We would drive into Belfast and the surrounding area. I stood out like a sore thumb. My work clothes consisted of blood red Dr Martin's boots and parallel Wrangler or Brutus jeans, a Ben Sherman shirt and a red lined parka coat. In winter I would wear a red and white Liverpool bobble hat and scarf. I was the only person standing outside a military establishment waiting for a works van to take me into Belfast; you could not make it up. I had to carry my military style Identity Card wherever I went it allowed me to get back into Palace Barracks after work. Writing this now, many decades later, I think what if anything had of happened to me in Belfast?. I was a sixteen year old English teenager with a Military Camp Identity card; it does not bear thinking about. Palace Barracks was frequently shot at from the main road outside of the camp - chance drive-by shootings and sometimes a bomb would be driven onto the camp.

In 1974 there was the Ulster Workers Council Strike; this was a political strike against the Sunningdale Agreement, regarding Power Sharing and the Council of Ireland. On the first day of the strike my lift turned up as usual. The van headed towards Belfast most workers could not afford to be off work. By the late afternoon there were loyalist paramilitary road blocks. Those manning the barricades were members of the Ulster Defence Association (UDA) and the Ulster Volunteer Force, (UVF) or the Ulster Freedom Fighters (UFF). The works van was heading towards Belfast to complete a construction job at RAF Sydenham, now known as George Best Belfast city Airport, just outside Belfast. It was heading towards a roundabout near the Sydenham bypass. The driver of the van informed us that we were fast approaching an armed barricade. He would do all of the talking. The person manning the blockade was dressed in jeans and an Army style jumper and a ski mask which covered his face with slots for his eyes and mouth. He was armed with a shotgun; we could see him as we approached the checkpoint. He had been instructed that he was authorised to take details of anyone approaching the road block. I thought that this was it - he would question me and find my military camp pass. The driver and the gunman were chatting and joking, and the gunmen let the van turn around and without further ado we drove off. The men in the back of the van asked why the gunman had not taken our details. The driver said that he knew the gunman and nothing further would be said. I thought 'thank god for that'. My heart was pounding ten to the dozen, even though those in the van had reassured me not to worry. No one would hurt me, you are with us. There would be nothing that my co-workers could have done to prevent anything happening. I always kept my thoughts and wits about me.

One 'job' in particular sticks out in my mind. The job was based at Moscow Camp in Belfast, where the company had won a contract to construct a Vehicle Workshop for the Army. Moscow camp was at the end of RAF Sydenham, situated at the far end of Belfast Lough. The weather conditions within the loch were always extreme, including the summer months. There would be sunshine one minute, then sleet, rain and snow all in a matter of minutes. The area was exposed to the elements, there were no natural features that could break up the foul weather. To get to the camp we had to drive into the Belfast docks area and onto the old docks road. There was security to get onto the road was because HMS Maidstone was tied up. The ship was used as a prison ship. It housed (Irish Republican Army), IRA. They were forever trying to escape from the Second World War destroyer.
As we approached the ship for the first time, it looked huge; it was a dark drab looking metal beast, tied up it looked imposing more so when approaching it in the fog. Once the van approached the ship in thick fog it seemed to suddenly appear out of nowhere. There were always Lorries off-loading cargo for the ship. The dock road to Moscow Camp was about three miles long; there was a sharp turning right for half a mile to the camp gates. The camp could be seen in the distance, and all around the area was barren waste land. Winter was one of the worst times to be working outside in the Belfast Lough area. Whenever it

rained, or if any sleet fell. It would feel like sandpaper on exposed skin.

Work soon started, by digging the foundations for the workshop. It took a few days to dig the foundations and place the framework around the hole so that the concrete could set in a nice neat square. Once the cement Lorries arrived we worked so hard to get the concrete out of the trucks and spread it around the mould and in between the reinforced iron bars. Once the concrete was roughly smoothed out, we used metal rods with an air pipe connected to a generator. We inserted pulsating rods into the concrete to ensure that the concrete had got into all the air pockets. We would use long vibrating machines which spread the concrete and levelled it. The company had to construct some hard standing bases around the work shop for the stores buildings. We successfully constructed the concrete bases and built walls, and another building company came in and start to build the side walls and roofs made of wood. These buildings were like the Second World War corrugated Nissen huts. During the bad weather some of us had taken shelter in the huts. Someone decided to set fire to some wooden crates and the straw. Needless to say it was nice and warm; there were no doors or windows in the building. The fire was blazing away, nobody took any notice of the flames or the ash blowing around. Someone outside shouted 'get out of the building - it is on fire'. He shouted, 'the roof is on fire'. We could see above us that it had indeed had caught on fire. A piece of ash must have got stuck in the wood and the wind had fanned the flames. It was practically burnt to the ground, and needless to say the bosses were not very happy, the company profits going up in flames. We were banned from all of buildings. This would seem like small fry to what happened later.

While building the workshop. I was mixing the cement used for the brick work, and it would be one shovel of cement to two shovels to sand in the cement mixer; there were a few of us apprentices. I looked after a small man, providing bricks and mortar he looked more like rod Stewart. In certain areas of the province he would wear Stewart tartan either a tartan scarf or tartan sewn onto his jeans, just like the seventies pop group The Bay City Rollers. If we travelled into Belfast to work he would not wear the tartan. The other brickie I looked after was someone known only as 'Billie'. He was very tall, with a full head of white hair. He did not say a lot he was a man of very few words. He was very alert and did not miss a trick. When he was in his early twenties he was a member of the Black and Tans; they were a force of temporary constables recruited to assist the Royal Irish Constabulary (RIC) during the Irish war of independence. He was in his seventies and kept himself to himself, he did not have an opinion about anything. I did know a little of what the Black and Tans had carried out in Ireland from my school history books. Billie seemed to be the sensible one on the site. The foreman and the bosses left him alone.

This was my first real experience of working on my own in an adult world since leaving school. I had started to come across people that had taken part in some infamous acts in history, depending on one's perception. I will try to cover some of Billie's background. Each day he was always dressed immaculately; there was never any dust or cement on his clothes. He always wore a white shirt under his dungarees. The dungarees were never faded, and he wore brown shoes always clean and polished and he was topped off by a flat cap. He taught me about the different types of bricks and the method of cutting them. He never spoke about his family life or of his background. The other brick layers and site workers talked about themselves all of the time. I had heard a rumour that Billie had lived in Canada for a number of years as a young man, prior to coming back to Northern Ireland. Rumour had it that he had served in the Royal Irish Constabulary (RIC) in the Republic of Ireland during the 1920's. Which would have made him in his seventies when I knew him. The infamous nickname of the RIC was the "Black and Tans". The background to the nickname was due to the uniforms that they wore. They were a mixture of black police uniforms and the Army Khaki uniform, hence "Black and Tan". The RIC was the idea of Winston Churchill it was setup to fight the Irish Republican Army (IRA). Many of those who made up the RIC were unemployed World War One veterans. Billie never spoke of his past, he did confirm that he was a member of the "Black and Tans". For various reasons it was better for him to "disappear", hence his move to Canada. He never mentioned his family. No one in the company knew anything about him or his family. He did have the appearance of a genial old man, I could imagine him as a six foot tall younger man dressed in uniform; he would have looked formidable to anyone having to face him.

There was another old builder. As a young man he had helped build much of the industrial buildings in and around the midlands. He would always be covered in mortar and brick dust. He seemed to have water dripping from his nose; his face was ruddy from being exposed to the elements. He was forever forgetting to do his flies up. - It was not too bad in the winter he wore dirty long johns. – In the summer it was a different matter altogether. The term "commando" springs to mind it was not a pretty sight; the foreman was forever telling paddy to do his flies up, especially if we were working near buildings that housed office workers. He was a prolific brick layer; he was never given apprentices to train as he would arrive at a site and put his head down and lay brick after brick just like a machine.

Getting back to the building of the workshop, at one stage I was told by the foreman to put more shovels of sand to one spade of cement. Billie and the other brickie complained to me about the coarseness of the mixture. At one point we all had to assist, and to evacuate the workshop to assist in raising the metal gables to be raised above each entrance to the workshop. The company had installed strips of aluminium which were to secure the roof to the walls. The roof was made up of a plastic material, which I have seen on swimming pool roofs. We helped the workers from the company who were installing the roof. The plastic was so light it was blowing everywhere, and it was becoming very difficult to slot it into the grooves within the aluminium struts. Once the roof was on and secured it was the Christmas break. We went back to work in between Christmas and the New Year and I got my normal lift to work. Billie was in the van and said "it was the cement". He went on to explain that the mixture was far too sandy. I thought "god what has happened".

As we got to the main gates of Moscow Camp, one of the guards snarled, "Bloody cowboys, you nearly killed us." The workshop looked like a bomb had gone off. At the workshop entrance the doors were twisted, and at the gable end a huge piece of steel was embedded into the concrete leading into the workshop. The inside was wrecked, the offices had files and paper blowing everywhere, and some of the walls had collapsed. We had to tidy up and repair the walls. It seems the company was not to blame, it was the fault of the roofing company. We repaired the gable end and raised the steel gable into place. After a week the carpenters started to install a wooden roof.

The Seventies

It was at Moscow camp that I came across the first Asians in Northern Ireland. We would visit a café on camp for chips and hamburgers and it was run by Asians they had a Belfast accent. When I first entered the hut I could hear voices in a rear room and two Asians came out saying, 'Wot about yer'. It was the very first time I had seen an Asian in Belfast talking with an Irish accent.

The company had a Bedford truck the driver of the truck was a member of the U.D.R (Ulster Defence Regiment). One of the more hair raising jobs was to help him deliver some sand, cement and timber to an Army base in Belfast at the Anderstown bus depot.
The company was converting the cookhouse and an eating area for the soldiers. This particular morning we were approaching the bus depot, and as we neared some shops we could see that a bomb had recently gone off. It had blown up the front of a shop. There was a crowd of people milling around. As we were approaching the damaged shop the driver told me to 'open the glove box'. I opened it and inside was a 9mm Browning pistol.
He had the pistol because he was a member of the UDR (Ulster Defence Regiment) and it was his personal protection weapon. The situation was becoming very serious. Here I was in Belfast near to where a bomb had recently gone off and in possession of a pistol. As we drove along, he told me to look calm, and just look straight ahead. This was easier said than done. I was with a member of the UDR driving through a Republican area of Belfast. Travelling to an Army base, with a loaded pistol, and me an English teenager whose father was serving in the Army. It could not get any worse. He was obviously very aware of the situation that we found ourselves in. The people in the street started to pick up bits of debris on the road and started to throw it at the truck. The driver told me not to worry; this always happens after

an 'Incident'. The small device may have been a distraction to lure the security forces. Whilst the terrorist were moving arms or people around the area. It was so surreal; it was as though we had travelled from a peaceful time to this hate-filled violent world, it all happened so quickly. We managed to get through without being harmed. We eventually arrived at the Army base. Inside the bus depot there were busses that were left many years before. There were lots of soldiers inside, readying themselves to go out on patrol, listening to their radio sets; they were talking about the explosion that had occurred nearby, and they were about to go out and patrol the area and support the police who had arrived at the scene. The bus depot was just like any other bus depot, a large concrete area for the busses, brick walls and a reinforced glass roof. It was a two storey building, the offices, radio and armoury at the bottom and on the top floor was the accommodation and cookhouse. Members of the company were patching up and converting some areas of the cook house. I noticed that in the darker areas of the depot there were shafts of sunlight streaming through the roof; the sunlight was coming through small holes in the glass roof. The holes were made by snipers, taking 'pot shots' at the soldiers. The snipers would fire shots into the bus station at night. As I was talking to some of the builders, a couple of soldiers picked up on my accent. They said "What the bloody hell is an English boy doing working in Belfast. "Are you trying to get yourself killed", they seemed very concerned.

I would to travel to watch Liverpool football club play most home matches. I would leave with a few people from work, and their friends, on a Friday night on the overnight ferry from Belfast to either Liverpool or Morecambe. Most football fans caught the Friday night sailings during the evening heavy drinking took place in the bar area. I will always remember a particular trip; we caught the Belfast to Morecambe ferry, which was a nightmare as we had to get from Morecambe to Liverpool on coaches. On this particular ferry trip there were Liverpool and Manchester United fans. It all started off well in the bar and there was plenty of drinks and football banter, and as you can imagine lots of people getting drunk. Last orders were called and that was it, it was like a red rag to a bull. The shutters to the bar were closed. The people in the bar forced the shutters up, they were buckled by the sheer use of force. There was fighting raging in and around the bar area. We awoke next morning feeling rough and, not having had too much sleep. As the ship docked an announcement came over the tannoy system informing all football fans that they had to remain behind while passengers left the ferry. As we were herded down the gang way to the quayside we could hear the police dogs barking, and as we approached, the dogs were straining at their leashes. Members of the ships company were pointing out the trouble makers. We were herded over to the coaches that were conveying some of us to Anfield, Liverpool's football ground. The Manchester United supporters boarded their respective coaches there was a lot of shouting from one set of supporters to the other, including lots of hand gestures. On the coach journey there was a lot of banter between the people sat at the front of the coach and the coach driver. The coach driver got his own back when he got to Liverpool; he parked the coach at Goodison Park, which is Everton FC's ground, Liverpool's arch rivals in the city. There were some Everton fans milling around the car park. They spotted our coach, and saw the red and white scarves, and started to throw stones at the coach. The driver must have realised that his plan had back fired and quickly drove the coach to Anfield, which was across from Stanley Park; which divides Everton FC from Liverpool FC. After the match we travelled back to Morecambe to get the ferry to Belfast. There were not as many Manchester United fans on the return trip. This time two RUC (Royal Ulster Constabulary) policemen were on the ferry. It was on this trip that I got talking to one of the truck driver's sons, he told me that he had been in the British Army for three years. I said to him 'just because I was English it did not mean that I was interested in the Army'. He was boasting and I was not at all interested. He said that he was going to release his brother from jail. I thought he was just bluffing; he was the brother of a terrorist.

I was working at a secluded house in County Down. The company had to build a substantial porch onto the front of the house. There were four working on this particular job. When the door arrived it was solid oak and a substantial size, it was very heavy indeed. One time when I was in the toilets I could hear voices. I told my friend who I was working with that I had heard voices coming from the garage, he said 'Don't be stupid, it's just a garage'. He went into the toilet block and said, 'I can't hear anything'. We went to the front of the garage and tried to open a door. We banged on the door, just in case someone was in the garage and may have needed help. When we got back to work we mentioned it to the other workers and they told us not to meddle and to stay away from the other buildings around the house. About an hour later a man came to the front of the house. He was smartly dressed in a suit, shirt and tie. Clearly visible were the scars on his face. He asked who was knocking on the garage door earlier. I said that it was me. As soon as he heard my accent he asked me what I was doing at the house. I told him, leaving out the important bits, as I did not know who he was. He said that he was a driver and he drove a judge around from Belfast to his home, which was the house that we were working at. The porch was for added security. We asked the driver how he got his scars thinking perhaps in a car crash. He said that his scars were caused by a bomb blast. Some members of his family had been killed in a bomb attack. It was whilst on this job that I came across the truck driver's other son. He was a dustman, and part of his round was at the judge's house, and as I mentioned earlier we all used to go to watch Liverpool play football. Also, his brother – the one in the Army. It was in the July that I found out that the brother the one who was a dustman had murdered a local teenager. The brother was a member of a banned loyalist paramilitary group. It turned out that he had murdered a sixteen year old boy. He had carried out a gross act of murder; the killer by all accounts was a member of the UVF (Ulster Volunteer Force) a protestant Terrorist Organisation.

The company carried out a lot of work at RAF Sydenham. It was during this period that I got into the group Super Tramp and bought their album Breakfast in America. Then there were no MP3's IPod's nor CD Players, some of the younger members of the company had radios and would play Radio 1.

On a Friday, those who lived in the town of Holywood - and myself, we would visit a particular pub and the landlord would cash our Giro cheques. He would only do it after we had spent a certain amount at the bar. In those days it would be a couple of rounds of Guinness or Harp Larger, one or two of the older ones would have a whisky or brandy.

One of the barracks, Kinnegar, was the main ordnance depot in Northern Ireland. The company had a contract to dig the trenches and concrete the heating ducts under the ground. One particular occasion we finished early. Everyone was in the works van, and as a joke the van started to drive off. I noticed it pulling off and I shouted and swore at them. They opened the back doors and told me to catch up with them. I forgot about the concrete trenches and fell into one of them, and my god did it hurt. I managed to hobble to the van, and everyone was laughing and some had tears rolling down their faces. Someone asked me in between laughs if I had hurt myself. I replied 'no' through gritted teeth. They told me that it was so funny watching me shouting trying to catch up, then all of a sudden disappearing into a hole in the ground. I thought 'yes very funny, I don't think so'.

I went to watch the first Northern Ireland versus England football match at Windsor Park stadium in Belfast during "the troubles". One the carpenters that I knew from work had a car. He drove the car through Leeson Street, which was in a staunchly nationalist area of the city. Most of the front doors to the houses did not have a front door, they seemed to have an internal porch. This was so that they either got more benefits or did not pay the full council rent, due to inferior housing. As we drove down the road people were chasing the car and shouting. The driver drove away very quickly I asked why did those people look angry, he said, "Look on the back window." Laid along the back shelf of the car was a loyalist flag. I felt physically sick; it was a very dangerous act of foolishness and stupidity.

There were many lighter notes living in Northern Ireland. Such as the time, at the height of fashion, wide lapelled shirts, flared or high waist trousers and of course the ubiquitous platform shoes. I thought that I looked "cool" and decided to walk into the local town wearing my shoes. I got half way into town and fell over, and there were people driving past and pointing at me on the ground and laughing. To them it must have looked funny, to me my pride had been severely dented.

On Friday afternoons it was always pay day, and the company Pay Clerk would travel around the various building sites and hand out our pay packets. Initially we were paid cash, but then the company switched to paying by GIRO cheque. When I lived in Northern Ireland I did not have a bank account. A few of us had to find a friendly publican where we could cash our cheques. There was only one stipulation: we had to buy a minimum of three pints each.

My father suffered his second heart attack at his place of work. He was transferred from the Military Hospital in Belfast to a specialist hospital in London. During his recovery period, he remained in England, as a family we were not moved back to England; this must have been a decision made by my father.
We were to remain in Northern Ireland, and till this day I cannot get my head around why he made that decision.

There was an occasion when we were working in Belfast; we were working on a small job in a security area. It was a Friday, and we had just got paid, and we all had some money. We would not cash the GIRO cheques in Belfast the van driver drove around and thought that he found a 'safe' pub to drink in. I had no idea which was a safe place in Belfast if it smacked me in the face. As soon as we stepped into the pub on the wall was a Republican Flag. We had walked into a Republican pub; I had no idea where we were. All of a sudden I felt vulnerable and alone, but deep inside of me I was sweating. I thought: oh my god, what the hell has happened here? We sat down and the others said to me, "You shut up, do not open your mouth, or we are all dead men"

I nodded my head; and I think that I was in a state of shock, we put our change on the table and someone got the round. He came back with the pints, and he said to me, "Do not knock it back, we are being watched." We finished our drinks and left, as the van drove off someone was stood in the door way. I felt sick, and someone was actually sick. We drove out of Belfast thanking our lucky stars.

After Northern Ireland my father was posted to a small German Hamlet called Viersen, in West Germany, the closest town is Monchengladbach. It is very close to the British Military Headquarters at Rheindahlen. At the time my father worked in one of the main stores depots in West Germany. There was a British Army Printing section based in the town as well. I eventually got to work in the printing section. It is where I met my future wife, and I know that this may seem a little corny she was the girl living next door with her parents. There were two elderly people in the house, whom I thought were her parents staying with her on holiday from the UK. I never did see the 'husband'. After a while my mum and dad said that she was the elder daughter of the old couple, her father was in the RAF working at the stores depot. The children were her younger brother and sister she had three brothers who were much older. At first she did not seem too interested in me, I found out that she was seeing a soldier in the Tank Regiment. I continued to work in the printing section; at least I had a wage.

My brother Michael decided to join the Army; he joined the Royal Signal Junior Leaders in Harrogate. Because he was a boy soldier my dad had to sign his enlistment papers, my mum seemed to be OK about it.

I met the girl next door's brother Stephen, he was in the Army. He came over to visit his parents, and I went into town a few times with him, chatting up German women and having a few beers. My dad was not too keen on him as Stephen was in the Army and, as he said, to me 'he is so much worldlier than you'. On a few occasions he took his sister out with him and I got to know her. She was very pleasant, we played badminton a lot, but her mum was very suspicious of me, and of my intentions towards her daughter. I continued to see her daughter we eventually became engaged, looking back we did not have a clue about the world; we lived with our parents and everything was provided for us. I was very naive, at this point we were just seeing one another.

While we lived in Viersen and I worked at my dad's camp I started working in the main store shed. Distributing stores around West Germany, there were many social functions and the opportunity to drink. On one particular occasion I had a few drinks and on the way home there was a chip van serving the traditional German Bratwurst and chips. I ordered some food as I have mentioned I had been drinking. I told the man that was serving me to get the money off my dad, he knew my dad, just then I felt a stinging sensation around my ear. I shouted 'who the hell is that'. It was my dad. He paid the man and clipped me around the ear again and told me get home.

The village was on the flight path of NATO (North Atlantic Treaty Organisation) military aircraft, the aircraft that stands out in my mind was the Lockheed F-104 Starfighter jet. It was a supersonic interceptor. The aircraft flying over the village were the German Air Force's Starfighters, and they made one hell of a racket.

The Germans nicknamed the aircraft, the widow maker, as a high proportion of them had mishaps - that is putting it mildly, and of course many of the pilots were killed.

I was moved to the printing section on camp and worked with a German chap called Franz. He thought that it was his mission to teach me German, I think that I frustrated him somewhat. We worked on the huge electronic guillotine and he was very safety conscious, and for a very good reason – I was working for him. When operating the guillotine there was an automatic safety feature. This consisted of a beam of light if the beam was broken it would cut the power to the guillotine. When Franz was out of the workshop I would use the guillotine. I would mess around with the guillotine and see if the safety beam worked, I did this by stupidly placing one of my hands under the blade and with the other, press the button to bring the blade down to cut whatever was on the cutting plate, I have to say I was a very lucky young man and a very stupid one.

It was in this year that the world news covered the North Vietnamese invasion of South Vietnam. Including the fall of Saigon in the south, watching film footage of the Americans and South Vietnamese being evacuated from Saigon.

I eventually joined the Army, and I also joined the Royal Signals. I was reluctant to join up; I did it because I wanted a career. My training was carried out in Catterick, near Richmond, North Yorkshire. My basic training was carried at 11 Signal Regiment, Helles Barracks Catterick Garrison. The name Helles is derived from Helles in Gallipoli, Turkey, the area was fought over during the First World War in 1915. Part of the Basic Training was to learn to march as a body of men and as an individual, field craft, fitness, and being able to fire a rifle. I am right handed but my stronger eye is the left. During training prior to moving onto the rifle Range. Everybody had to learn about the Self Loading Rifle (SLR). This consisted of learning to strip the Rifle and to clean it, I also had to carry out dry training including how to use the rifle having various stoppages to the rifle. For me it was routine until the troop moved onto live firing. It was at this point that I learnt that I could not shoot using my right eye. During the first live firing I decided to swap the rifle from my right shoulder and place it into my left shoulder. I used my right hand and tried to move it over to the left side 'cack' handed. It was at this point that the range staff started swearing and shouting. One of the range staff approached me and said, "What the fuck do you think that you are playing at?" I said, "I cannot fire it with my right eye, it is too weak." After a few more days we were taken back on the range and the Warrant Officer kept an eye on the 'difficult children in the troop', which included me. When I was on the range and I could hear the Warrant Officer saying to me, "Don't shoot any fucking sheep." I kept my eye on the targets and fired off all of my rounds, I remember a large white thing move at the back of my target. I let off a round and the white ball of fluff, soon started turning red, and whatever it was crumpled to the ground. The Warrant Officer went ballistic with me I thought he was going to burst a blood vessel. I said "what the fuck was that"? He said, "That my son was a dead sheep". I knew I was in the mire. The Range Warden stepped out of his hut and said to the Warrant Officer he should be using a left-handed Rifle; you cannot blame him ...During my twenty two years of service I was never issued with a left-hand rifle. I adapted and learnt to shoot with a right-handed rifle, I still used my left eye. The weather in the summer of 1976 was one of the hottest on record, temperatures in some places it rose to 27C (80F) – 32C (90F). During the troop exercise phase of training, the streams on the moors had dried up. There were dead sheep and animals in and around the dried up waterways. They had tried to access what little water remained at the bottom of the stream. It was easy for an animal to get into the gully or river bed it was impossible to get out and in the end they perished.

The room that I shared with others during my military training had a mixture of people that were from all walks of life. There was someone whose father worked in the diplomatic service and had travelled from Cyprus. Someone from Lincoln, and I think he worked for a short while on fishing boats. There was someone who must have been in his thirties when he signed up, he obviously lied about his age. He struggled to complete any physical training, including drill and other physical aspects of the training. During the coffee and cigarette breaks he would collapse on his bed and have a quick sleep. At lunch time and tea time he would lie on the top of his bed and drop off to sleep completely exhausted. He looked much older than he was.

One afternoon we got back to our room and he was gone. We were summoned to the Officer Commanding's office, there was a civilian policeman and a Royal Military Policeman present. We had to write a statement regarding everything that we knew about the soldier. The police were interested in every aspect of what he had told us over the past few weeks, it was not a great deal. We were told that he was on the run and wanted for criminal activity in Manchester.

I look back on this time and think that I have two children and grandchildren of my own. I would never have put any of them in the same position that my parents placed me in. I realise how dangerous the situation was. I count myself very lucky that nothing ever happened to me. I am also glad that the people of Northern Ireland are living in relative peace.

Chapter 4 - My Moves In and Around West Germany

As soon as I had completed my trade training I was posted to 2nd Armoured Division and Signal Regiment. The Regiment at the time was based in West Germany, close to a small town called Bunde.

There was nothing much on the entertainment front in the town, apart from drinking beer or visiting the town's brothel. As I was engaged to be married, the latter was definitely off limits. The camp was surrounded by farmer's fields. There was one German pub nearby, it was a mile from the camp. There was a farmer who lived close to the camp. Everyone knew that he would try and encourage the Army Air Corps helicopter pilots to skim over his crops. Rumour had it that he would frequently submit claims to the authorities for damaged crops. I once had a ride in a gazelle helicopter. The pilot skimmed alongside the autobahns (motorways) and sailed across the fields. It was like flying in a goldfish bowl. The view of the outside from inside was absolutely amazing.

The accommodation on camp consisted of single storey buildings, and at the end of every second block there was a bar, one for each squadron. I would frequent the three bells club, which belonged to Three Squadron. On the first day of my arrival I reported to the guardroom. This is the focal point for any new arrival. No-one knew that I was arriving and subsequently there was nowhere to stay or to report to in the morning, I was housed in the transit accommodation. In the Headquarters (HQ) squadrons transit accommodation. The room was a mess, and it smelt of decaying food.

On the Monday morning I reported to The Regimental Headquarters (RHQ). I reported to the Orderly Room, the main administration department within a regiment, and was informed that no one knew why I was posted to the Regiment. Eventually I had to report to the Superintendent Clerk, who was a Warrant Officer Class 1 Clerk, and he was the most senior clerk in the Regiment. I marched into his office, and he asked me the same questions as everyone else had; what was my Regimental number and where was my posting order, this consisted of a piece of paper with my posting details. I produced it and it clearly showed that I was posted to the Regiment. He informed me that they did not require another Electronics Draughtsman, as they had recently had two posted to the Regiment, one from basic training. I had come across him during my training and the other one was posted from 7 Signal Regiment based in Herford, West Germany.

I had to report to the Squadron Sergeant Major, (SSM) of Headquarters Squadron. I went to his office. He was a Gordon Highlander attached to the Regiment. He ordered me into his office, and I smartly marched in. He shouted at me, he had such a strong Scottish accent I did not catch everything that he had said, I got the gist of what he was saying. When he finished, he asked me if I had any questions, I had lots, I said "no Sir". "Good, get out of my office and report to the Guardroom immediately." I can remember him telling me to report to the Guardroom or at least the word Guardroom was mentioned, and that is what I did.

The Guardroom was to become the focal point for me during those first couple of days in Bunde. Once I arrived at the guardroom a Corporal shouted, "What do you want?" I told him that I was to report to the guardroom, what I should have said was I needed to report to the Regimental Police Sergeant, RP Sergeant. I told the Corporal my story, I would have to repeat the same story time and time again, he said, "OK you are on the Night shift. You start next week, you have a week off before you start, get settled in and find your way around the camp." On a notice board outside there were a few photographs of important people in the Regiment, along with their names. He told me to study the pictures and the names. I looked at him and thought that he was joking so I took a cursory glance and walked off.

I unpacked my military kit and starched and ironed my uniform, ready for a week of night shifts. On the Wednesday there was a loud bang on the door of my room (at this point I still had not met my room-mates). It was the RP Sgt (Sergeant) with the Corporal from the guardroom. The Sgt barked, "Where the fuck have you been, I have been, looking for you, for two fucking days." I replied that the Corporal had told me that I was on the next RP night shift. In front of the sergeant he denied that he had said anything of the kind. I learned very quickly that not everyone was as honest or trustworthy as I was. I was ordered to get changed into my uniform and to report for the day shift. Commanding Officer's (CO's) orders were taking place that day and the RP staff needed everyone they could muster for escort duty. Escort duty is required for anyone found guilty of a misdemeanour and is sentenced to a period of time in jail. When I got to the Guardroom the RP Cpl told me, "Anymore messing around and I would find myself on CO's orders, and not to drop him in it again." Over time I got to know him better and I never trusted him. I met up with him many years later and he was still a Corporal. I settled into the RP, Regimental Police, way of life and it was a totally different existence from the other soldiers in the Regiment. One morning there was a room inspection it was carried out by the HQ Sqn SSM. I found out that the people sharing the room were Army Chefs working at the officer's mess at the Divisional Headquarters in Lubecke. There were always salvers of food under their beds and it was starting to rot and smell. On one occasion the door opened and it was the SSM I stood by my bed, the SSM went ballistic over the state of the room. I got both barrels from him, every time I saw him something was wrong, and if anything was out of order or incorrect he would target me. I was in his sights. I did not like it at all; it was a very uncomfortable feeling.

During this time there was a spate of soldiers being attacked during the night in their beds whilst asleep. I was informed that one of the vehicle mechanics was in hospital with a serious head injury. The assailant had accessed the room via an open window and smashed the mechanic over the head with a hammer. Over the next few months the perpetrator went onto assault a couple more people. He was eventually caught and court martialled and jailed for a considerable length of time in a civilian prison in the United Kingdom.

By now it was Christmas 1976; I had to stay on camp due to my RP duties. I did not see my fiancée or my family over that particular Christmas. On New Year's Eve 1976 I was working the day shift everyone who was on the day shift on 1 January 1977 went out on New Year's Eve. It was a full on drinking session, and we ended up getting a taxi into Bunde Town centre. It was the fashion for men in the seventies to wear jewellery, bracelets and gold chains. During the evening it got to the stage that we could not pay the bar bill. The landlord asked for the various bits of gold that we were wearing. He was satisfied that he had enough to pay the bill and have a bit left over for his troubles. We ended up walking back to camp. We eventually got back to camp in the early hours of the morning. As we entered the camp the night shift, were shouting out of the windows of the guardroom. Yelling at us not to be late relieving them from duty in the next few hours. The next morning everyone turned up for guard, albeit with hangovers. I may have looked smart, but inside I felt like shit. We were inspected by the guard commander, who was a corporal. He inspected the guard prior to the Orderly Officers inspection. The Orderly Officer inspected the guardroom and read the diary of events which the guard commander and the second in command of the guard would have to complete. The next working day one of the guard commanders would have to take the Diary of events to the Regimental Sergeant Major (RSM). The Orderly Officer inspected the guard he made a comment about how we all stank of booze. Since this was the day after New Year's Eve he would let it go. He said that he wanted a nice quiet day. I was chosen for the first guard stint because the guard commander thought that I was the least affected by the booze, how wrong he was. He should have chosen someone else. I may have looked less drunk than the others but I felt as rough as hell.

The entrance to the camp had two very large iron gates that were closed at midnight and opened again early in the morning. During the day the main gates stayed open, about fifty meters away from the main gate there was a set of swinging gates which allowed the guard to check identity cards.

My moves in and around West Germany

Early on New Year's morning we thought that it would be quiet on guard since no one usually came onto camp, especially early on New Year's Day. I began to swing on the barriers to amuse myself and my hat fell off. I was just picking it up and placing it back on my head. When the RSM drove onto the camp. I made the mistake of saluting him; the only people you salute in the Army are officers, definitely not the RSM. He pulled into the Guardroom car park, did not look happy at all. He strode into the guardroom. The sliding window opened and I could see the guard commander and the RSM looking towards me, the RSM was pointing in my direction. The guard commander looked petrified, and I then realised that I was in deep manure. I watched the RSM leave and get back into his car and drove off. He looked bloody angry I could see steam escaping from his ears. I finished my two hour shift and was relieved by someone else, who looked even rougher than me. He had been woken up, after having two hours to sleep off the booze. I entered the guardroom and the guard commander said, "You're in the shit the RSM is not impressed with you. You have to report to him on Tuesday the 4th of January.

I prepared myself for the worst and ironed my "best kit", which was the khaki No2 dress uniform. I bulled my boots (notice that there is a lot of bulling and shining of boots in the Army). I made sure that my best hat was immaculate. The first morning back at work I stood outside the RSM's office, and I was petrified. I turned up early and made sure that I did not crack the polish on my bulled boots. I was the first in line outside his office. The RSM entered RHQ and I immediately came to attention. The RSM went into his office, and shouted, "You have any of the guard commanders turned up yet"? I shouted, "No sir." "What's your name?" I replied, "Hearn Sir." "Hearn, go next door and make me a coffee NATO standard, (which meant) white two sugars." "Yes Sir," I replied. I went next door to the Orderly Room. The Orderly Room Sergeant was there, (ORS), and he reminded me of Sgt Wilson in Dad's Army. I told him that the RSM wanted a cup of coffee. "Dear boy," he said, "the brew kit is over there do help yourself". I took the coffee to the RSM and remained stood outside his office. The guard commanders began to turn up, and the one that was on guard when I was caught by the RSM saluting was outside the office. The RSM called them in one by one. They had to explain what had happened during their tour of duty he checked the diary of events. Soon I was the only one left. He shouted, "Hearn, March in, and make sure that you do not salute this time." He told me to explain myself and my actions on New Year's Day, and then he balled me out. There was a desk across from him in his office he ordered me to stay in his office. He left and when he returned he said, "From now on you are my Clerk, The RSM's Clerk." Becoming the RSM's clerk meant that I had to maintain his discipline books, for those who found themselves on Commanding Officers Orders. I had to make sure that the Squadron clerks had typed the charge sheets correctly, and that the conduct sheets were together. The RSM would take the book, charge sheets (AFB 252's) and conduct sheets into the CO. Those on a charge had to march into the CO's office with the RSM. Lined up close to the RSM's office would be the soldiers, Officer Commanders (OC's), Sergeant Major's (SSMs) and the RP Sergeant and members of the RP staff. They were there to march anyone away who had been sentenced to a spell in the Regiment's jail. I was also the CO's exercise clerk. I collated his maps that had to be put together for the various exercises. I completed the tasks so well that the Superintendent Clerk had to supply a clerk to the RSM and CO whenever I was on holiday. Most of the clerks dreaded me going on holiday.

My moves in and around West Germany

During this period of time in Germany the British Army did not arm the guards with rifles; instead they were armed with pick helves, which is the wooden shaft of a pick axe. If we were shot at, the guard commander could authorise the issue of rifles. We had been briefed that there had been a spate of fires on the parade square where the Royal Corps of Transport (RCT) had their mobilisation vehicles parked up. The vehicles were packed with fuel and ammunition, ready for a Russian/Warsaw Pact invasion of West Germany. All of the Regiments in West Germany had pre-determined war deployment areas to move into, prior to any invasion of West Germany. Getting back to this particular guard duty; I was guarding the gate, the main gates had been closed and locked. The gates were always locked at midnight. If anyone arrived at the camp there was a pedestrian gate with which they could enter and show their identification. Before the main gate there was a swing barrier and a guard hut. I was stood near the swing barrier in the early hours of the morning. Suddenly I could hear a Stalwart amphibious vehicle (stolly) start up, the engine has a deep throaty sound when it starts. The Guard Commander opened the window and shouted, "Stop the next vehicle trying to leave camp." I could hear the vehicle approaching the gates. It seemed to be travelling very fast. I was stood on the pavement, the guard commander shouted, 'Hearn, stop it.' I thought, 'What, with a bloody piece of wood?' Anyway, it drove past me, and smashed through the main gates even though the gates were closed. The gates were written off; they were a pile of twisted metal and rubble. The guard commander came running out and was swearing and ranting at me, "Why the fuck did you not stop that vehicle?" I looked at him in total disbelief, he blurted out, "You're on a charge in the morning!" I said, "What for?" He replied "For not apprehending the person who just stole that military vehicle. Oh, and for not jumping in front of the vehicle and using your pick helve." The vehicle is a five Ton piece of motorised metal. He was having a laugh, bloody idiot. Common sense prevailed and the charge was eventually thrown out.

In 1977 I married my fiancé and it was a quiet affair in Rheindahlen West Germany it was in the Garrison church, both of our families attended. It was a church wedding, for some reason I could not smile. There was no honeymoon we moved immediately into a private hiring instead of a Military Married Quarter. This was due to lack of points; the military at the time had a points system for allocating housing. I had been in the Army for less than a year, I was only a Signalman (Private), and my rank was not sufficient for many points. I qualified for a private hiring; these were Ministry of Defence (MOD) approved Local German housing or flats/maisonettes. I was allocated a maisonette near to one of the Army Housing estates. It was convenient as I could get a lift to camp. I managed to get a nice maisonette in a local German's house. The owners lived in the downstairs part of the house, and we had part of the upstairs and our own entrance to the maisonette. One evening the owners invited us downstairs and introduced themselves. We were sat on a settee and the owners sat in separate chairs. I noticed a photograph of the man in a German police uniform; he had been the local village police chief before he retired. My wife nudged me and nodded towards another picture at the other end of the sideboard. It was the owner in a black and white photograph; he was much younger, he looked about twenty. He was wearing German Army uniform during World War Two. He had a metal plated necklace (gorget) which indicated that he was in the Military Police. His cap badge had the skull and cross bones and lightning flashes on the collar of his jacket. He was dressed in the uniform of an SS (Shutz Staffel) soldier. He noticed that I was looking at the picture. He said "there were lots of good men in the SS not everyone was bad". I thought try telling the poor souls who had the misfortune to cross their path. After the war he came back to the village and joined the newly formed West German Police force.

Every month the majority of the Regiment had to attend the Regimental Sergeant Major's (RSM's) Drill Parade. The parade format consisted of the Squadron Sergeant Majors (SSM's) and all other ranks. It was to instil discipline. It was the RSM's big day. One has to remember at the time I was the RSM's clerk. Back at the flat I had prepared my boots, they were bulled up and they looked immaculate, I was wearing my best uniform, and my Number Two dress hat, best peaked hat. I had my boots on, which were highly bulled, there was a knack to walking in the boots to stop the polish from cracking. I asked my wife if she could trim my hair as I thought that my hair was a little bit too long she used a pair of very sharp scissors. As she cut around one ear, she said "Oops, I am really sorry'. I could feel the warmth of the blood trickling down my ear. I got a towel and put it against my ear. She showed me the scissors, and on one of the blades was the skin from the top of my ear. This was not an excuse not to go parade. I got a plaster and placed it over the cut, and cleaned up the blood on my ear and neck. Luckily the blood had not dripped onto my shirt. I got into the car to take me to camp, and the driver said, "That looks bloody sore." I told him what had happened and he said, "That would not excuse you from attending the parade, especially as you're the RSM's clerk". I said, "Tell me about it." When we arrived at the camp my Squadron had formed up outside the HQ Squadron office. The SSM called out our names. He marched the squadron to the parade square.

Before we attempted any drill the RSM shouted out the squadron he was going to inspect and this time he chose the unit that I was in, HQ Squadron. There was a murmur in the ranks, 'bloody hell he has chosen us'. I thought 'Now I have had it'. During the inspection the Provost Sergeant was present including some Regimental Policemen, RP's staff, and the HQ Squadron's SSM. I heard the RSM shouting at people as he inspected them. Any soldier who was not up to the required standard, would be marched off the parade and detained in the guardroom. Before marching the soldier off the parade ground, a member of the Provost Staff had a wheelbarrow, and the soldiers' rifle would be collected and placed into the wheelbarrow. It was my turn to be inspected by the RSM he stood in front of me with his pace stick; he went behind me checking if everything was in order, things like the length of my hair and if the uniform was ironed and clean. He looked me up and down, then pointed his pace stick at my ear that was covered by the Elastoplast he shouted, "What the bloody hell is that?" I did not answer him, as he had not told me that I could answer. He was still pointing at my ear. Then the Provost Sergeant shouted, "Hearn, fall out". He was about to March me away to the guardroom, the RSM shouted, "Stand still, Hearn, you're not going anywhere. I asked you what the bloody hell have you done to your ear." I told him, "I have cut the tip of the ear off, Sir." I thought that this was it. He said, "You are not going anywhere; I want a nice hot cup of coffee on my desk when the parade is over." The Regiment remained on parade and marched around for nearly an hour.

In Germany there was an operational requirement for the married personnel to be notified of any operational or exercise call outs, it was known as Active Edge. The results of the call outs were passed onto higher organisations. It was the Divisional

Headquarters who would collate the operational call outs in the Divisional Area and forward them to 1 (British Corps), 1 (BR) Corps. They then forwarded the Corps area data onto Headquarters British Army of the Rhine, HQ BAOR. The data was very important. The data would show how quick the Regiment could deploy on a war footing should it ever arose. When I took up the post as the RSM's clerk it was only one of the roles I took on. The call out was previously maintained by the Regimental Orderly Room, but it was not working very well and it was roughly 65% efficient. Since the RSM had gained a clerk, the role was transferred to the RSM, and I subsequently maintained the call out lists. I went through the home addresses of all of Regiment's married personnel. I had to nominate a person in the street or block of flats. They were responsible for waking everyone up. I came into camp one morning and Regimental personnel were dressed in combat gear, looking as though they were going on exercise. I saw the RSM near some vehicles and he bellowed, "My offices, and stay there, do not move and do not pass go." I arrived at the RHQ and went into the typist office and made a cup of coffee. One of the clerks then said, "You're in the shit, there was an Active Edge called early this morning." The penny dropped; I had not added my name on the call-out sheets! I returned to the RSM's office and checked the call-out list that I had prepared. I knew that my name was not on the list.

The RSM came back and marched me into the CO's office, and I thought 'God, I've had it now." The CO said, "Well done, Hearn, the Regiment had a 99% call out this morning. I am extremely pleased with your work, it is a pity that we did not have a 100% call out. I am sure that you will eventually put your name on the list." I replied, "Yes Sir, I am sure I can manage that." I saluted and was marched out of his office. I got back to the RSM's office and he said, "You were bloody lucky that we had 99% call out." I had to type out a new list, which included my name and address. In those days there were no photocopiers, everything was typed on 'skins' and then printed on Gerstetner machines. As I entered the Orderly room to get permission to use the Gerstetner. The clerks were talking about me having been marched into the CO's office. I took the sheets to the guardroom to put them into the Active Edge drivers' folders and placed a new sheet with my details on them. The Provost Sergeant was there with his side-kick. "Ah, Hearn, I would not have liked to have been in your shoes this morning, and I bet you got a right bollocking from the RSM and CO."I just said, "Oh yes, it was such a bollocking." Whenever the Regiment deployed on Exercise (Manoeuvres), I went out and worked with the Regimental Operations team. This was manned by the second in command of the Regiment, RSM, and The Regimental Yeoman of Signals. The Commanding Officer would come and sit in at certain points of an exercise. I remember one particular exercise when the Regiment was housed in a dense wooded location. I was asked to help some of the Squadron who were setting up the Headquarters complex in the woods. They were struggling with a generator on a trailer. It was so difficult manoeuvring it we moved it by hand. The Corporal in charge was a bit of a jobs worth, and he was meant to be guiding the rest of the group who were holding the tow hook.

He was at the front guiding us, the generator was so large we could not see in front of it. He managed to direct the generator down a slight incline, the generator was so heavy that the incline was like a sheer drop. We could not control it anymore, and let it go. The corporal was panicking as he realised what was happening. He shouted, "Hang on for dear life." We watched as it bounced down the hill, it was bouncing off trees, watching bits of metal being ripped off the generator; it was pretty obvious that it was write off, it looked damaged beyond repair. After the exercise there was a Regimental Board of enquiry.

It was on the same exercise that I was asked to sit with a detachment commander in a Radio Relay vehicle. These vehicles normally had a three man crew, as the crews were operating twenty four hours a day. I tried to chat to him but without any joy. I suggested that if he got some sleep, he would be fit enough and refreshed to drive. I said that I had worked out the basics of the electronic equipment. He said that he could not sleep. He told me about why he was sad and quiet. At the start of the day there were two of them. The second crew member had a fatal accident. He explained that the pneumatic mast equipment was not working correctly, so the mast had to be winched up by hand; these were substantial masts, the crew member had to somehow hand crank the mast up. Bearing in mind the vehicle was in a dense forest, the mast came in contact with some overhead live electricity cables. He was winding the mast higher and higher and was unfortunately electrocuted. I stayed overnight and the next morning until another crew turned up to relieve the detachment commander, who was taken off the exercise; I went back to the operations Cell. No one said anything to me; they knew what had happened, and they had not told me before I left.

In 1978 my daughter was born. At the time I was on exercise deep in the German countryside. The Superintendent Clerk at the time turned up in a wood in his civilian car. His car was a bright yellow Renault and it stood out a mile. I turned up at the hospital dressed in my exercise kit I got there just in time. I was sent to the maternity ward and my wife had been moved to a single room next to the delivery room. The film The Exorcist had just been released. The film was about a poltergeist taking over

96

someone's soul and a priest was going to perform an exorcism on the person. My wife shouted "what the hell have you done to me, I am never going to let you near me after this". I thought blimey, 'I had better hold her hand and comfort her'. I grabbed her hand, and she was in labour, not that I really knew anything about it. I was holding her hand when she had a contraction and nearly broke every bone in my hand; I did not realise she had so much strength. It was then that I thought if she could twist her head around three hundred and sixty degrees she would look like the main character in the film. Anyway, she was taken to the delivery room at the end of the corridor. I sat on a chair in the room, thinking 'That's it, my job here is done'; at least I made it to the birth. A nurse came to get me and I was ushered into the delivery room. As I got closer the noise was getting louder and louder. I thought to myself what the hell is that all about? I was about to find out. I was told to hold my wife's hand, remembering what had happened earlier when she nearly broke my hand, she shouted 'hold my bloody hand'. This time I was lucky, no bones were broken. My wife gave birth to our lovely daughter. She was long and had a grey colour to her skin. I also noticed that she had a lot of dark hair on her shoulders, and that she had a full head of jet black hair. My daughter was wrapped up in swaddling and handed to my wife I noticed that one of the nurses had picked something up. Whatever it was it looked quite large she took it to a table near the window and was examining it. I thought that it may have been another baby and mentioned to the nurse "is the baby OK"? She looked at me and laughed, "You idiot, it is the afterbirth." That is when I started to become rather green and felt a little sick. I came back to the hospital frequently to see that my wife and the baby were OK. One afternoon I got to the maternity ward and she was asleep, and my daughter was not in her cot. I was about to wake my wife up when a nurse told me that she was in the nursery. She showed me the nursery I went inside and picked up my daughter up and started to undo her baby grow. The nurse said, "What do you think you are you doing?" I said, "I am making sure that she is not a wolf child." She replied, "It was only downing on the skin. Some babies have it for a while then it naturally drops off. I spoke to my mother in-law about regarding my daughters jet black hair she said that her family were from the west coast of the Republic of Ireland. She told me a story of the Spanish sailors from the ships of the Spanish Amada as it broke up on the west coast of Ireland. Many of the villages took the Spanish soldiers and sailors in and hid them in fishing villages. Some of the Spanish eventually made their way back to Spain many years later, some remained in the villages, which may account for my daughters olive looks and black hair.

After a year I was still working for the Regimental Sergeant Major (RSM), one morning I was called into the Adjutant's office present was the Adjutant, RSM and the Superintendent Clerk. They informed me that I would be one of the Prisoner Escorts during a military court martial. The person whom I was to escort was someone that I knew, not very well. He was married with a couple of children and they lived on a different housing complex. It had been generally believed that he was on a course in the UK. In fact he was imprisoned in another Regiment's Guardroom. He was placed into our Regiment's Guardroom overnight and would be driven to the Court Martial Centre that morning. I was not informed why he was on the court martial, I was only informed to be at the guardroom the next morning dressed in my best uniform. The Court Martial Centre in Munster was quite a distance away. The Adjutant informed me that there was no other clerk that they could trust; I was only a Signalman, a Private in the Army. When we arrived at the Court Martial Centre I noticed a Staff Sergeant from my Regiment, I knew him quite well. I acknowledged him and he saw me, he quickly turned away. I thought that was a little odd as we used to play rugby together, he was normally quite a jolly person. I wondered what he was doing here. The escort and the prisoner formed up in the corridor; I was stood in front of the prisoner and there was someone behind him including the Regimental Provost Sergeant. My mind was ticking over now, I was very nervous. The main door was opened and the Provost Sergeant barked out the words of command and we marched smartly into the main court martial room. I could see in front of me some very senior Army Officers, all sat at a large table. They were wearing their dress uniforms including medals. It was all extremely formal, much like the TV series about the First World War Black Adder. We were brought to a halt and I sat on a chair in front of the prisoner and the other escort as sat behind him. As the charges were read out I felt sick. My head was spinning; the prisoner had molested a little girl. No wonder no-one told me why he was at the court martial. The Staff Sergeant who I had seen outside earlier stood at the witness area, it was his little girl had been molested. As he gave his evidence I felt sick - I had a young daughter of my own. To be honest I did not hear what the defendant had to say, many thoughts were going around my head. It was all a bit of a blur the evidence was so shocking. To this day I only remember what was said in the first hour, after that I cannot remember a thing I switched off. After the first morning the court adjourned for lunch, I had lost my appetite. I went outside and smoked as many cigarettes as I could. After lunch we took our places in the Court Room and once again we had to march in with the accused, just as we had in the morning. When the afternoon session was over, I was instructed to sit in the car with the prisoner I refused, the Provost Sergeant went back with the accused. He knew that it was a massive shock to me. I was not prepared for what I had heard. The soldier was found guilty and was remanded into civilian detention in the UK.

Writing about the episode regarding the court martial reminds me of a prisoner I had to escort to the Military Corrective facility in Colchester. I was selected because I was travelling back to the United Kingdom on my own attending a course. I met the prisoner and the escort from his unit, he was based at BMH Rinteln, and he was one of Army nurses based at the hospital. There were four of us including the prisoner; it was very unusual for a member of the Royal Army Medical Corps, RAMC, to be sent to the Military Prison. On the flight over the Sergeant who was escorting him, told me why the prisoner was sentenced. The prisoner looked so weedy, I wondered what the hell could he have done, a very bizarre story began to unfold. He had a canary that he kept in his room. Somebody had killed the bird and put it under his bed sheets with its head popping out and resting on a pillow. He came into his room saw what had happened and went crazy. He poured petrol around the single accommodation and set fire to the block; the fire took hold and destroyed a few rooms, thankfully no one was in them. I was relieved when he was dropped off at the prison.

After successfully completing my course I got a lift into work from the camp barber. I knew her very well. I also knew her husband as well; he was one of the drivers from my squadron. She said that her husband had not come home after work. She said that she was pissed off with him'. As she drove through the camp gates we saw a man in uniform climbing out of a window in the single accommodation block. The soldier was her husband it was a surreal scene. A naked woman was shouting after him. It was like looking at a giant cinema screen, watching a comedy film. The hairdresser drove her car off the road and onto the grass verge in front of the building. I shouted, "What are you doing"? She was attempting to run him over. She lost sight of him and drove back onto the road. She eventually dropped me off outside of the RHQ building; I thought no one would believe me if I told them what had happened to me on the way into work. A little later the RSM came into the office and said, "Ah, I believe that you have been involved in a domestic." I explained the story to him; I had a feeling that he already knew. For the next couple of days the hairdresser's husband was seen repairing the damage to the grass verge. They eventually patched things up and remained, blissfully, married.

Whilst serving in the Regiment we were on exercise (manoeuvres) for much of the year. The Regiment was forever being deployed on exercise. Somewhere on the 'Tank' plains of West Germany, It was where the Soviet Union's tanks would theoretically pile through onto the plains of Germany – it was ideal tank country. I went to see a Bundeswehr anti-tank destroyer on the West German plains to see how they operated on a war footing. It was an impressive setup. During this phase of the exercise we were operating out of a farmer's barns and the out-buildings. The Regiment's communication vehicles were camouflaged and hidden under trees. One of the roles of the NATO Air Force, was to over fly the exercise area and take aerial photographs. This would show up any vehicles and soldiers on the ground, they would also fly past using the opportunity to simulate an air attack on military installations. There was an incident involving an American soldier in the Operational Headquarters. I was manning the Signal Operations Desk (SigOps), with the Regimental Yeoman of Signals. An American soldier entered the building with his M16 Rifle, complete with a magazine of live ammunition attached to his rifle. He started to carry out pokey drill, the same style of drill that can be seen at any American Military tattoos. As he was walking through the Operations Complex he was swinging his rifle around. The British General Officer Commanding (GOC) of 2 Division, General Frank Kitson. The soldier was ordered off the exercise. The soldiers Commanding Officer complained, stating that the General could not authorise such an action as he had no jurisdiction over American Forces, he too was duly 'sacked'.

During the same exercise I was sleeping in one of the out buildings, on a military bed called a camp cot; they were easy to pack away and setup they were an American manufacture. To obtain one, you either had to barter with the American Forces or steal one. Both the day and night shift personnel shared the beds; each individual had their own sleeping bags. On this occasion I was asleep when I felt something run over my face. As I started to wake up it was on my mouth and nose; it was furry and warm, I realised it was some sort of animal. As I became more awake I realised that it was a dirty big hairy rat. I don't know who was more scared me or the rat. I don't think it was the rat. The camp cot was balanced precariously on a table, and I shot off the bed. The bed tumbled after me and both the bed and I landed with a thump on the floor. There were others asleep in the building and of course I had woken them up with my screaming and shouting and the noise of me falling off the table. Everyone saw the funny side except me. One of the old sweats asked me why I was sleeping on top of the table. I explained that someone had told me that sleeping on top of a table would be safe as rats did not like heights. I was a naïve young soldier at the time, not much has changed since then!

During the same exercise, the order was given to move to the next location, I had loaded all of the detachments equipment onto the vehicles. It was very early in the morning, the sun was starting to appear in the sky. I had been watching an old lady moving milk churns up and down the farm in a wheeled contraption. She moved the churns to the side of a road on a hill, suddenly out of the woods came one of the Regiment's Bedford Radio Relay trucks. It turned onto the same road as the churns. The truck crashed through the carefully placed churns and the milk and churns flew everywhere, the milk spewed out and flowed down the hill. The old woman was shouting at the driver I am not sure what she said I did understand the word "schwein".

During another Divisional Exercise it had rained non-stop for a couple of days. The exercise was eventually called off. We drove into a holding area and waited for a message to end the exercise. It was pitch black, a torrent of water was running everywhere; the area was a river of mud. As we drove into the location there were vehicles of every type. There was a British Main Battle Tank parked up. I think that it was a Chieftain Main Battle Tank. There were orange lights flashing and lots of people running around getting soaked, there was another tank with a crane. We thought that the tank was waiting to be-repaired. When we awoke we noticed that the tank had been removed. Someone informed us that there had been a nasty accident during the night. Two soldiers had decided that it would be better to sleep beneath the tank. The tank had sunk into the mud and crushed the pair of them underneath. It was always drummed into us do not sleep under any vehicle, as this type of tragic accident could happen.

Part of the introduction to the regiment of any newly arrived soldier was a visit to the Inner German Border (IGB). It was also known as the Iron Curtain which sliced Eastern and Western Europe in two. The border was patrolled on the Eastern side by approximately 50,000 – 60,000 East German Border Guards. The border ran for 1,393 Kilometres or 866 miles, and it ran from the Baltic to Czechoslovakia. The border consisted of high metal fences, walls, barbed wire, alarms, anti-vehicle ditches, watchtowers, automatic booby traps and mines, all formidable obstacles. People from East Germany were still prepared to take the risk and try to cross the border; many failed and paid the ultimate price with their lives. On the Western side of the border there were tens of thousands of North Atlantic Treaty Organisation (NATO) troops. Ready for a war with the Warsaw Pact soldiers on the Eastern side of the border. To observe the Inner German Border we travelled to the British Frontier Service post at Helmstedt. The British Frontier Service was a British Government Organisation that was responsible for border monitoring duties in West Germany. Its role was to assist the movement of British military personnel and their dependents, monitor the border regions, and to defuse any border incidents. The reason why the British Military had to travel to either Helmstedt or Luebeck to see the IGB. Was to ensure British units did not commit any border violations. The Frontier team took us to a viewing platform close the border. We could see into a small village on the other side of the border, the village had been divided by the iron curtain. There were killing zones, a minefield, electric fences and watch towers. We could see the runs for the guard dogs, and could hear the sounds of the dogs. The only sound on the East German side of the border was the barks of the guard dogs. Once we were on the viewing platform the Frontier service personnel gave a briefing on what was going on in the eastern border zone. A watch tower nearby had guards in the tower with binoculars and one or two had cameras with long lenses. The Frontier guide informed the group that all of our pictures would be in Moscow within hours of the photographs being developed. We could see border guard's trucks moving around. As far as I could see there were no civilians. We moved along the border to a very rural setting, looking across the border into East Germany. I saw a farm house; it looked immaculate from where we were standing. The signs along the border gave warnings about mines and being shot on sight. The farm land was well kept, one of the Frontier guides informed the group that all was not what it seemed. In fact it was not a working farm it was an East German Military Establishment.

Eventually my wife and I were allocated an Army Married Quarter; it was a flat in an area where most of the British personnel were housed. I did not drive and would sometimes catch an Army bus that took everyone to Birdwood Barracks. Sometimes someone who had a car would offer a lift. I was never one who was dependant on others for a lift. At least if the Army bus was late I could blame the driver. On one occasion I got a lift from one of the Orderly Room clerks. It was mid-winter and the country roads had not been treated and there was black ice and snow on the roads. The camp was in the middle of nowhere, the Army had its own snow clearing Lorries they had not reached this particular road. As we were travelling the car was picking up speed and the driver seemed unconcerned about the conditions. He did not slow down, he said, 'you look nervous just relax, I am a good driver and I have driven in far worse conditions than this lad'. I thought 'Yes, famous last words', I could see that he was not concentrating on the road. As we approached a bend I heard him say 'Oh shit' and the car left the road and flew over a snow covered bank into a field. He was cursing and shouting at me to give him a hand to get the car out of the field; we must have been ten metres away from the road and well and truly stuck in a field. Just then one of the Regiment's trucks turned up and pulled the car out of the field. An hour later the truck had returned to camp and the driver had told others about what had occurred. Word soon got around camp and, yes, he did have the 'Mick' taken out of him. The same stretch of road also held some very sad memories. The Regiment would send people on adventure training; skiing, mountaineering, yachting, and outdoor pursuits in an organised environment. There was a soldier who was part of a sub-unit, within the Regiment. I believe he went on one of the skiing trips. He arrived back to Bunde with a broken leg. Normally if you are injured you invariably end up doing the squadron typing, mail or working in the squadron stores. Because of his injury he was employed as the squadron gofer, he collected the mail and picked up various orders. Even though he was on crutches. When his leg had healed he went back to working at his trade. He was a single man earning the extra money for serving in Germany. He owned an opal mantra car; it was sporty and very fast. The Regiment had just returned from exercise, there was a corporal who was married to one of the Women's Royal Army Corps (WRAC) she worked as a typist in the Regimental typing pool. I had been on the same exercise and was dirty and smelly just like everyone else. The RSM was always dressed smart even though he had been on exercise. I entered the Orderly Room and the typing pool. A corporal came out having told his wife that he did not need the family car as "John" was giving him and another NCO a lift back home. They all squeezed into his car with their exercise 'kit'. As the car approached a bend on the road the car was catapulted and the car left the road and "flew" into a tree. The passengers survived sadly he was killed; the driver's side of the car took the full impact. The car was eventually returned to camp and members of his squadron removed the military equipment from it and any other personal effects.

On a much lighter note, the weather changed for the worse and in the afternoon it started to rain and as the rain hit the ground it froze solid. All the cars were covered in ice as the rain froze. The Commanding Officer decreed that no military vehicles or civilian vehicles would leave camp as it was too hazardous to drive. Some people had slipped over and had sustained various injuries. All of the squadron bars were opened early and the Regiment had sanctioned bar tabs as there were no cash point machines in those days, or mobile phones. We did not have a phone in the flat so I could not inform my wife that I could not get home. Most of the Regimental Headquarters personnel were in the HQ Squadron Bar, the beer was flowing and everyone was happy; I wonder why. I went to the toilet and when I returned it seemed very quiet it was too quiet. I thought 'Something is not right here'. My wife was stood at the bar, and I slurred 'what the bloody hell are you doing here, how did you manage to get to camp?' She had got a taxi which had snow chains on its wheels. I tried to explain, having a skin full of beer and everyone egging her on I was on a hiding to nothing. One of the clerks who lived nearby said that he would give us a lift back to the flat, as we travelled back home I received such an ear bashing.

Having an ear bashing has reminded me of an incident that involved the Vehicle Workshops Staff Sergeant (SSgt). Once again I was part of the Regimental Guard. The Senior Non Commissioned Officers (SNCO's) Mess was having their annual summer's ball. The guard commander and Regimental Orderly Sergeant briefed everyone on guard to be alert and smart and to be aware that the RSM would be attending the function. It is not good to have the RSM on camp when you are on guard duty, as I knew from my previous experiences. Sure enough, later that evening the RSM drove into camp with his wife. He parked his car next to the guardroom; he was wearing his Mess kit. He entered the guardroom, checked that all was well and shouted out my name. "Yes sir," I responded. He said, "Make sure you do not drop a clanger tonight." I replied, "Me sir?" "Yes you Sir". Everyone on guard took the piss out of me, shouting 'Fucking RSM's pet'. The evening was quite until a large lady entered the guardroom she was demanding that her husband should be locked up. She was wearing a ball gown, she had been attending the summer ball with her husband. She began to shout "My husband has thrown me into a trench full of mud." She was dishevelled, obviously having had a few drinks; as she was shouting she had managed to wake up the remainder of the guard. We noticed that she was covered in mud. She saw members of the guard staring at her and demanded that we were sent outside to look for her husband and to arrest him. At that moment someone tried to open the main door to the guardroom, it was open, but whoever it was trying to gain entry was pulling the at the door handle instead of pushing. One of the guards opened the door and the Workshop Staff Sergeant fell in, drunk as a newt. He admitted that his wife had been in the trench. He said they had been walking near some pipe work. They both had decided to take a short cut across the works area and they fell into an open trench. His wife fell in first and he landed on top of her and her being a large lady took the impact of both of them. It was at this point that he started laughing, his wife was not amused. He could not stop laughing every time he tried to explain what had happened. Eventually a taxi arrived and his wife was threatening to end the Guard Commanders career. It was all very laughable and amusing it was the only entertainment of the evening.

I was the duty clerk over a weekend, and my wife had recently given birth to our daughter, and we were settling into life with a baby in the house. On this particular duty (I do believe that it was a Sunday duty) the Adjutant (he was responsible for the organisation, administration and discipline of the Regiment). He entered the Regimental Headquarters, followed by the RSM, Superintendent Clerk and the Commanding Officer. As duty Clerk one of my tasks was to enter their details in the Duty Clerks diary of events and of course to provide tea and coffee in the CO's office. Just after they had arrived the Royal Military Police (RMP), most people refer to them as "Red Caps", arrived with German civilian Police. I then knew that something serious had happened. All of the Regimental hierarchy were in the CO's office with the police. After a while the Teleprinter started up. It was a noisy machine and there is a distinct start up noise on these particular printers. All 'signals', messages, had to be logged into the Duty Clerk's dairy. As I was logging the signal into the book I realised why so many senior people and police were in the CO's office. The signal was about the death of a baby in a military house belonging to the Regiment. I thought that I ought to place the signal and the copies into a sealed envelope. Suddenly the superintending clerk came out of the CO's office and asked for the signal. I think that the CO must have received a phone call informing him that the signal was on its way. I gave him the envelope, he asked me if I had read it. I confirmed that I had he said 'It goes without saying that the contents are sensitive'.

1977 was a busy year for the majority of the British Army in Germany. This was due to the Queen's Silver Jubilee parade which took place on the 7th July 1977 at the Sennelager Training Area. The Regiment were to provide supporting communications from Sennelager to the rest of the world. 4th Division was chosen to be reviewed by the Queen. The division I was with set up the communications vehicles behind the scenes, immediately behind the main stand. There was rehearsal after rehearsal and the dust was everywhere. There were soldiers trying to hose the ground where the vehicles would travel close to the main dais where the Queen would eventually review the troops. During the lead up to the Queen's visit. Permission was given for all of those attending the parade including the support troops to have an evening off. Most of the soldiers I was with only had their uniforms. Most of us headed for the NAAFI bar on the camp; it was a large building. The time soon came to closing the bar the place was heaving with soldiers. The Orderly Officer and the guard turned up to empty the bar; the Orderly Officer was a young second lieutenant and he looked like he had just come out of Officer training at Sandhurst. He was dressed in the uniform of a Scottish Regiment; he had no control of the situation nor did the guard. He was being jostled; there were hundreds of drunk and tipsy soldiers. I was with a group of soldiers from my Regiment and one of the 'old and bold' amongst us said 'Come on, let's get moving, we are leaving".

As we were leaving we could see that the young officer had pulled his ceremonial sword out of its sheaf. Why he was wearing his sword God only knows. We were close to the main doors and saw him disappear and being flung out of a large window. The bar was on the ground floor, which was lucky; none of those who threw him out of the windows would have known which floor they were on they were so drunk. In the distance we could see the RMP vehicles pulling up outside of the NAAFI. When I got to work the next morning the RSM asked me if I had been to the NAAFI bar the night before? I confirmed that I had.

He told me that a number of soldiers had been arrested. Some were in hospital, including an idiot who was so drunk that he decided to go for a swim in the outdoor pool. Unfortunately the pool had been emptied of water.

The parade rehearsals were amazing; I could not get over the amount of vehicles and manpower that was used to stage the Queen's review. The Gazelle helicopters flew so low over the parade, the dust clouds were horrific. The vehicles were covered in dust this was a frequent occurrence. Every morning the parade area was hosed to reduce the dust, during the rehearsals. There was a car accident on the same route that the Queen would take the following day. Someone had crashed their car into a tree it was a fatal crash. The wreckage including the damaged tree was immediately removed. If anyone drove past the crash site they would not have known that an accident had ever occurred.

It was not long after this that I attended my clerk's course and was promoted to Lance Corporal. I was nominated to become the Regimental Classified Security Clerk working with the Second in Command of the Regiment (2 I/C). The Adjutant shared the same office as the Second in Command, and inside the office was a secure room that housed the classified material. The person who had the position before me had long since left the Regiment long before I took over. On my first day I checked the classified material against the ledgers that recorded each individual classified document. I found that most of the ledgers had red lines in them including the signatures of the second in command and the last security clerk, which meant that the classified material had been destroyed and had been verified that it had been destroyed. I came across a lot of classified material that should have been destroyed. I spoke to the second in command, informing him of what I had found. His face turned bright red he asked me to go back into the secure room. He double-checked and confirmed my findings. I told him that I would start burning the material immediately. He realised that he had dropped a big clanger. He should have ensured that the documents were destroyed as his signature were on the ledgers certifying the destruction of the material. It took both of us nearly a week to destroy the documents. One morning the CO asked the 2 I/C to pop into his office. At one stage when he had CO's orders the accused were staring out of his window. They were distracted by the 2 I/C and I wheeling documents in a wheelbarrow and burning masses of papers in an oil drum, in a field behind the CO's office.

In West Germany at the time there were Russian Military teams called SOXMIS – Soviet Military Mission. In Russia there was British Military Missions called BRIXMIS, both deployed a few members of military intelligence and support staff. The official stance was to monitor and further better relationships between Russian and Western occupation forces. All British forces had to carry a 'yellow card' called a SOXMIS card. It contained information about what should be displayed on a Soviet vehicle and what should be carried out when a Russian vehicle was ever seen and a contact telephone number. All of the units I served with in West Germany carried out checks for SOXMIS cards and of course our own personal ID card, MOD F90. It was normally a chargeable offence not to carry either card.

In 1979 my next move was to The Joint Headquarters British Army of the Rhine, JHQ HQ BAOR; the largest nearby city was Monchengladbach. Rheindahlen was the area that housed the Headquarters. The HQ buildings and support buildings were housed in a secure compound. Included within the complex was the HQ of Second Allied Tactical Air Force (2 ATAF). Rheindahlen was a military village containing married quarters, messes, schools, cinemas, swimming pools and shops. There was a satellite married accommodation a few miles away there was a military bus to take service personnel to work at the Headquarters; lots of people had their own cars or could cycle or run to work. Most people were housed at the satellite accommodation prior to being allocated married accommodation in the Rheindahlen village; Military personnel very rarely moved directly into Rheindahlen.

I worked at the Communications Branch in the 'Big House', as the Headquarters was fondly referred to. The Branch was made up of mostly Royal Signals personnel. It consisted of one Major General, Commander Communications, British Army of the Rhine, BAOR. I worked for the Technical and Equipment side of the Branch with a sergeant. I arrived as a lance corporal, hoping to eventually be promoted to corporal. The Chief Clerk worked in another large office with the two female clerks. The other three and I worked within a secure room. I worked with a sergeant who was always coming to work smelling of alcohol and occasionally arriving late for work. Within the Headquarters there was a German canteen, and all of the German workers used it, and it also sold beer. It only sold German food; I particularly liked the German cheese and brown bread. This particular sergeant would always get the orders for lunch as he spoke fluent German. He would have a bottle of beer and chat to the Germans in the canteen. It was normal for German workers to drink beer in the mornings. He lived at the same satellite accommodation area that I lived in. He never wanted to move to Rheindahlen village, he was happy to stay where he was. I did not know him socially and I never met his family, I knew very little about him, apart from when he was at work. I had recently moved to the area and I was having some family problems; I was trying to move out of our current flat, since the flat had some disturbing things happen in it before we moved in. The previous occupant's wife had died in the living room. One day I got home from work and my wife was not her normal self. In fact she was very quiet she told me that she had taken the covers off the couch. The colour of the couch underneath should have been white; this one had huge bloodstains on it. She said, "Something terrible has happened in this room, I can feel it." I spoke to the neighbours and asked them if anything had happened in the flat. They told me that the previous lady had been complaining of headaches. Her husband had gone to work as usual. Sometime during the day the woman must have lain down on the couch and had sadly suffered a brain haemorrhage and died. The information freaked my wife out; she wanted to move there and then. I spoke to the appropriate authorities, to see if we could move flats. They said that we would to stay put. They would only change the couch. When I broke the news to my wife she said that she would not stay in the flat and that I needed to get something done.

One morning the sergeant that I worked with did not turn up for work. I noticed that his desk had been cleared and so had all of his personal items. All of the ledgers that the classified material was recorded in were missing. I spoke to the Chief Clerk and he informed me that we were to use new temporary ledgers for the time being. There were three men in suits in the branch. I noticed that the Staff Assistant was not in his office, he was in the Chief Clerks office; the three men were using his office. The General's PA asked me to pop into the General's Office. One of the colonels was in the office including the Staff Assistant and the

Chief Clerk. The General informed me that that the sergeant that I worked with would not be working in the Branch anymore; I thought that it may have been due to his drinking and subsequent unreliability. I was so wrong. He informed me that I would be interviewed as would everyone in the Branch. Then I was hit by a bombshell. It transpires that the Sergeant had been passing classified information to an East German spy. The spy was a female who worked in a bar close to where he lived. He regularly frequented the bar, it was not a bar that many service personnel would frequent. He had been running up large bar bills. He was also borrowing money from her and it was a substantial amount. He was also having an affair with her. She began to blackmail him; he was up to his neck in it. Obviously, she was a spy, who was being run by the KGB in Moscow and East Berlin, they knew everything about him. I believe he was copying and taking photographs of sensitive material. The General briefed everyone in the branch to the fact that there had been a gross breach of security. They were trying to find out how damaging the material he had been supplying was. The woman had already travelled back to East Germany. The Sergeant had immediately been moved to the UK. He had confessed to everything, including how he did it and how long he had been doing it for. The Chief Clerk informed me that there would not be a replacement for him for some months. After a few weeks I was promoted to corporal, I was covering the work that the sergeant undertook. The Chief Clerk looked after the Colonel so that I could cover the remaining tasks.

I eventually got a move of married quarter to a flat across the road, which alleviated the pressures at home.
The other sergeant in the office was an old and bold soldier and he was coming towards the end of his service in the Army; this

was his last posting. In the Army there are many mandatory Military Training Tests that every soldier has to undertake annually. One of the tests was the Basic Fitness Test (BFT). The test consisted of a three mile route. It was a run and it was broken down into two stages. The first stage was a mile and half run as a squad, it was completed in a pre-defined time. At the mile and a half point, everyone would set off at their own pace as individual best effort. On one particular test, 'Jim', the old and bold sergeant, was at an age where he could opt for two methods of completing the test. He could run with the squad and complete the second part in his allowed time. Or he could run the three miles at his own pace and in his age time allowance. This particular day he chose the latter. The time that he had to complete the task was long he could have strolled around the course. As we started our BFT we could see Jim in the distance. He was walking and it looked like he was smoking. Someone in the squad said 'I am sure he is smoking'. When we finished, he had just completed his run and was finishing off a King Edward Cigar.

During my time at Rheindahlen there was a building within the compound which housed the Intelligence element of the Headquarters. Every now and then a courier would visit the Branch with classified documents that only the General was to read. There was a change in the courier and a rather large lady who was a member of the Women's Royal Army Corps, (WRAC), would bring the documents to the branch it was only a short walk from her building. She would turn up huffing and puffing, red faced, and sweating profusely. She always turned up at the Chief Clerks office in a mess. She had a reputation as a heavy drinker and she frequented the clubs on Rheindahlen, the clubs were the Marlborough Club and the other was the Queensway Club. One morning there was news that a new born baby had been found in a street bin. The baby had been discovered by a cleaner who had cleaned an office close to the female accommodation block. The cleaner had opened the lid and some paper had blown away and exposed the baby. At first the cleaner had thought it was a plastic doll until she touched it. When the police searched the female accommodation block they found out who had given birth to the baby. It was the courier, she had carried the baby the full term without anyone suspecting that she was pregnant. As I mentioned, she was quite a large woman. It was subsequently found that she had given birth in a bath in the accommodation block over the weekend. She hid the baby in her cupboard as she knew the council bins would be emptied on the Monday morning. She had placed the new born baby into a dustbin at the last minute. No one would have known what had happened if it was not for the cleaner. The cleaner had emptied an office waste paper bin into the street bin. The baby was close to the top of the bin. The woman who had given birth was obviously disturbed. To have given birth on her own and then to have disposed of the baby in that manner. The last I heard she was being treated in hospital and returned to the United Kingdom for further medical help.

One of the duties that were frequently carried out were the Anti-Terrorist Patrols and guard duties in the 'Big House'. The 'Big House' duties were carried out wearing slippers, as the duty was carried out wearing trainers. The duty consisted of walking around the building, checking that the hundreds of office doors were locked and secured. The checks were timed by a very bizarre system of keys, and within the guardroom there was an electronic monitoring board and it was a basic system of lights; red, white and green. The Mixed Service Organisation (MSO) also known as 'mojos'. It consisted of Ex-Eastern European and displaced military after the Second World War. They were captured by the Nazis and imprisoned in Germany. Some were offered service with the German Army to escape the harsh conditions in German Prisoner of Camps, many refused. After the War they did not want to go back to their homes in Eastern Europe as their countries were occupied by the Russians. Some of the MSOs thought that it was too risky to return home as they would be imprisoned by the Russians. Others knew that their families had perished during the war. The British Army offered the prisoners of war work, mainly menial work, and they became interpreters, store men, clerks and guards in some military installations. The outer perimeter of the camp was patrolled by the MOSO guards and guard dogs. The Ministry of Defence, (MOD) guards manned the entrance. During silent hours there was only one entrance to the building. Inside the building it was manned by members of the British Army. We were not armed when patrolling the corridors. Within the guardroom there was weapons and ammunition. Close to the guardroom was The British Army of the Rhine, BAOR Duty Officer. He dealt with any compassionate cases, security issues and any information that affected soldiers and units in Germany. Out of hours he was directed by the MOD (Ministry of Defence) in London.

After a year or two of working at the Headquarters there was an incident during one of the guard duties. I had completed a set of security checks. When I got back to the guardroom the guard commander said "we have got ourselves a situation", talk about an understatement. A member of the guard had taken a rifle and a magazine of live ammunition. He said that he had informed the BAOR Duty officer, whom he stated had just shut the door and locked it. Before he locked the door his last words were "let me

118

know when you have resolved the situation". The guard commander said that they had tracked the guard to the cellars. The soldier had placed magazine of live ammunition onto his SMG. The guard commander told me to take two other members of the guard and to monitor the situation. Do not provoke him, the guard commander did not want any dead heroes. We all laughed at him. The guard commander said that he would report the incident to the Joint Military Police post within Rheindahlen Garrison. As I and two other members of the guard entered the cellars the renegade guard was walking towards us. He gave himself up; I took the rifle and made the rifle safe, taking the magazine off and making sure that there wasn't a round loaded into the breach of the rifle. We took him back to the guardroom. The RAF Police have a nickname in the Armed Forces, it is 'Snow drops' due to their distinct white peak caps, they had just arrived. They took him into custody, I handed the rifle and magazine to the guard commander. The RAF police took both items as evidence. The guard spent the next hour or two writing statements. The senior 'Snowdrop' spoke to the Duty Officer, and we heard him say to the police that he had everything under control and had despatched the guard to find the renege soldier.

Outside of the Headquarters perimeter fencing there were three single storey buildings, which contained the 'NATO' Bars. There were Dutch, Belgium and German Bars. The bars had drink and food from their respective nations. The Dutch, Belgium and German soldiers were in the bars all hours of the day, but the British mainly visited after working hours on a Friday. The Dutch military were the only soldiers who were allowed to wear their hair long, they had their own union.
One particular Friday I decided to ride my bike into work. That evening I ended up in the bars, or several of them. In the early

1980's there were no mobile phones. We did not have a phone in the flat. Therefore I could not let my wife know where I was or not to worry. It was one of those balmy summer evenings, and in those days you could wear your uniform off the base. After a skin full of beer I decided stupidly that I would try to ride my bike back home. Germany has cycle paths running along-side the pavements, the down side is the cycle paths butts up close to the roads. I managed to ride out of the Rheindahlen village complex without any dramas. I was heading towards a small village. There was a cemetery on the left hand side of the road. I recall thinking 'poor sods', and the next thing I remember was waking up in a ditch. I had ridden into a drainage ditch. I woke up just as the light was starting to fade. I got to the next village and the traffic lights were out of order, there was a policeman directing traffic. There were about three or four cars in front of me and they managed to get past as he directed them to drive on. He saw me and put his hand up to signal for me to stop. I immediately thought 'I am for it now' just as in the UK there are penalties for riding a bike whilst intoxicated. It was now my turn to move on he signalled for me to ride on. The bike refused to budge, I looked down and the front tyre had got stuck in a gap between some old tram lines. I pulled it and twisted it, the policeman started to come towards me, and I thought I am going to get stopped here. Just has he got close to me, I managed to pull the bike tyre out and sped on, shouting over my shoulder in English 'thank you' as he let me pass. That was so close. I got home and it was getting dark, and obviously my wife was worried; she said that she thought that I had an accident.

We eventually moved onto Rheindahlen village, into a nice three bed roomed house, by this time my wife was pregnant with our second child. The house was situated at the far end of the village,

Colchester Walk. It was such a nice leafy area with a nice big garden for our daughter to play in. It was worth the wait. It was close to a small shop and it was handy for the family.

My wife and I did not drive at the time, we would travel back to the UK by coach or aeroplane. While at Rheindahlen we got to see a little of Germany, there was an occasion that some friends of ours offered to drive us to the Rhine river near Koblenz. It was a warm day and we took our daughter with us, and by then she was twelve months old. My wife and I decided to go for a paddle in the Rhine. The neighbours said that they would keep an eye on our daughter. As we were paddling a doll, it looked just like a doll, floated past, we stood in disbelief, to our horror it was our baby. We pulled her out of the water and immediately got her to the river bank by this time she was chocking and the water came gushing out of her lungs. I berated the couple who were supposed to be looking after her. The journey home was decidedly frosty. My wife and I blamed herself for what had happened.

One of the other duties I had to carry out whilst serving at Rheindahlen was referred to as "the Anti-Terrorist Patrols". The patrol consisted of a sergeant and a mixture of corporals and privates. The duty was only carried out whenever the security level was heightened. The duties were normally over a twenty four hour shift. There was one particular patrol that I recall as being eventful. We collected our weapons, aging Sub Machine Guns (SMG's) including live ammunition from the Garrison Armoury as normal. The sub machine gun, SMG, I was issued with was dirty it did not look as though it had been cleaned since it was last fired on the ranges. I made a comment regarding the state of the weapon the sergeant of the patrol and the armourer shouted 'Just shut up and sign for it'. I was issued with a magazine and it was damaged. The lips of the magazine were bent. I was issued with my ammunition. I told both the patrol commander and the armourer that I did not want the magazine as it was damaged, I was told to just sign for it and stop moaning. They would not issue a replacement magazine as they were allocated for this particular duty. I asked for the armoury comments book. I noted the date and time and made a detailed record of the state of the SMG and the damaged magazine. The armourer and the sergeant signed the book. Both of them said, 'There, satisfied. Now piss off'. This would come back and bite them later. When I put my ammunition into the damaged magazine I marked the last round with a red marker pen, which could be seen at the top of the magazine. We had completed the anti-terrorist patrol late at night and we were entitled to have a hot meal in the RAF canteen or mess hall. It was far more sophisticated than anything the Army had, and it was open twenty four hours a day as the RAF had various duties which were carried out of normal hours. I checked my magazine in my ammunition pouch and I could see the red bullet in the magazine. We had our meal and went back to the billet. It was at this point that I checked my magazine again and I found that one bullet was missing. I panicked and removed the remainder of the bullets and counted them. I couldn't believe it, there was one round missing. I searched my ammunition pouch and it was not in there, I checked the room and I could not find it. The Sergeant asked 'What's wrong with you? I explained to him what had happened, we searched high and low. We went back to the canteen and searched everywhere. We asked the duty cooks they confirmed that nothing had been handed in. The Sergeant informed the Duty Officer who informed all organisations by Signal, that a 9mm live round was reported missing. When I got to work the following Monday. On my desk was a copy of a Signal (military Telegram). It was regarding the loss of live ammunition. I handed it to the Chief Clerk. He looked at me and said, 'You are on your own'. I had that sinking feeling. I was soon on a charge; my crime was Negligence, loss of a 9mm live round. I walked to the, Garrison Sergeant Major's, (GSM's) office. He read the charge out to me. Then declared that "in five minutes I will march you into the Garrison Commanders Office". To be charged with the loss of ammunition. The GSM said "you will only be able to speak when the Garrison Commander tells you to, understand.'" I replied, "Yes Sir." Minutes later I was stood outside the Commanders office. The GSM barked out his words of command. I marched into the office, saluted the Garrison Commander. He read out my charge of 'negligence' in that I had on Sunday negligently lost a 9mm round. The Commander said, "Well do you have any mitigating circumstances?" The GSM snapped, "It is a straightforward case, sir." I countered that there were mitigating circumstances. "If I was negligent then I would not have reported the damaged equipment issued to me." And I told him of the response by the armourer and patrol sergeant. The commander asserted, "None of this evidence had been brought to my attention. GSM march him out of the office then come back in". A moment or two later the GSM dragged the armourer in to the Commanders Office. The Patrol Sergeant turned up and went into the GSM's office. Soon after they were lined up in the corridor and were both marched into the Commander's office. I was then again marched into the commander's office and I noticed that the armourer's faults book was on his desk. He said, "Hearn, you have got away with the charge." I was about to say something the GSM barked, "It is not your turn to talk." The commander pronounced, "Case dismissed." I was marched out and into the GSM's office. He snarled, "Hearn, you have got away this time. I was so sure we had you from now on I will be watching you." When I got back to work, my bosses called me into their office and asked me what had taken place. I told them and they asked why I had not informed the Chief Clerk. I replied that I had, but he had been totally disinterested and told me that I was on my own. He also received the telephone call from the GSM and sent me down to the Garrison Commander. I did let it slip that the GSM had advised me that I was a marked man. When you are in deep mire up to your armpits, you soon find out who your true friends are.

One of the sergeants that worked in the Branch lived close to my house. In those days all of the mail from the UK was delivered to the soldiers work address. I remember taking the sergeant's mail to his home address. He answered the door and I gave him his mail. He was not impressed at all; he stepped outside and closed the door behind him. He said, "I did not ask you to bring the mail to my house whilst I was on leave, do not do it again." I was young and I suppose naïve I was happily married and did not have any secrets from my wife.

In 1980 our son was born. He was also born in a military hospital, the birth went according to plan but he had problems breathing, the doctors smacked his bottom and there was no immediate response. I could see that he was turning blue, his cord was cut and he was rushed into a back room and after a while I could hear him screaming, I thought thank god for that. His mum was very worried I kept saying "don't worry it will be alright".

During April 1982 Argentina invaded the Falkland Islands. I was working for two majors who were responsible for equipping the

124

British Army in Germany with the latest radio equipment. It was a long slow process. News broke of the invasion and one of the majors informed me that the three of us may have to go to UK to assist with issuing the latest radio equipment. In the end we were to remain in Germany and continue with equipping the British Army units based in Germany. Since there may have been a case for units from Germany having to deploy to the Falkland Islands. No one had any idea of where the Falkland Islands where. One morning I was sat at my desk looking at some cartoons depicting the War. Suddenly everyone stood up the General had walked into the office. He was waving a British tabloid newspaper. He opened it up to the centre pages and asked, "Hearn, do you buy this paper?" I replied that I didn't. He retorted with a sharp 'Good'. He placed the paper on my desk, within the centre pages there were two Royal Signals Corporal's. They were stood on the quay side at Southampton docks. They were saying farewell to their respective wife and partner. It was my two younger brothers who were both serving soldiers in the British Army. He enquired, "How many brothers do you have?" I replied, "Two, sir." He snapped "You are not going anywhere. How could the Ministry of Defence explain to your mother if anything happened to all three sons? This will be one war that you will not be taking part in. Too many Hearn's in a war zone is recipe for disaster." Happily both of my brothers survived the war. One was immediately sent to the conflict in Beirut, for six months, within seven weeks of the end of the Falklands war and within two weeks of his marriage.

In the October of 1982 I was posted to 249 Signal Squadron Allied Mobile Force Land based in Bulford. My next move to England would be quite an eye opener.

My moves in and around West Germany

My time in West Germany was for me enjoyable I was married and had a young family. My career was heading in the right direction.

Chapter 5 - Bulford

This chapter has been very difficult to write, it has opened up old memories and feelings that had lain dormant for decades. Prior to arriving in Bulford my career was progressing in the right direction. I was being promoted at the right times, and I was 'picked up' at twenty five for my promotion to sergeant. I arrived in Bulford "on the up" and left in a very dark place!

When someone in the Armed Forces moves from one regiment, barracks or country the term used is 'posted'. In October 1982 I was posted from West Germany to the United Kingdom, to Bulford Camp near Salisbury. As my wife and I were travelling up the hill approaching Bulford Camp. We could see some Married Quarters on the left hand side they looked like dilapidated concrete boxes. I had a sinking feeling in the pit of my stomach when I saw the houses. Arriving at the Headquarters building of the unit to which I was assigned to. I was told that the address of my house was Quebec Gardens. I thought "well the name sounds good, especially with 'Gardens' in the name." We arrived at the house and disappointingly I realised that it was the same houses that we saw on the hill. Entering the house, we found that it was constructed of four solid concrete walls and one concrete slab on top as the roof. There was a 4ft x 10ft tarmac "garden". Our first night that we spent in the house was a cold October evening. The house was so cold the central heating and the electric fire made no perceptible difference. My wife was not impressed. Eventually the removals truck arrived with our personal belongings. We found that we could not hang any pictures on the wall using the conventional hooks. I had to use a drill to put holes in the walls to hang the pictures. The walls were so hard. I kept reassuring my wife that things could only get better; I thought to myself - who was I trying to kid. It was a miserable start to what should have been an upward journey in our married life. The UK was still feeling euphoric after the Falklands victory earlier in 1982 and our military was still deploying around the world.

Three months into my tour and I deployed on exercise to take part in an Artic Warfare Survival course in Norway. It would not be the last time that I would be away from the family. In the September of 1983 the unit deployed to Denmark. It was a short trip and we came back in the October only to deploy again to Norway in the January. It was a continuous cycle of training in the UK preparing for the next deployment.

During the periods that I was not travelling around the world I would try to make the time spent in the UK as family orientated as possible. My wife and I tried to make the house look and feel as much of a home as humanly possible. However I could sense that things were not ideal on the home front. I contemplated moving away from the unit although I knew it would be detrimental on my future career as I was likely to be promoted during or at the end of my tour. I didn't pursue the opportunity and thing were about to turn from bad to much worse.

It was around this period that my brother-in-law, Stephen, who I had known before I joined the Army, and his wife had moved to the Married Quarters in Bulford. He was in the Royal Artillery based in Ward Barracks. The children would see their uncle and aunt frequently. My wife and Stephens wife would go into Salisbury for a 'girls' night out. Stephen was happy and I saw no reason to suspect anything untoward. Stephen would drive them into town and drop them off and they would get a taxi back home. I would look after the children. I thought that it was healthy for my wife to go out with her sister-in-law, we trusted one another, and I had no reason not to trust her. She began to change and she was not as warm and open, she was not as affectionate, she was not the person that I knew and loved. I asked her if everything was OK and she said yes, she was just a bit tired.

The Squadron deployed to Turkey on the eastern border with Russia. The major problem with having family problems in the military. Especially during a deployment it is very difficult to find the time to iron out any marriage problems. Early 1984 I was in Norway again. I wrote home about once a week keeping the family informed of what was happening on the exercise. I very rarely had a reply. I returned to the UK at the end of March of that year. Easter was fast approaching, and we took the children out on day trips and visited her mum and dad. I continued to ask her if all was alright, was there anything we could do to sort out any problem; she just said all was OK. In the September I deployed yet again to Denmark, and this time it was only a three week exercise, and we returned to UK in the October. I deployed to Norway in early 1985, and I was informed that I would be promoted to Sergeant in early 1986. It was about the March of that year I was informed that I was to deploy to the Falkland Islands on a six month tour. I informed my wife and of course she was not impressed. I had already been away for nearly three months. Soon I would be away for six months but this time I would be eight thousand miles away. I think that this news was the straw that had broken the camel's back.
Unless I said no to the Falkland Islands I had a feeling that my marriage would be over. I tried telling her that I would get

sergeant's pay and it would better for all of the family and that in early 1986 we would be in Germany. I told her that when I returned we would buy a new car. I knew that it was a form of emotional blackmail, and it is something that I had never used before.

I convinced myself that it would work and eventually deployed to the Falkland Islands. However I was proved wrong early into my deployment I received a letter from home it was from my wife. As I read it, was as though it had been written by another person. She said that she had got a part time job cleaning on one of the many camps in Bulford. The cleaning job covered the period that the children were at school, and she seemed to be writing as though she was single. Concurrent with receiving the letter I was summoned to telephone call from my unit in Bulford. At the time the calls were via satellite and cost a small fortune the calls had to be cleared at a high level. The caller informed me that my wife was having an affair, with someone from another regiment. My mind went blank, I felt sick. I said that I wanted to come back to UK, sod my promotion; my family meant everything to me. The call was short, not too many details, it was the words 'having an affair', they went round and round in my head. I lost a lot of weight and could not concentrate on anything. A week or so later I received another letter from her explaining she was aware the unit had informed me of the affair. She also phoned me in the Falkland Islands in an attempt to stop me ruining my career by coming back home early. I told her that I did not care; I thought saving my marriage was more important. If you are blinded by what you deem as love, then you cannot see what is in front of your eyes. Logic goes out of the window. She then proceeded to tell me that she had broken off her relationship with the other person. I was an emotional wreck but remained in the Falklands.

Never a Dull Moment

I arrived back in the UK a few weeks later hoping that things could return to where they were prior to arriving in Bulford. Instead I found out that the children had been either staying with her brother and sister-in-law or with friends or at my mum and dad's while I was away.

My wife was a completely different person. I needed some leave to try to sort things out, things were out if control. Somehow we were both living in the same house and sleeping in the same bed. Since finding out about the affair our physical relationship had stopped! Lying in bed that night she started to tell me everything. This outpouring consciously convinced me that everything would just be the same. I was kidding myself. It was never going to be the same as before. I just could not trust her. That night she explained the soldier with whom she had an affair had taken her to his parents in Manchester. She had been shocked. The house was dirty and his family were from a different world to that which she was accustomed. On one occasion she went with him and his family to a local pub. They were all looking at her and saying to him "You've done alright for yourself". She told me that she still loved me and for the sake of the children it would be better if we stayed together and moved to Germany. As I listened I got more depressed and angry and got up and slept on the couch.

Yet again I convinced myself that things may change even though deep down I couldn't bring myself to trust her. Stupidly I ordered a brand new expensive Escort Diesel from a local garage. A few weeks later and the squadron were taking part in ten mile run ending with a shoot on the ranges. On the way back from Tidworth to Bulford we had to run on the main road linking the two towns. Someone shouted 'It's those women in the red car', and as they went past it was my wife and some friends. After work I spoke to her she said, 'Oh we were just driving around.' Yet again things seemed to be deteriorating. The arguments were frequent and on one occasion she informed me that her activities outside of our marriage had caused her some medical problems. I thought that things couldn't get much worse and I know that I should have walked away. I just felt she was "taking the mick" and I was falling for it every time. Finally we moved apart, she living with the children in our married quarter while I moved into the military single accommodation.

Christmas came and went it was now 1986, the year that I was due to go to Germany in the April. Prior to leaving for Germany my wife confirmed that I could pop back to the house. This would enable me to pack my stuff and see the children before I left. That night the Chief Clerk and the WO2 (Yeoman of Signals) took me to the Durrington Working Man's club for a few drinks. I was to sleep on the settee and was just getting ready when my wife came downstairs and started arguing, goading me about the new man in her life. I learnt that he was only a teenager, and she started to taunt me about his abilities. I finally flipped, and even though I still feel anger about her affair, I remain hugely embarrassed for what happened next. She was standing near the stacked hi-fi unit, I did not realise that she was stood behind the glass door of the hi-fi. I went to push her away but instead I pushed my hand through the glass door and badly slashed my wrist. There was a lot of blood all over the place. Splattering across one of the living room walls. She meanwhile had moved closer to the couch and went on and on, I grabbed her and pushed her onto the couch. I started to shake her. I have hated myself ever since for grabbing her, since it is not in my nature to lay a finger on a woman. I quickly released her as I came to my senses.

132

I realised what I had done. She ran out of the door, and drove to the barracks of her lover. Seeing the blood he took her to the Royal Military Police (RMP) station and reported an attack on her. I remained in the house only to be startled by the door being smashed down by the RMP. They had their pistols drawn, and told me to put my hands in front of me. This was nigh on impossible with blood spurting from my wrist. But I did as they asked. The result being two military policemen being covered in blood. I did not have much sympathy. Handcuffed I was placed into the back of a Land Rover. In the back was the Orderly Sergeant. He said to me that this was his last Duty in the Army, and that he had completed twenty two years of service. He said "I thought that this was going to be a bloody quiet duty". They took me to the Main Guardroom in Ward Barracks where the handcuffs were removed and I again tried to stem the flow of blood. Instead I was told by the Orderly Officer to stand to attention. I tried to tell him that if I did there would be blood everywhere. He said, "Just do as I tell you". The result being another soldier and wall being covered in blood! Blood was also now pooling on the floor and I was beginning to feel lightheaded. I heard the RMP corporal tell them that I was under arrest for assault. My wife and her "boyfriend" had arrived at the police station and was demanding that I should be charged with assault. Thankfully a civilian police sergeant and a constable were visiting the RMP police station they had listened to what my wife had to say. She told them what had happened, and apparently her friend started to shout at the police to charge me. They had far more experience with these matters and they dropped the charges. Unfortunately, the military can be vindictive at times and I was informed that while the civilian police said I was a free man. I could not be released until the Orderly Officer gave permission. They then proceeded to suggest if I was not an attempted murderer then I must be suicidal. They dragged me off to the local military doctor, not to fix my wrist but to see if he would sanction me. Fortunately, he had more sense and proceeded to sort out my wrist, incensed at the poor treatment that had been metered out, but equally pretty powerless to do anything. Back at the barracks and after I had my breakfast I was marched to the Orderly Officer's office. He signed my release and then laid into me; he said that if he had his way I would be charged with attempted murder. He informed me that from now until I was posted to Germany I was banned from going anywhere near the married quarter. Given the dreadful situation of the previous night, and prevented from seeing my children and departing to Germany, it was not an option. I knew someone who served in my unit and lived close to me, and he said that he would speak to my wife whenever I wanted to see the children. A few days later he said that he thought he saw some-one else in the house. When he approached the door it was a few minutes before my wife came to the door, a little dishevelled and adjusting her clothing. She said that she was celebrating Keith being out of her life. She did however let me have access to the children and sometimes I could have them at the weekends. Not being able to drive we would travel by bus to my parents in Swindon. The children were a little quiet whenever I picked them up from their mum's. I felt; this was understandable, it must have been so hard for them to adjust to such a huge change in their lives. My parents kept telling me the marriage may be over, but my wife was a good mum, I would have to accept that the marriage was over. It was difficult to take this advice on board as I thought that I was in love with my wife. I could see the hurt in the children's eyes. I was about to be posted to Germany, the Army would not cancel the posting since hundreds of soldiers in the Army were in the same position as I was. My wife said that she would drop the children at my parents at weekends whilst I was in Germany, and she did. My parents kept me up to date with the progress of the children and sometimes I would get to speak to them on the phone; it broke my heart.

I was able to return from Germany on a fairly frequent basis and one day I was stood outside the door of the Married Quarter we had occupied together. I saw the 'boy' with whom she was now living with. It appeared his regimental Families officer had provided permission for him to stay at the married quarter. Apparently my wife and her boyfriend were going to marry in the very near future. At the time his regiment were preparing to move to Northern Ireland for a two year tour of duty. This was going to complicate my relationship with my children and I came home from Germany on an extended compassionate leave. I was staying at my parents and the children were to be dropped off at my parent's house. When the children arrived they were very quiet, they seemed withdrawn. I had not seen them so thin, and it was very disconcerting to see them like this. I was about to face one of the most harrowing periods of my life. I asked the children if there was a problem, they started to tell me a very horrific story. I went to the Amesbury police station and reported the incidents. The police doctor examined the children and confirmed what the children had told me. He also commented that the children were underweight and malnourished. The children gave their statements, and as we were leaving by the front of the police station a police car pulled into the car park. In the car was my wife. From that point on the children remained with me at my parent's house. They were not to stay with their mother she could visit them at my parents on her own. My wife and her boyfriend were now facing very serious charges.

Bulford

During the wait for the court case against my wife and her partner I made a serious mistake, yet again. My heart ruled my head. She made contact with me and assured me that her latest boyfriend was banned from the house. She wanted to see the children and could they stay with her over the next weekend.

I had a blazing row with my dad he told me I was a fool. What did I think that I playing at, she and her boyfriend had been accused of child abuse (physical). At this point nobody had informed me that my wife had been charged by the police for any offences. One Friday I took the children to their mum's house, and they seemed genuinely pleased to see her. I said that I would pick them up on the Sunday. She seemed fine and the children looked OK. When I went to pick them up, her boyfriend was in the house the children were very quiet. It seems as though they were being told to withdraw their statements to the police. It had been a deliberate ploy to get the children to tell the police nothing had happened to them. The story was that the boyfriend, had just been playing rough outdoor games with them. My wife also refused to let the children go, and I should never have placed the children in this predicament. It was a very careful planned situation, a car pulled up, a woman came over to me and asked if I was Mr Keith Hearn. I confirmed that I was, and she showed an identity card. She asked if she could enter the house, and I was invited in; my wife had phoned a social services department and informed them that I had dropped the children off with her and her boyfriend. The children were taken away to a safe house'. I did not know where to go what to do, and apparently my wife and her boyfriend had been charged by the police on cruelty charges. In hindsight I should never have taken the children back to the house. My wife and I should have met in a public area, a restaurant/pub or coffee shop. In the heat of the moment many things were twisted around and allegations were made, including that I could not cope with the children. I did it out of compassion for the children and their mum.

During the social services investigations I was interviewed on the premise that I was in the Army and without a partner to help me raise the children. My wife seemed to be encouraged in pursuing her relationship with her current boyfriend, as it would be in her favour. I said to the social worker that the pair of them had been charged with child abuse. I was told that they had not gone to court and it was highly unlikely in the eyes of the social workers that she would be sent to prison. The social worker informed me at a meeting that they were going to submit their findings to the court. On one court appearance for custody of the children, the social services solicitor read out part of a statement from my wife. "I loved Keith more as a brother, not as a lover or husband. He was a means to enable me to escape from my stifled, religious life with my parents. As soon as he fell in love with me I told him anything that he wanted to hear." It was such a shock. In court I was allowed to respond to the statement, I just said, "Why did she have the children? Why was she so cruel in allowing me to think I was living with someone who I thought loved me; my life and the children's lives up until then were a tissue of lies." It was such a devastating revelation, or was it another lie? My solicitor added that if she can deceive my client into believing he was in a loving marriage for so long, she is capable of any amount of lies.

The dreadful outcome was that the children were placed in foster care, in Salisbury, and it broke my heart. I went to visit the children with my parents, and the sight that met our eyes was mind blowing; it was a Council run foster home, and it was horrific. There was nothing that could remotely be equated to a safe friendly home. The whole system was about control and going through the motions with the minimum amount of emotional care. I had to get them out of the foster home and after engaging a really good solicitor, for whom I will always be grateful. I finally got part custody of my children. The state had the other part. It was better than before but, for many years I was looking over my shoulder for any interference from care workers or social workers.

During this period my wife and her boyfriend were found guilty of child abuse (physical); I and the children were never asked to give evidence. I do not know the length of jail sentence they received. My wife was sent to Holloway Prison and he was sent to a youth offenders institution initially and then onto an adult prison.

I look back on this period with fear and wish that I could change this period of my life. I love my children dearly and can only hope they will forgive me for my part in this horrendous period of their lives. I knew that my absences were putting a strain on our relationship and I perhaps should have done more to help my wife in coping. I now realise that trust is what makes a relationship endure and it needs time to nurture. I am not blameless in what occurred I should have faced up to a broken marriage and tried to make the best of it. Instead I continued to try to hang on and hope, probably knowing it wasn't the right thing to do but convincing myself I didn't. It made things worse. We arrived in Bulford as a wonderful happy family and left destroyed and broken. I never got over the events until 2012. The children will never have forget the events.

Chapter 6 -Norway/Turkey/Denmark

Norway is a country that has had a profound impact on me. I only got to visit the country during the winter months care of the British Army. During the winter it can be a very inhospitable place; however, the people are very friendly. Nothing ever seems to happen outside of the main cities during the winter season.

I was serving with 249 (AMF (L)) Signal Squadron based in Bulford, Wiltshire. The AMF L stands for Allied Mobile Force – Land, a quick reaction Force. When I served with the unit it deployed to Northern Norway, Germany, Denmark and Eastern Turkey. The squadron would deploy to Norway during January to April; we would either travel by ship from Marchwood near Southampton or by air from RAF Lyneham in Wiltshire. If the unit flew to Norway, it was the most frequent way of travelling, we would land at Bergen Airport or Oslo Airport. I only ever travelled by military ship to Norway the once. It was not one of the most pleasant of trips and it was nothing like the cruise packages advertised in the media. We travelled on a RFA (Royal Fleet Auxiliary) ship. We embarked at Marchwood docks near Southampton. It was a slow sailing and it seemed to take forever, in reality it only took a few days. Part of the way across the North Sea we had to carry out safety drills. It was during the early hours, it was pitch black and the drill was to simulate either a missile attack, aircraft attack or a ships fire. It was freezing cold on deck. The North Sea wind ripped through everyone's clothing, the sea spray soaking our clothing. After the habitual roll call and accounting for everyone we were allowed below decks. Everyone was cold and thoroughly wet through, and below decks there was nowhere to get warm or dry. There was a Royal Marines sergeant on board. He was travelling to the same exercise area. He was as sick as a dog, we took the mick out of him. He said that in all the years of service in the Royal Marines travelling by sea was by far the worst form of travel. The remainder of the journey was uneventful. We were housed deep in the hull of the ship, and if you were one of those unfortunate people sleeping near the bulk head. They were lucky if they got any sleep next to the bulk head due to the noise of the sea smashing against the sides of the ship. On the mess deck there were Chinese chefs from Hong Kong, as well as stewards. They understood English but if anyone did not like something or you wanted something else to eat they would only speak in Chinese, most of soldiers said 'oh forget it'. The tables had what I would describe as a wooden lip to stop the plates falling off in rough seas, and by heck the North Sea was very rough.

The unit was the only fully trained Arctic Warfare Signals Squadron in the British Army. Most soldiers completed a three year tour of duty with the squadron. Most, like me, had not skied before; it was a shock to the system and a huge challenge. There was a continual turnover of personnel who were required to be trained in Arctic survival and warfare skills. Every year the squadron ran a Basic Arctic Survival Course and an Artic Warfare Course. The Basic Arctic Survival course was a lesser course, but none the less it was an extremely taxing course.

During my first deployment to Norway I attended an Arctic Warfare course. It stood me in good stead for future deployments. It would also show other members of the unit that even though I had to carry out my clerical duties. I had completed the same training as everyone else; over the years I

140

attended the course a couple of times, to ensure that I was up to date with new ideas and methods. In Norway there were no family distractions. Most of the time I deployed with the squadron we were billeted at the Stalheim Hotel, in the Naeroyladen Valley near Voss. The training and exercises were dry, meaning the consumption of alcohol was forbidden. That was until one evening, which I will cover later in this chapter.

Apart from a refresher survival course, I remained at the hotel. I was part of the unit's rear echelon. I am sure that sometimes they would think, 'bloody lucky sod; sat in his warm office'. There was one particular incident that happened to me, that sticks in my mind. There were personnel from the unit learning how to herringbone. I was the second one to traverse the hill. The snow had stopped falling, and the snow that had settled was fresh and soft on the ground, and there was a stillness in the air. I was about halfway down the hill when my left leg gave way. I tried to stand up, but I could not bear any weight on the left leg. I took my Bergen off and looked down at my leg. It was at a very peculiar angle. I could hear people shouting from the group above. Someone skied down to help me. They knew something was wrong, especially when they saw me crumple and was struggling to stand up on my legs. I could not feel the pain and at this point I thought that I had only sprained my ankle. I subsequently found that I had snapped my tibia and fibular. I had severed the nerves leading to that part of my ankle. I was soon carried off the hill. I felt such a fool having to be carried to the hotel. There was an Army medic based there. At the time one of my brothers was serving with Alpha Troop 244 Air Support Signal Squadron. The troop had a similar role to my unit. His troop was formed up for a nominal role check and head count. He could see that it was me being carried; he shouted 'Are you

OK?' I informed him that I would be OK; I just felt a little stupid and had only sprained my ankle. There was a small medical unit from the Royal Army Medical Corps (RAMC) based in the hotel. The corporal in charge checked my ankle and he declared that he was not happy about my damaged ankle. He carried out some basic checks, I kept on insisting that I was fine, it was only a sprain. He maintained he was sending me to the main Norwegian Hospital in Voss, it is the closest town. He said that he would inform the RAMC Captain in charge; he was based at a large Norwegian Military Camp near Voss. I was virtually thrown into the back of the Land Rover, and my legs fell across a camouflage net that was covering the vehicle's spare wheel. There was someone else already in the back of the Land Rover, he asked me what I had done. I replied "nothing much, I think that I have only sprained my ankle. I will be back skiing in a day or two". I enquired why was he going to hospital, to me he looked perfectly alright. I soon realised that he had part of a ski pole sticking out of the left side of his temple. The pole had been cut by someone and there was about six inches of pole protruding from his head, it seemed to be deeply imbedded in his skull. He also had a huge black bruise spreading around that part of his skull and covering part of his face. I said to him, "Bloody hell that looks sore." I could not get over his composure; he was as calm as anything. He just said, 'No not really'. It was so bizarre travelling to the hospital with him having part of a ski pole sticking out of his head. He was chatting away as though it was quite normal to have a ski pole sticking out of his head. When we arrived at the hospital the RAMC Captain was already there. I knew him from Bulford he was there to liaise with the hospital's medical teams and to make sure that the correct paper work was processed. Obviously I needed to have my leg X-rayed. I informed the driver that I had only sprained my ankle and would be going back with him. Later I could see the Medical Officer (MO) walking towards me with what I could only assume were my X- rays. He had been consulting with the Norwegian Medical Staff regarding the results. The MO said to me, "Corporal Hearn, what do you think that you have done to your leg?" I said to him, "In my professional opinion I have sprained my ankle." He responded, "That's why you are a clerk and I am a bloody doctor, you have broken your tib and fib." Before I could reply the driver said, "Keith, that's a good one; proves how much you bloody know". I replied "bugger" I wanted to get back to my unit. The longer I remained in Norway I would keep the extra money. All the military personnel were receiving extra payments for being on exercise in Norway.

I was placed onto a trolley and left somewhere in a dark and dingy area of the hospital and fell asleep. It was some hours later when I was awoken by a hospital porter. He was very agitated and shouting at me. It transpired that at some point whilst I had been asleep I had been moved to the cellar area of the hospital. I found out later that I had been missing for about four hours. The hospital shifts had been changed during the period that I was asleep and I was subsequently overlooked, the story of my life. I was moved to the pre op room. The anaesthetist was about fifty or so and she spoke perfect English. Not like my Norwegian, and she told me that she went on holiday once a year to Kent in England. She explained that before the operation she would give me an epidural. This would make me feel numb from the waist down. She said that she was having a problem finding a good spot to inject me in the back. My back had thick muscle tone, as a result of skiing with sixty lbs of weight strapped onto the back. The body soon tones up. She eventually found a decent spot to administer the injection; it would take five to ten minutes for it to take effect. I kept telling her that I could still feel my legs and toes, I had not lost any feeling. She took a pin and was sticking it into my legs and toes to test if I had any feeling. I fell asleep and I awoke briefly during the operation, to the left I saw a monitoring screen. I could see a lot of red skin and what looked like bone. I sat bolt upright and I could see four people surrounding me I looked down and realised that the picture on the screen was my leg. I looked down and passed out. Very brave of me! I woke up on a ward. I had no sense of time. I could see that it was light outside; I knew that it was the next day, which meant I must have been in hospital for at least eight hours. A nurse approached me and I asked if I could have a bath or a shower and clean my teeth. She said "not just yet". She explained that I should not to try and get out of the bed suddenly; as the flow of blood to the lower part of the leg would be very painful. If I wanted to go anywhere I was to ask one of the nurses. She informed me that I had a prescription for painkillers. I told her that I was not one to take pills, and that I felt OK and did not require any pain killers. I thanked her for her concern. I wished that I had taken her up on her offer, she must have thought that I was a bit of a fool. Later on in the night I woke in pure agony; I was sweating like mad and it felt as though my ankle was on fire. Needless to say I required some painkillers, and very quickly. A nurse said that a few of the other nurses had wondered just how long it would take for the pain to kick in. She explained because I had a few epidural injections before the operation, the affects had lasted a long time. Obviously the affects had worn off at this point and boy did I know about it! When I woke up the next day I was feeling so much better. I noticed that there were three other soldiers on the ward. One of the soldiers was from my brother's unit, he moaned, moaned and moaned; he was moaning for the sake of moaning. I could see that he was running the nurses ragged.

Once again I asked if I could get a shower I was starting to feel rank. The nurses checked with the duty doctor and he told them only if I thought that I was up for it. The nurses advised me that I should not just 'throw' myself out of bed. I should gradually ease my leg down, the reason being to stop a sudden rush of blood to the bottom half of my leg. I swung my left leg out of the bed, and I have never felt so sick, the pain was excruciating. I had to grin and bear it, I had to get used to using the leg again. The leg was throbbing like mad. A nurse wrapped a plastic bag around the dressing. I was given crutches and I made my way to the shower room; the showers in the hospital were like small wet rooms. Needless to say it was fantastic to clean off the muck. I managed to get back to the ward on my own unaided, washed and cleaned. It felt so good feeling human again. Once I returned to the ward, the moaner was still complaining to the nurses that he had not had a shower since he was admitted. He wanted the nurses to arrange a shower just as they had done for me. The way the nurses looked at one another when he demanded a shower, told a thousand words. I told him to stop moaning and to get off his bloody lazy backside and help himself.

The Army Medical Officer came to the ward to see if we were OK and to provide a report to the Officer Commanding of each unit. Keeping them abreast of the medical situations concerning each soldier. He informed me that the surgeon had done the best he could on my ankle. He said that I was lucky that I had been admitted to a Norwegian hospital as they were used to these types of breaks. They had pinned and inserted a metal plate to secure the tibia and fibular.

My brother Michael and some of my mates had managed to visit me; he asked the nurses if he could move me to the lift area. The

145

moaner instructed Michael to come back for him. Michael told him to 'piss off'. My brother explained that he was a shirker; he did not like hard work or the Artic Warfare Training. As I have said before it is mandatory, no one gets out of attending at least one of the courses. Michael explained that when he started his first day of Artic Warfare Training the moaner had complained of a bad back, and therefore had ended up in hospital. Once I got to the lift area there were five people, some from my unit and some from Michael's. They had also brought my equipment from the Squadron, they realised that I would have to be medically evacuated (MEDIVAC) to the UK.

On the day that I was released from hospital I was to fly back to the UK in a C130 Hercules aircraft. The aircraft was 'parked' away from the main terminal and close to some woods. Once I had boarded the aircraft there were ten others already on the aircraft. I recognised some of them from the Parachute Regiment based in Bulford. I noticed a large plywood box in the middle of the aisle. Some of the Para's were playing cards on the top of the box. Someone asked me what I had done and so I explained what had happened. There was a roar of laughter at my predicament. One of the group told me to rest my leg on top of the box, which I did; and it was very comfortable, as my leg was throbbing like mad. During the flight the pain was shooting through my leg. I got talking to some of the Para's that I knew. I asked why they were going back to the UK. Were they attending a course? One of them replied that they were part of a regimental burial party; I asked whose funeral was it. They told me that it was a sergeant in the Regiment. I had heard that there had been an 'accident' on the mortar live firing range. A mortar round had been dropped into the tube it had not ignited. Another round had been dropped on top of the previous round within the tube. This action caused both rounds to ignite in the mortar tube. This is referred to as a double drop. The fragments of metal flew around the firing point, seriously injuring those around the mortar. They said that it was carnage on the range site. I could well believe it. The sergeant, who was killed, was struck by a small piece of red hot metal. If it had hit any other part of his body he may have survived. The piece of shrapnel penetrated his heart and killed him instantly. His body was in the plywood that box we were sat around. The Hercules touched down at RAF Lyneham in Wiltshire. I was transported to The Military Hospital at Wroughton outside of Swindon. I stayed there for a couple of days to have my leg checked. I was determined to get back to using my leg as quickly as possible. At this point the squadron was still deployed in Norway, so I had ample time to return to fitness.

After a short period of time my body began to reject the metal in my ankle. I began to see the outline of the metal plate and the screw heads; they appeared on my skin as red outlines. I was eventually sent to the local military hospital to have them removed.

For me these were memorable times, but for my family I doubt if they found this period very memorable. I did care about my family, I tried to put them first they were always on my mind whenever I was away. It was my career, and the only other option available would have been to leave the Army. It was not an option I wanted to take. I had a very young family to provide for.

During a particular deployment to Norway there was much unrest with the soldiers within the squadron. The Officer Commanding ruled with an iron fist; in the armed forces the officers are the leaders, and the majority of them are capable of leading their troops. This particular deployment, the pressure from above was relentless. I realised that during the deployments to Norway that there was a lot of hard work to be done. There was the odd period to relax (I do not mean getting drunk and being rowdy or letting ones hair down). These exercises were normally 'dry' (no alcohol), which the members of the squadron were aware of. I meant, by relaxing, that it was to have time to maintain personal equipment and military equipment and time to wash any laundry and write home, receive mail and to have some time to relax. The Norwegian Liaison Officer attached to the Squadron kept the unit in its place regarding winter survival. There was one particular night exercise in a valley; we were very lucky during this particular night. As a squadron we skied up into the mountains surrounding the valley. We were learning the skills required for night time ski conditions. Carrying the equipment that we needed to survive an attack by enemy forces and whatever nature had to throw at us. During the trek as we headed towards a valley we heard a loud cracking noise it sounded louder in the quiet night sky. It was apparent that the Norwegian Liaison Officer knew very well where it was coming from. People began to make up their own minds about what was happening, and the Norwegian Officer was getting agitated with our Officer Commanding (OC); they seemed to be arguing. The majority of the squad could see the Norwegian Officer ski off the mountain. Rumour had it that there was an argument between him and the OC, the OC had told the Norwegian Liaison Officer that he knew what he was doing. As a squad we skied along a ridge above a valley. We heard a tremendous rumbling sound coming from the rear of the group. We instinctively knew that we had skied over an avalanche area. We had no idea of how large it was or how close we were to it before it cascaded into the valley. Any avalanche was bad enough, especially when there are a hundred or so men skiing in the vicinity or possibly over it. It is believed it was why the Norwegian Officer had left. I am sure that he had no idea that we would be skiing so close to it. He reported the incident to his superiors and they subsequently reported the incident to the NATO high command in Norway. On the way back to our base camp, the Squadron had been spilt into sections. Earlier in the day we had to clear the snow and build banks of snow to form rudimentary walls. The roof was made up of 'tent sheets' these were individual sheets of tarpaulin. They had metal holes sewn into them so that the sheets could be bound together with cord to form one large tarpaulin. This was fastened with tent pegs to form a roof. Inside our equipment was stored. A member from each group was nominated to stay behind and cook a hot meal. It normally consisted of what can only be called a form of stew in a large pressure cooker. During this period the Army used multi fuel stoves. We were using a fuel called naphtha, it is heavier than air. If too much fuel is pumped into the cooker before igniting the fuel it would lay on the bottom of the shelter. As we skied back towards the base camp some of the skiers could see a fire in the distance. As we got closer we could see it was the squadron camp. As we skied closer to our section we could see that it was our shelter on fire; the person cooking the meal had pumped too much fuel before lighting the stove and the fuel lying in the shelter caught alight. A few of the tent sheets were on fire. We got back in time to put some of them out. Some of the sheets were singed others were badly burnt. In addition, some of the sleeping bags were burnt. I can say that we were not impressed with the person who set fire to the shelter. This type of accident does have a massive effect on morale, and we knew that some of us had burnt sleeping bags and even less 'tent sheets'. We were miles away from the hotel; we had to carry on as best we could. One of the survival training techniques for surviving in the outdoors was to build emergency 'snow holes'. One particular time it was late afternoon, of langlauf (cross country skiing) and tactical military ski drills; I think that we must have travelled for about five hours. We were divided into groups of around four or five (one of the reasons of being split randomly was to ensure that different people could work together as a team). This particular time, the temperature was dropping rapidly. It soon plummeted once the sun had gone down. It was approaching minus fifteen; everyone dug the snow into square blocks with our snow shovels. Normally we dug into a bank of snow, and then dug down to create what is referred to as a 'cold hole'. This would trap any cold air during the night. We had to make blocks of snow to create a rough igloo. Inside there were shelves dug deep into the bank to form sleeping platforms. The skis and ski pole were stuck into the roof to form a gap to allow carbon monoxide and condensation to escape. Too much condensation would eventually collapse the roof of the snow hole and possibly bury everyone in there. The skis and ski poles would hopefully indicate our position to those searching for any survivors.

One particular night everyone had eaten a hot meal and were fully clothed in their sleeping bags to keep warm. For safety reasons there was a candle watch, which meant that we all took turns during the night to stay awake with a lit candle. Never put ones legs into the cold hole, believe me. Even wearing snow boots tucked inside an arctic sleeping bag the cold eventually penetrates into the legs and feet. The cold keeps you awake. We all took our turn, one person decided that it was too cold during his candle watch. He pulled his feet out of the cold hole and snuggled up in his sleeping bag and fell asleep. Most of us awoke at the same time, to water dripping onto our faces and our sleeping bags were soaked. I remember looking up and there was no candle light. I found an emergency candle in the dark and lit it to find that the roof of the snow hole had dropped and it was literally inches from my face. The water was dripping off the roof, the ice was melting and the roof was collapsing due to the heat from our breath and our body heat. The person on candle watch had fallen asleep. He had gone to sleep early on during his stag (slang for guard duty). We quickly dragged everything out of the shelter, and woke up the remainder of the team, we could see just how low the structure had dropped. The individual who had fallen asleep on his watch, as a punishment he had to do all of the dirty tasks for the rest of the training period.

There was a period of heightened tension within the unit. The Officer Commanding was losing control and respect of the men he commanded. There are very strict rules regarding Military Training in Norway, from an environmental and safety aspect. There were two incidents that I remember that crop up whenever I meet someone who served with the unit at the same time. One was a shameful incident which could have been deemed mutinous. During subsequent military reunions, people have asked a handful of those who served in the squadron during this period if we served in the unit during the 'mutiny'. The infamous period in question began with the soldiers having a dry exercise, the officers and senior Non Commissioned Officers had a bar which served alcohol. It was part of the build up to a flash point. The Officers and SNCO's had a games evening, it had degenerated into a full on 'piss up'. I was on duty and manning the 'reception area' of the hotel. Which had the telephone system and the dedicated phone for UK. I also manned the Rear Link

Radio link back to Bulford UK. There was a lot of noise coming from the 'bar' area. In the hotel foyer there was a flight of stairs which came from the bar area and ended close to the reception. I heard a lot of shouting and swearing coming from the steps. I saw the Motor Transport Sergeant, MT Sgt; he was in charge of the vehicle requirements of the Squadron. He was walking down the steps when the Quartermaster, who was a Captain, jumped onto his back they crashed onto the ground. There was a lot of shouting and other people trying to pull them apart. They were taken back to their respective rooms. The Squadron Sergeant Major (SSM) tried to find out what had happened. I had started to write up the events book. As twenty five year old corporals we were not deemed responsible enough to have a couple of beers and relax after being on exercise for weeks on end. The SSM spoke to me and asked me what I had seen. I told him what I had observed, I did not know where or how it had started. However, I had seen that the QM was on the back of the MT Sgt and both of them ending up on the floor. He ordered me to type up my statement. He said that I would not be relieved from my post in the morning. I had to remain to type up the various statements regarding the events that had taken place. He said that everything that I hear or see would be in the strictest confidence. The Officer Commanding eventually turned up. The SSM briefed him on what had apparently happened during the evening. The OC stated that nothing must be said to other members of the Squadron. What he meant was I was not to blab my mouth off to anyone.

In the morning, everyone was coming down for breakfast. They had heard about the "punch up" the previous evening. After breakfast the OC called me into his office. He said that he had been informed that most of the squadron knew about the events

152

that had happened the night before. How did the rest of the Squadron find out? I told him that it was not from me. He said that he knew that it had not come from me. If it had I would be sacked and on a flight back to the UK. The squadron hierarchy seemed to be closing ranks. It does seem as though the OC had come to some kind of agreement with the QM and MT Sgt. Nothing more was said the paper work was destroyed.

The resentment between the Other Ranks (ORS), and the hierarchy began to bubble away. During the night, someone had moved all of the Officer's and SNCO's ski boots and equipment to different parts of the Hotel. Later on in the morning the Squadron was on parade outside of the hotel. The SNCO's and Officers were shouting at the squad about discipline. They were wanting to know the name of the person or persons who had messed the equipment around. Obviously No-one owned up. Overnight it had snowed there was fresh snow on the ground; the snow was the light fluffy type, it came midway up our legs. We were made to run with Ski boots and ski equipment on, less skis. We ran for a distance, and wearing so many layers of clothing the sweat was pouring off us. We were physically fit; our lungs were burning due to the cold temperature and the effort of gulping the cold air into our lungs. There were more than one hundred people running in boots that were totally inadequate for the job. The snow was deep and people were falling over, eventually we got back to our start point. The SNCO's and Officers were waiting. Once again we were asked which one of us had messed around with the artic equipment. No one replied. The Norwegian Liaison Officer looked very uncomfortable at the way that we were being treated. Again he may have reported the incident to his superiors, and I am sure he did. We carried on with light training around the local area. I remember a group of us skiing on the white wasteland, and there was nothing but white everywhere. It just looked like a large field. There were quite a few of us in the ski group we had skied over the roof of a farmhouse.

As we skied back to the hotel, we were travelling on a very icy road. I could not stop I had hit a patch of ice. I went whizzing past all of the others, and I think that some of them thought 'wow, Keith's a bloody good skier'. Far from it, I could not stop and I was picking up more and more speed, the road was quite steep, and I was petrified. In front of me I could see what looked like a fresh bank of snow, I thought that it would stop me. I hit the snow, what I did not realise was that hidden in the snow there was a brick wall. My skies bent and snapped, I was thrown onto the road, everyone curled up laughing. We got back to the hotel everyone seemed more relaxed and in good spirits. We were told to report to the cookhouse and wait for the OC's address. He came in and told us that we were all punished due to someone's stupidity and we were read the riot act. He announced that the squadron would have the bar open that evening. On hearing the news everyone was very happy. At the time there was a saying going around the unit, it was "be there or be square". I was going to be square because once again I was manning the duty desk. I had not seen my room for almost two days and I needed some sleep. That night the booze flowed. Some of the Officers and SNCO's stayed for a little while. Most people were pretty drunk, the majority were wary of the situation, and they thought that it was some sort of trick. Later I was relieved of my duty, and I had a few beers and noticed the 'Be there or be square' gang were knocking back the beer. I noticed the Yeoman of Signals, a Warrant Officer, was still in the bar.

Never a Dull Moment

The next morning at breakfast I heard stories about the Yeoman in the bar the night before. He had been trying to jump from one table to the next he had slipped and banged the side of his head near his eye. I heard another story about someone trying to get to the OC's bedroom. They had a knife, he was prevented when he was restrained by some others in the OC's corridor. At breakfast in the cookhouse, two soldiers started to fight and pushed each other through the fire-proof partition wall within the cookhouse area. On parade that morning the squadron took no notice of the instructor's words of command, the SSM took control and barked out orders of command once again no-one moved. It took the OC to shout out the words of command and he threatened to charge anyone with mutinous behaviour. This was still the aftermath of the QM's incident the SNCO's and Officer's drinking debacle. The OC had made his point no one was disciplined. It was a period of ill-discipline within the squadron and the Officers and SNCO's losing the respect and control of the OR's.

There was an incident involving a helicopter. Close to the hotel we had dug and cleared a helicopter pad, every morning someone had to make sure that the area was cleared of any debris. One morning a senior officer was going to visit the unit, but most of the squadron was out training. I grabbed a black plastic bin bag. I arrived at the helicopter pad and I could hear the helicopter. It was gazelle, which can carry four passengers. It is a reconnaissance helicopter. I placed some snow into the bag. I was crouched facing away from the down drought from the helicopter. Hats were never to be worn as the downdraught from the blades could suck the hat into the blades or engine. I could just make out the shape of the helicopter as it landed. I looked again and next my face was a bright light. Then the pilot played a

155

trick just before he landed he nudged the helicopter forward and gently knocked me over. Then he touched down, the helicopter was so manoeuvrable.

As the main clerical support during the squadron deployments to Norway. Sometimes I had no choice but to be based in the hotel whilst the squadron deployed on exercise or during military ski training. It was not too bad as the rest of the squadron knew that I had attended the Arctic Warfare courses. I was manning the reception area when the QM came into reception; he was laughing his head off. The QM and the SQMS had been out skiing. They always went skiing wearing their civilian gear, whereas the rest of the squadron used the military equipment. The skis that we were issued were called 'NATO Planks', virtually lengths of wood, with the ski boot cramps to hold the boots into place. They both were using civilian skis. They were right posers, especially the SQMS. He had a nickname of Yorick, a character from Hamlet, a Shakespearian play, as he had a very thin face, almost skeletal. The QM told me to write an entry in the Events Book stating that the SQMS had disappeared down a hole near the hotel. I asked, "Shall I get people out looking for him?" He replied, "No, he will be along soon." Within minutes the SQMS strode through the hotel doors. We could smell him before he got anywhere near us, he absolutely stank and was covered in brown excrement. He had fallen into one of the hotel's cesspits. He looked a fine sight with his designer GUCCI ski kit covered in muck. He sheepishly walked on. The QM told me to enter another event; "Found SQMS, smelt to high heaven." It was a very comical site.

When the squadron returned to Bulford, the whole squadron was on parade. The QM instructed everyone to take their jumpers off as there had been reports of needles being found near the single accommodation blocks. The squadron was on parade, the Medical Officer was there with members of the Royal Military Police. Once the jumpers were off we had to roll our shirt sleeves up. These shirts at the time were called KF Shirts, horrible uncomfortable scratchy shirts. As a result there stood a motley variation of uniform. The MO came along looking for needle marks on our arms, but luckily none were found. When the MO and RMP left. The QM instructed the SQMS and other QM staff to go up and down the lines, taking details to charge people for new shirts and jumpers.

We had a Run every day and every Friday was the OC's parade. The run consisted of a ten to fifteen mile run, sometimes over Salisbury Plain or on Wireless Ridge or over to Tidworth and through Shipton Bellinger village.

I will always remember two Signalmen volunteering for 'tests' at Porton Down, which is the Nuclear, Biological and Chemical Warfare establishment (NBC). This establishment were always sending out requests for human volunteers for testing. The soldiers would get 'extra pay' for taking part in the tests. The two signalmen set off. They were there for a week. When the soldiers came back to the unit they told everyone they had been tested on flu viruses or the common cold. These two came back and said that they had been given droplets on their skin, they said it was easy money. When they deployed to Norway one year, I think it was about twelve months later, they had to be sent back to the UK; their skin on their arms exploded in sores and all sorts of rashes. The story goes that the tests that they were subjected to were designed to react to freezing temperatures.

157

Hence in Norway, when they deployed, it was always going to be -20 to -45 degrees. The laboratory knew that the unit deployed to Norway. As they had volunteered for the tests they had not been forced into taking part.

249 Signal Squadron (AMF (L)) had many soldiers applying for the Special Air Service (SAS) and we had a fairly high pass rate. The unit was a good grounding for applying for selection to the Special Forces.

During Officer Commanding Orders, this was the time when he would summarily hand out justice for any misdemeanours. The corridor to the OC's office would have the troop commander and the troop Sgt, with responsibility for that soldier. If the soldier was awarded so many days in the Guardroom the SSM would march the soldier out of the office and into his office with the Troop Sgt following. The SSM would phone the Guardroom to inform them that someone from the squadron would be staying with them for however long. The Troop sergeant would have to escort the soldiers to their room to make sure that both his equipment and his uniform was packed. Before marching the soldier to the local guardroom. One particular time the troop sergeant came staggering out of the accommodation block looking quite dazed, with a lump on his forehead. He told the SSM that the soldier had placed his steel helmet in the bottom of a long army issue bag, and then filled the bag, (nickname sausage bag because it was long), with his other equipment. The bag is very heavy when full. The solider swung it around and clouted the Sergeant. He was knocked out for a period of time. It was the helmet at the bottom of the kit bag that caught him. The soldier ran for it and got into his car and drove off camp, and at that point most of the barrack area was open and at the time there were no security gates. The RMP were informed, and the soldier was a bit of a mother's boy and lived in Manchester. A local RMP unit were waiting for him and brought him back to Bulford. He was put on a more serious charge for hitting the Sergeant and escaping custody.

Turkey

One of the exercise deployments whilst I was serving with the Ace Mobile Force Land (AMF (L)) was to Turkey, Eastern Turkey; the nearest city was Erzurum. When the squadron deployed, the city was cleaning up after an earthquake. The exercise area was near to the then Soviet Border, close to Armenia. The area has been fought over for centuries. There are old forts and fortifications from a bygone age scattered over the border area. We were a few hundred kilometres away from where Noah's Ark was said to have come to rest after the biblical floods, Mount Ararat.

The Squadron flew from RAF Brize Norton, in Oxfordshire. We flew by C130 Hercules aircraft. When the aircraft was approaching Erzurum Turkish airbase, there were severe storms, lots of rain and thunder and lightning. The lightening was cracking around the aircraft; the sky was the colour of gun-metal grey, punctuated with the sound of thunder and the bright streaks of lightning. The aircraft was full of soldiers, our kit and Bergen's were piled up in the front of the aircraft. Suddenly the aircraft was lit up by a blue hue and a loud bang; everyone looked at one thinking that someone must have packed some prohibited items in their kit. The front cone of the aircraft had been struck by lightning and the lightening had damaged the Radar. The load master entered the cockpit and threw the burning Radar unit into the area of the plane where we were sat, it was a worrying sight. We were informed that the aircraft was going to start to dump fuel as a precaution. The pilot then started the descent towards the airfield. When we all disembarked from the aircraft, a crew member took us around to the front of the aircraft. We could see that the black nose cone had been ripped apart and there was a gaping hole. It was where the radar equipment was housed and the lightning had hit. Seeing the damaged aircraft in this state certainly focused the mind.

Everyone who landed at the airfield had to wait in a tented area on the airbase, to wait for the vehicles that had been loaded onto ships at Southampton. They were to arrive in a port in southern Turkey and would be moved by rail to a railhead in Erzurum. The drivers were taken by bus to the railhead. We would crew the vehicles and move off to the exercise area. We had heard that due to the weather, that part of the exercise start point had been washed away. The Turkish Army had to dig a new route. Whilst we were waiting in a tented area a Belgium Sergeant Major, who was a short and bull-necked man. He was a member of the Belgium Parachute Brigade, he informed us not to drink the water unless it had been boiled and purified. He said some of the Belgium soldiers had become ill drinking the water. He pointed out two Turkish soldiers who were delivering the water; they were also slopping out the latrines, hardly a reassuring combination.

The vehicles eventually arrived; we loaded our personal equipment including our rifles onto the vehicles. We travelled through Erzurum; there was a mix of traditional dress and western. We noticed lots of armed Turkish soldiers lining the route through the city. They were heavily armed, and they wore a blue camouflaged uniform with a blue beret. I believe that these were a highly trained section of the Turkish Army.

We travelled for miles on a highway towards the Armenian border; these highways were the artery for the Turkish Military to get to the various borders that they had to defend if there was ever an outbreak of hostilities. The Turkish Military Police patrolled the highways, ensuring that no one attempted to blow them up. We travelled through a military garrison town. As we drove through we could see the Military Police escorting ten people in handcuffs to a large parade square. More about this later on. We could see that they had been moved from a prison, which was close to the main road.

We were in a holding area waiting to move to our war positions to start the NATO exercise. The SSM informed me that a couple of officers and men had to attend a parade before the start of the exercise; the parade consisted of members nations of NATO. When the SSM returned he told me that the ten men who we had seen the previous day were hanged during the parade. He said that they were hanged in the vicinity of the parade by the Turkish Military Police. Eventually we moved to our exercise positions. Again, it was a few hour's drive into the mountains and we moved into the Turkish Army's pre-dug positions. These were dug out frequently, so that they were ready to use if required in a war situation. We passed some remote villages; in one of the villages there was an Old Russian fort. Some people lived in caves, and they had mud brick frontages and chimneys cut out of the rock. The roads were dirt tracks, and near one village a huge vicious looking dog attacked a Land Rover. It had a huge mouth with vicious looking teeth. One of the vehicles in the convoy was attacked by the dog the driver had his arm hanging out of the open window. The dog leapt up and sunk its teeth into his arm. A local famer shot the dog the driver's arm was in such a bad way he had to be taken to a field hospital. He was sent back to the UK for further medical treatment.

At our final location we were based high up in the mountains, the air was very thin and the sun was very strong. During our deployment a couple of American jeeps turned up and they had trailers, which were full of flowers. It was a slightly bizarre as they were asking if we had come across any poppy fields. The SSM took down the vehicle number plates and told them to stay where they were, they drove off. He used the radio to send the details of the incident which were sent to the American Liaison Officer attached the British HQ.

I decided to sit under the trees and use the radio without my shirt on. The exercise did not last very long; it was one of those NATO exercises which was meant to demonstrate to the Soviets that NATO was deployed along the border. Later that day my back was one huge blister. I was aware that in the Army sunburn is classed as a self-inflicted wound and is a chargeable offence. I also knew that the burn on my back was serious and I managed to get a lift to the field hospital. I was still carrying my rifle, and even though it was a military hospital they would not allow any weapons or ammunition to be brought into the hospital. I knew that one of our unit's radio vehicles was providing communications to the hospital; I got them to look after my rifle. I went into the hospital and the hospital staff assessed the blister on my back. They took me into one of the treatment rooms, and on the floor was a sheet of plastic. I took my shirt off. I suddenly felt something sharp cutting into my back, I heard a splash on the plastic sheeting; it was fluid from my back. They cut the rest of the skin off my back and smeared it in cream and stuck what I can only describe as tin foil onto my back. I took a look at the floor and could see the fluid and skin from my back. I was embarrassed for being so stupid as to get such a serious sunburn. I also knew what the consequences were. I signed the release documentation and collected my rifle. I had no idea of how I was going to get back to my unit. Just at that moment, another one of our vehicles arrived at the Radio Vehicle, and they said that they would take me back to my last location. I was lucky that they had not moved. I was in incredible pain that night I could not lay on my back.

The next morning the exercise ended and the squadron moved to a thick wooded area which was run by the Turkish Army. As we drove into the woods there was a log cabin guardroom manned by Turkish Military Police. They checked everyone in, counted how many people were in the Landover and the registration number. As I worked with the SSM he told me that he knew all about my hospital trip. He said that he was ready to charge me for a self-inflicted wound. He told me that because I had stayed at the hospital for treatment and not been admitted I was fortunate not to be charged. Later that night shots rang out in the nearby woods, everyone stood to thinking that it could be a rogue Turkish soldier or a terrorist attack. We had rifles but we did not have ammunition. Not like the Americans, they were stood to with their M16 rifles and magazines fixed onto their rifles. A message was sent to the troops that a Turkish Officer of the guard had found one of the guards asleep on duty; supposedly he had woken the guard and shot him dead. Allegedly the story is that Turkish Officers could shoot dead so many Turkish soldiers without an enquiry. It could have been a myth.

We eventually headed back to the airfield at Erzurum, and once again we travelled out of the mountains onto the flat plains of North-East Turkey, along the highways. Our convoy was overtaken by a couple of American tanks travelling at high speed. When travelling in a convoy there is a set speed limit, the tanks were travelling flat out. A few miles further on one of the tanks was off the road and had flipped onto its turret. We could see bodies around the tank it looked like someone had been cut in half, it was a very dramatic sight. One of our radio vehicles stopped and radioed for a helicopter and medical assistance; it was too late for at least one of the soldiers. We passed through a military garrison town, and we were a little subdued from the previous experiences and the events which had unfolded a few days previous; we could see prisoners in the exercise yard of another prison. We eventually arrived back in Erzurum. We parked the vehicles up and set up the tents, we were in a different area. The soldiers in the blue camouflage uniforms were around the area. I can only think that they were based at the airfield because they had finished escorting the NATO units and lining the streets of the city.

There was a football pitch in front of the squadron's vehicles. Some of the Turkish soldiers were playing football members of the squadron challenged them to a game. Everything seemed to be going OK, until one of the squadron tackled a Turkish soldier the soldier took offence. Some of the other Turkish soldiers picked up their rifles. The SSM could see what was unfolding and intervened. The Turk's unloaded their weapons and the SSM got everyone off the pitch. Another International Incident averted.

Denmark

The Danish people seemed very friendly. I will try and cram everything in that I remember about my military visit to the country. On one of the trips to Denmark the Squadron had to travel to Harwich in Suffolk and to load onto a civilian roll-on/roll-off ferry. We set off from Bulford early one evening ready to catch the ferry. There were four convoys on the road. In the convoy that I was with contained the Technicians (tech) Electronic Repair Vehicle, ERV. This truck was normally driven by a couple of Tech Corporals. It was a very heavy truck, full of technical instruments and stores to repair the Squadron's radios and electronic equipment. We were the last convoy to leave Bulford; the MT Sergeant was in the same convoy and the Light Air Defence, LAD team. They would repair any of the convoy vehicles if they broke down, or tow the vehicles to the docks. The MT sergeant spotted that the WO2 Foreman of Signals (F of S) had got into the driver seat of the ERV; he was not permitted to drive that vehicle. I believe the F of S pulled rank and the convoy set off. Everything was straightforward until we arrived at a small village outside of Harwich. The ERV took a wrong turning off the main road and headed into cul-de-sac a number of other vehicles followed the ERV. The truck had nowhere to turn around it drove through the front garden. The residents were not impressed. Luckily, the other vehicles were Land rovers and they remained on the road and did not plough through the gardens. When they got back onto the main Road, the RMP (Royal Military Police) and the civilian police were waiting. The FofS tried to blame the corporal in the cab, but everyone knew that he had been driving the truck. The police took statements from all of those involved.

We eventually arrived at the docks. The driver of the Land Rover that I was travelling in kept droning on about not liking boats and how he hated ships as they could sink. After a few drinks he sounded like a stuck record. He spoke to the Sergeant Major (SSM) about being sea sick. The SSM told him that the best thing for sea-sickness was to be at the highest point of a ship. It was just a passing remark. Later on in the evening there was an announcement over the ship's public address system; "Can someone in charge of the British Army on board the ship please report to the captain". The OC, the SSM, and other unit's hierarchy reported to the Captain. The SSM returned and told me that 'our driver' had tried to climb up on the ladder on one of the funnels of the ship. He was caught near the bottom of the funnel by a member of the ship's crew. He blamed the SSM for telling him the best way to beat sea-sickness was to climb the highest point of the ship. Nothing more was said.

The base camp in Denmark was located in a Danish Army Camp, which was in a town called Ringsted. The accommodation was brick buildings, and they were like large barns with bunk beds. Within the camp there was a soldier's bar. As the squadron were not on exercise at that time, we were allowed to frequent the bar, providing no one kicked the backside out of it. If we did we would be banned from using it.

Whilst on this particular exercise, one of the squadrons soldiers who had deployed on exercise in Norway a year or two before had gone absent without leave, (AWOL). He had handed himself into The Norwegian Border Police. Who in turn handed him over to members of the Royal Marines They ascertained which unit he was with and they knew that the squadron was on exercise in Denmark. The Royal Marines got in touch with the British

166

military attaché in Oslo. There was a Royal Marines radio detachment adjacent to our location. They knew the whereabouts of our SSM and gave him the signal from the Royal Marines and the Military Attaché in Norway. It informed the squadron that they had picked up Signalman X. The Marines in Norway were taking part in the exercise in Denmark they brought him with them. The Royal Marines SSM marched him in on orders in the OC's tent it doubled up as the Squadron Office. The soldier was dealt with by the OC and he was remanded for Court Martial.

On one occasion, the SSM and I had to attend a movement's conference in another part of Denmark. As we drove back into the camp at Ringsted Camp, there was a soldier bouncing off the walls of a building. He was in the British Army, I recognised him straight away. It was my middle brother, Michael. He was drunk. The SSM snapped, "Cpl Hearn, arrest that man." I replied, "I cannot do that, sir, it's my brother." He said to me "just get him to his detachment and we will say no more". Both of my brothers, Michael and Garry, were deployed on the same exercise with 30 Signal Regiment. I got Michael back to his vehicle and he collapsed on his camp cot, I told the others to keep an eye on him. I went to my youngest brother's vehicle and Garry was making a stew for the rest of his detachment. I told him about Michael and he replied that he would pop over and see him a later.

As the exercise progressed there were thousands of conscripted Danish soldiers taking part in the exercise. I think that the exercises were to enable the Danish Military to mobilise their reserve forces and to monitor how efficient the mobilization was. When the exercise had ended we travelled through various towns and villages. There were many soldiers on their bicycles in uniform with rifles slung over their shoulder heading for home it really was a bizarre sight.

Once we were back in Ringsted Barracks, I was billeted in a large barn transit accommodation blocks; I was on the bottom of a bunk bed, when I heard a few Army Air Corps pilots. They had been drinking in the bar on camp. They came in making such a noise, some of the others sleeping in the block told them to be quiet. After about half an hour there was a sickening thud on the concrete floor and a lot of moaning and someone in so much pain. The lights were switched on and a siren was heard outside an ambulance crew were trying valiantly to transfer the pilot onto a stretcher. He must have been in a lot of pain. We awoke in the morning to find blood and teeth on the floor; apparently he had rolled off the top bunk and onto the concrete floor. It was not a nice sight.

Chapter 7 – London 1986 - 1989

There are events that have happened during a person's life that can shape and have a huge influence over a person's life. I had not realised until very recently the true impact that some of the events in my life have had on me. The children and I moved to 238 (London) Signal Squadron at the time the squadron was based at Chelsea Barracks in the heart of London. Initially I was allocated family accommodation within Ingliss Barracks, Mill Hill, North London; fifteen miles away from Chelsea. Every day I would travel by tube to work; I eventually got a move to central London during the summer holidays. I did not have time to register the children at a local school I had to report immediately to my new unit. I was lucky that I found myself an "un-official" child minder, I could not leave them on their own while I went to work. I had been placed in a very difficult situation, it may well have been a 'test' of my will power and determination that would stretch me to the limit. I was desperate to have somewhere to live closer to my place of work.

After much wrangling I eventually got a different place to live; it was in one of the two thirteen-storey blocks of flats in Chelsea Barracks. It was a three bed roomed flat, and the children were allocated a place at the local school St Gabriel's in Pimlico.

Eventually I had an appointment to see my case worker at Westminster Social Services; the children accompanied me to the meeting. We sat around in a waiting room, it was full of all sorts of people. Our turn came to see the social worker, as we sat in his office he looked harassed and under pressure; he had files piled high on his desk. He introduced himself, and asked who the children were, and they looked at me in disbelief. I think that it was his idea of a joke or to try and break the ice, the children did not laugh. They were tense because they thought he was going to make a decision as to whether they could stay with me. They were extremely worried, they did not fully comprehend why I had to report to a social worker. He asked them some fairly basic questions, they happily answered his questions without being prompted; he wrote some notes in a file. He asked me what employment I had, he obviously knew that I was in the Army; I told him where we were living. He said that he was not going to take the case any further, the Army would not let anything happen to the children. The children had somewhere to live. They were also visiting both sets of grandparents. He said that it was a balanced situation for the children. He told me that he had some horrendous case files. Which were more complicated than mine. In his opinion the case file was going to be closed. The children looked at me and I think that they were thinking the same as me, we were all relieved.

Before the house in Bulford was vacated by my wife, I was asked if there was anything that I wanted. I asked if I could have the washing machine, fridge freezer and some other electrical items. The duty transport went to the house and picked up the electrical items. I thought it was 'a blessing in disguise'. The white goods were delivered and everything looked fine on the outside. On closer inspection the cables had been neatly tied up to stop them dangling. I untied them and found that the wiring had been cut. Luckily enough there was an electrical repair workshop on camp, and one of the technicians repaired the electrical radio equipment within the unit. I explained to him what had happened. He said that he would repair the items. It was such a relief I had been doing the washing in the bath.

We lived on the eighth floor. There were four flats on each floor. Immediately across from our flat lived the Provost Sergeant and his wife, they had no children. I think it was his second marriage. Next door was the chap who looked after the Regiment mascot, 'Connor' The Irish Wolf Hound. The family had children; the dog had its own bedroom. It also had its own Regimental Number and pay book. I cannot remember who lived at the other flat.

I did not realise that this tour of duty was going to be such a roller coaster ride. Not a fast ride, but certainly an up and down one. I was the Chief Clerk of the squadron, the work was fairly straight forward. It helped as I had to care for the children. As I have mentioned the children attended a local primary school in Pimlico, St Gabriel's it was an old traditional school it was sandwiched between several blocks of flats. I was able to use the duty vehicle for a lift in the morning to drop the children off at school and to pick them up after school. I had my military duties to attend to as well. I know that the situation regarding the children was not ideal, but I had no other choice I needed work to support the children I had no other alternative. Almost every weekend we did something, even if it was just visiting Battersea Park. The children must have visited all of the museums in London more than once, including London Zoo and of course the other tourist sites in London.

I was not an angel, far from it, the pressure got to me and I would have heavy sessions of drinking. I would drink when the children were staying with my parents during the school holidays. I would frequent a number of drinking venues. One of the more upmarket places was the Pheasantry Night Club on the Kings

171

Road, it was just around the corner from Chelsea Barracks. I once went there with my Squadron Sergeant Major, Gus. He hailed from Yorkshire, and he asked for a pint of bitter he was told that the establishment did not sell bitter because it was not a pub. He asked for a pint a lager he got the same response. We ended up drinking Bacardi and coke, and we tried to make it last for a long time. There were some elderly ladies loving being chatted up by some young men. One particular night a man dressed in authentic guards uniform appeared and was there as a 'birthday present' for one of the elderly ladies. Gus, being a Sergeant Major, was going to ask him for his military identity card as he thought that he was in the military. He could have been but I doubt it, you never know; another one of life's great mysterious.

One evening while drinking in the Royal Court Tavern pub, RCT, in Sloane Square, there was a commotion outside close to a restaurant; someone was singing and he was a little boisterous. Someone in the pub took a look outside and informed the rest of us that it was the actor Peter O'toole. He had obviously had a nice meal, he was not being aggressive. He was saying goodnight to the other diners in the restaurant and was having a bit of a sing song whilst waiting for his taxi. I have a sing song in my local pub every Friday!!

It was in Chelsea that I saw my first mobile phone; a lady was carrying one, literary over her shoulder. It consisted of a shoulder carrying case for the batteries and a curly wire connecting it to the receiver it looked huge. She was also carrying a very large Filofax, a personal organiser. There was a term used for these business people, it was 'Yuppie' - Young upwardly-mobile professional.

Never a Dull Moment

Another drinking hostelry a number of the unit would frequent was The Orange Brewery. As its name suggests it was a small brewery. The brewery was in the cellar of the pub and the landlord would brew a particular beer each week. It ceased to brew beer in 2001.

London on a Sunday morning was deserted, with hardly any road traffic, I would take the children for walks along the footpaths along the Thames.

The couple living immediately across from our flat seemed very nice. They had no children, the lady was from London and she liked my children and would invite them into her flat and spoil them rotten. Her husband was serving with The Irish Guards, he was employed as the Battalion Provost Sergeant; he was the head of the Regimental Police within the Regiment. They had recently married. He was doing well in his Army career. Then all of a sudden he seemed to go downhill. One evening the doorbell rang. I asked my daughter to answer the door and when she returned she said it was the lady from next door. "The lady has black eyes and she was covered in blood". I came to the door to see for myself. The ladies face was black and blue, and one of her eyes was so swollen that it was closed and bloodied. Her face was so puffed up and her lips were covered in dry blood. It looked as though her jaw was broken, it was such a sad sight for anyone to see. She came into the flat and I took a look at her injuries and she told me what had happened. Her husband had been drinking heavily. When he got home he went on the rampage, smashing furniture, and then he took things out on her and used her as a punch bag. I went to one of the neighbour's flats I knocked on the door of the person who looked after the Battalion mascot the Irish wolfhound. He entered my flat and took a look at our neighbour's injuries. We both agreed that she needed immediate medical treatment he and his wife took her to the Regimental Medical Centre. The doctor said that she needed to go to Westminster Hospital, The Irish Guards Duty Officer turned up. He said that he would prefer a Royal Signals Driver to take her to the hospital. The Signal Squadron Duty driver was only eighteen, I informed him and that he was going to have to drive a lady who had been beaten up to Westminster Hospital. When he saw my neighbour he took a sharp intake of air; it had obviously shocked him seeing her in such a dreadful condition. The doctors at Westminster hospital had reported the incident to the civilian police, and the police wanted my neighbour to press assault charges against her husband; she said that she could not press any charges against him. Meantime The Irish Guards Duty Officer and members of the guard force had broken down the door to my neighbour's flat. The Orderly Officer asked me to go inside with them because I knew my neighbour and I may might be able to calm him down. The sight that greeted me was a little comical if it was not so serious. He was laying on his back on the floor. It looked like he had tried to take his life. He had tried to take an overdose there were tablets all over the carpet. A Medical Orderly was pushing his fingers down his throat. I warned him to take his fingers out, and by the time he shouted "why" he found out the hard way. My neighbour bit through the orderly's fingers. It looked as though he had bitten thorough the skin and into his bone. The guard had brought a stretcher into the flat and they were attempting to get my neighbour onto a stretcher. They picked him up and rushed him out of the flat, smashing against the walls of the flat and through the splintered front door. To get him into the lift they tied him onto the stretcher and literally threw him into the lift. He was later placed on a charge and was on Commanding Officer's orders; I had to write a statement regarding the events. Everyone involved that evening also had to submit statements. My neighbour was later demoted to the rank of corporal; he remained working in the guardroom with the provost staff. His problems did not end there. His wife came back to live with him again. Soon the arguments began again and he slipped back to drinking heavily. His wife began staying more and more at her parent's house in London. One morning on the ground floor there was a car stuck between two pillars at the main entrance to the flats. I recognised the car as being owned by my neighbour. He had jammed the car tight between the pillars, the doors and the body work were scraped, dented and the paintwork had been scraped back to the base metal. It was my neighbour who had been driving the car, he had been drinking heavily. I went to work as usual, it transpires that during the day he had locked himself in the flat. He had barricaded himself in. It was said afterwards that he thought that the Army would deploy the SAS (Special Air Service Regiment) to break into the flat and arrest him. There were negotiators from his Regiment trying to persuade him to let them gain entry to the flat. They eventually got him out and he was subsequently arrested. He was discharged from the Army. His wife came back to the flat to pick up some of her possessions and she showed me the destruction within the flat; everything was smashed to pieces. She eventually divorced him, and his mother blamed a bump on the head that he had when he was a baby.

The Irish Guards deployed on exercise to Canada. The Signals Squadron were tasked with providing manpower to cover the Battalions rear party duties within Chelsea Barracks. It was agreed that the Signals would run the guardroom with only Royal Signals personnel. I was on duty as the guard commander. The barracks had CCTV, Close Circuit Television, coverage on the camp they covered many blind spots along the perimeter fence. The perimeter was made up of high brick walls and barbed wire on top and wrought iron fencing. The public could look through the iron fencing and observe the soldiers on the parade ground they could watch the guards practicing drill. On St Patrick's Day, the late Queen Mother presented shamrocks to the Irish Guards and to Connor the Battalion Mascot. One early summer morning the CCTV operator had observed a package close to the fence. The package was not there during the previous foot patrol. I called the Irish Guards Orderly Officer, and he took a look at the package with the CCTV and zoomed onto the package. He called the London District Duty Officer, who then informed the Metropolitan Police. A cordon was setup and the traffic outside of camp was stopped. The flats on the camp were evacuated, Chelsea Barracks had been targeted by terrorists in the past. Before the Metropolitan Police and the bomb squad turned up, The Irish Guards Quarter Master turned up at the guardroom. He was taking over as the on-coming Irish Guards Duty Officer. He walked up to the package, and at that point I told the CCTV operator to record everything, even if the package exploded. The QM kicked the package, and most of us in the guardroom expected it to explode, but luckily for the QM it was not a bomb. As we were opening up the main road to traffic, the Met Police turned up; they asked me what had happened I told them. The Irish Guards Orderly Officers gave their account of events, the police asked to see all of the CCTV footage and they wanted a copy of the video. The QM asked why they wanted it. They informed him that they wanted it for evidence and they would also use it for training purposes.

The pressure of looking after two young children was starting to tell on me including the children. I felt that the second in command of the Signal Squadron did not approve of me bringing up two young children in an Army environment. The Officer Commanding was very accommodating, and he allowed me to take a car and take the children to school and to pick them up afterwards.

Saturday the 19 March 1988 was a terrible day. I was watching the television and a news flash appeared, and it was regarding two soldiers being killed in Andersonstown Belfast. It was the murder of the two Royal Signals corporals Howes and Woods. On Monday 21st March 1988 I had to visit Headquarters London District. The car park on Horse Guards parade was packed. I could see in the distance emerging from the direction of Number 10 Downing Street the then Secretary of State for Northern Ireland Tom King. He may well have been coming back from a meeting regarding the weekend's events with the Prime Minister, The late Margaret Thatcher, a civil servant was running to keep up with him. The civil servant was carrying a large table lamp, in any other circumstance it would have been comical but not on this day.

The children's school was close to the Westminster Children's hospital. At the time the hospital was studying children's growth disorders. When my son arrived at the school I believe the school's nurse forwarded his details to the hospital. I was asked to come to school and talk about his size and weight etc. There was a specialist from the hospital who asked if they could monitor his height, weight and food intake. At first I agreed, at the end of the observations and data gathering period, I was called back into the school. The doctors recommended a growth hormone treatment, my son was aware of what was happening to him regarding the tests and the hospitals involvement. I refused to allow the treatment, as many of our family members on both sides of the family were of small stature. The driver who drove the car to school said "whatever you do don't go through with the growth hormone treatment". I heard many years later that he had passed away to Creutzfeldt-Jacob Disease (CJD), that horrible colloquial term of mad cow's disease.

The flats within the barracks were sometimes used by the soldiers to abseil from the roofs to practice their abseiling skills. They carried out the abseiling on behalf of various Armed Forces charities. Many years after leaving the Army I was sat watching a TV programme with my son, it was about Battersea Park. There was an aerial camera shot of the park from taken from above the roof of the flats. My son said, "I recognise that view." I said, "You could not have seen that view from our flat as it did not face Battersea Park it faced Victoria Railway Station." He said that he could squeeze through the bars to the roof of the flats. As an eight year old he would dangle his legs over the roof and look at the park and surrounding areas. My stomach turned somersaults. I could have lost him all those years ago. It is not worth thinking about.

It reminded me of the time that I had to go to the shop on camp. The veranda door was always locked. I returned to the flat and walked into the living room. I asked my daughter where her brother was she said that she did not know. I noticed movement out on the veranda. I rushed over and looked down and it was my son hanging off the Balcony. I quickly grabbed him under the arm pits and pulled him back over. I was trembling I felt my legs go to jelly, I shouted at him, I just did not know what to do.
If I had been a few minutes late I could have lost him. My life would have been so empty.

Never a Dull Moment

I was always aware that I was walking a tightrope between bringing the children up in a military environment and carrying out my duties to a professional level.

If the children did not visit their grandparents in Ipswich they would use the pay phone near the flats to speak to them. I would dial the telephone number. One afternoon as they were talking to their grandmother. My son spoke to his Grandmother, and he suddenly became very quiet and handed me the phone. I spoke to her and asked her what she said to the children. She said "I told them that they had a brother." I said, "No, they do not have a brother." I put the phone down and suddenly there was the sound of breaking glass. I looked round to see where my son was he had smashed a car window. I do not need this. The soldier whose car it was came out and he was screaming and shouting, about keeping control of my kids... I was lucky he allowed me to pay the damage each month.

During our time in London the great storms of 1987 had hit the United Kingdom. The following morning the children and I were travelling to Ipswich by train from Liverpool Street Station. We got to the main gates of the camp and on the way to the tube station we could see that lots of trees had been blown over in the Chelsea Hospital grounds. We walked towards Sloane Square to catch the tube, and there was scaffolding erected around an estate agents office. During the storms the poles had gone through some car roofs and through the bonnets of some of the cars. We travelled to Ipswich, and at some point we had to change to coaches for part of the journey due to trees on the tracks. During 1988, a pop group called 'A tribe of toffs' released a song called 'John Ketley is a weatherman'. He was the unfortunate weather man on the BBC who gave the weather forecast predication that there was nothing amiss for that night. Of course the great storm of 1987 broke that evening.

Every year the squadron provided a public announcement system to a canoeing event being held in North Wales, it was part of the K.A.P.E. Keep the Army in the Public Eye. It consisted of a team of four soldiers running the public Announcement system. On the last day of the event the sergeant in charge allowed one of the soldiers to visit his home. The soldier lived in the Manchester area, the sergeant told him to be back before the team set off for London. Needless to say he didn't turn up. When the sergeant returned to London he reported the soldier as being absent without Leave, (AWOL). A few days later the soldier returned to the Barracks, of his own accord. The squadron had an out of hour's duty room. As I lived on camp I was called in to charge him for being AWOL. He explained that he had not returned to the canoe site because his girlfriend had been attacked, and that during this time he had married her. When I saw him he was wearing a gold ring, it was not a wedding ring it was a large signet ring. I noticed that his knuckles were grazed and that he had some blood on his clothes. I wrote everything down in the events book. I warned him for OC's orders, the charge was for being absent without Leave. I phoned the Squadron Sergeant Major, who lived elsewhere in London. I clarified with him if he wanted me to place the soldier in detention. He informed me not to place him in the guardroom, and that he would deal with the soldier the next morning. The next morning the soldier was on OC's orders. The OC deferred awarding him a punishment for further evidence, the soldier had told the OC the same story that he had related to me. That evening I was called back into work, it was about eight pm, and I was told to report to the OC's office. He informed me that the Manchester Police had turned up and had arrested the soldier he had been charged with murder. In the corridor I saw the soldier in handcuffs he was between two suited burly policemen. They took the events book with them as evidence I had to write a statement. They went with the SSM to the soldier's room in the accommodation block. They took everything out of his lockers and placed the items into evidence bags. The SSM said that he had clothing covered in blood, I said that I only saw him in a particular top. The SSM replied that his jacket was also covered in blood; I told him that when I saw him he was not wearing a jacket. The same evening he was taken back to Manchester. A few months later I received a summons from Manchester Crown court to attend his trial and to give evidence. In the court I was sat with the police and others that were giving evidence on behalf of the prosecution. On the other side of the court building were his friends, and some people that were giving evidence in his favour. The trial was took place during the winter. Most people were well wrapped up against the cold. I looked over at the people who were giving evidence for the defence, and his friends. They were either wearing t-shirts, track suits, and some were wearing flip flops! A girl came over to the police, she must have only been eighteen or nineteen, and she was wearing a t-shirt and flip flops. Her feet were dirty and she looked frozen. The police knew her and she came across to them. She asked one of them for two cigarettes, one for her and one for her boyfriend. The police said that none of them smoked. She asked me and I also said that I did not smoke. One of the policemen who sat next to me said "see that old man over there" there was a man who looked fifty he may have been younger he looked a mess. He said, "That's her boyfriend." I was speechless. The policeman said "these are the people who are going to give the lad a character reference". The police were called forward to give their evidence; I was called forward and my evidence was straightforward. I could see the accused in the dock, he looked like a child. The prosecution and defence were interested in the ring that he had been wearing. Including the blood that I had noticed on his clothes, and the explanation that he gave for the blood on his clothes. They read out the entry in the dairy of events and sections of my statement. It was soon over and I was allowed to go back to Chelsea Barracks. The soldier and his friends had gone out on the town and were drinking in a pub. They had spent all the money that they had between them. The soldier had noticed that one of them had put a five pound note into his pocket and didn't want to go with the rest of them. They left the pub and apparently they were all hungry. They had no money for chips, the solider told them that the lad in the bar had five pounds in his pocket. They piled into the bar, took him outside to the pub's court yard. It had white painted walls. The soldier hit the man over the head with a rounded bar, similar to a scaffold bar. He smashed his head so hard that the bar bent and the walls were covered in blood. This was the reason why his top was soaked in the victim's blood. They then walked calmly away and bought several bags of chips. They never checked on the person that he had battered, mind you I suppose having been hit so many times you would instinctively know if someone was dead or not.

Whilst in Chelsea Barracks the Signal Squadron carried out a BFT (Basic Fitness Test) test in Battersea Park. We wore our green lightweight trousers, Army boots and a civilian t-shirt, no military identifications. It was a strange course. Obviously we could not chase the civilians out of the park. There would be other joggers and people riding their bicycles and some people pushing prams around the park, even early in the morning, trying to get their babies to sleep. In the middle of our particular route were the public toilets. Scattered throughout the park were large rhododendron bushes. Many a soldier on the BFT would hide in the bushes and wait for the last person to run past. On the return route they would join the last person or group of people and then start sprinting past the last runners.

The Squadron was entered into the London District Minor Unit's swimming competition. The team would train in the Pimlico swimming pool, we were doing very well, and confidence was on the up. We got through to the London District Finals; these were to be held at the Swimming Pool at The Royal Military Academy Sandhurst, RMA Sandhurst. The problem was that a lot of the team could not make the finals due to courses, leave or illness. The team was decimated. I had brought the children along to watch and the other members of the team had brought their families along too. I managed to earn a silver medal for the breaststroke; I thought I did really well. There were points for every place a team member entered an event. We soon realised that we did not have a team in the butterfly event. I had only just finished the breaststroke final, and I was trying to recover from the race. My daughter said "my dad is really good at swimming he can do the butterfly" and so I ended up entering. I started the race fairly well, but my arms ran out of energy and I was virtually drowning. I thought earning a point was something, but sadly I came in last, I was exhausted. It took me a few days to recover from my swimming excursions.

There were many informal and formal visits by the Royal Family to the resident battalion, and at the time was the 1st Battalion the Irish Guards. Its role was to carry out ceremonial duties at Buckingham Palace, Windsor Castle, St James Palace and The Tower of London. The late Queen Mother would frequently visit the battalion. One of her many roles she carried out when visiting would be to present shamrocks on St Patrick's Day to members of the battalion. I remember on one occasion during the lead up to Christmas in the barracks; the Royal Signals Officers invited the senior non-commission soldiers to the Irish Guards Officers Mess. In the men's toilets were cartoons of the Queen mother inspecting the Irish Guards, I suspect that she was fully aware and briefed.

A lot of marriages break up in the Army, there was a couple that worked in the Communications Centre, COMCEN, at Headquarters London District, COMCEN LONDIST. They did not have any children, and they moved into the single accommodation within the barracks after their divorce. There was a separate female accommodation block within the barracks and they saw one another quite a lot at work and socially. One night the ex-husband got very drunk and decided to try and access the female accommodation block. He climbed onto the ledge that ran around the male accommodation block. He dropped onto the cookhouse roof and then into the cold store, which was made up of reinforced glass with wire inside the glass; he fell through the glass, and landed onto some of the large fridges and freezes in the cookhouse cold storage room. No one was aware of what had happened, someone from his room noticed that he was missing. His roommate searched the accommodation block but could not find him. He went over the female block. At the door there was always a female soldier on duty to ensure no male personnel gained access to the female block. She woke his ex-wife and she confirmed that he was not in her room. They alerted the guardroom that something may have happened to him they searched extensively, when they entered the cookhouse and could hear moaning coming from the cold store. Someone noticed blood coming from under the door. They took a fire axe and hacked through two doors to get to him. He was in a bad way, an ambulance was called to ferry him to hospital. He had massive problems with one hand, mainly the thumb area. The wire in the glass had acted like a cheese cutter and had nearly severed part of his hand and the whole of one his thumbs. The doctors saved his hand. He was able to continue in his trade, he had a lot of problems with his hand.

The Signal Squadron had an underground car park for military cars and motor bikes. The squadron had white Triumph motorbikes. These were used by Buckingham Palace and Number ten for invites to the various embassies in London and any state visits. The bikes had to be kept immaculate. If there were any major issues with the bikes they were taken by Triumph in Birmingham and repaired at the factory. One morning there was a thumping sound coming from the underground car park and flames shot out of the car park area.
A soldier could be seen running through the thick acrid smoke. The bikes were in such a mess. Triumph came to London and picked the bikes up, when the bikes were returned they looked good as new. The soldier was placed on a charge, he admitted that he had used petrol to clean the bikes and had left two petrol cans open. He decided that he had worked very hard to make the bikes gleam. They looked the part for an upcoming ceremonial duties. He decided to have a cigarette, all hell broke loose.

There was an Officer who was a staunch Royalist, bordering on the extreme. His name was Grey. He eventually got married and I am sure that his wife is a very nice lady. One morning he appeared at the Squadron Admin Office to have his marriage published on the military record system. When checking the marriage certificate his surname appeared as Windsor-Grey. I queried the surname with him and he produced a change of surname by deed poll document. As mentioned he was a staunch Royalist and had the surname "Windsor" added. Thereafter he was known as Windsor-Grey. One of the typists in the administration office placed a calendar on the wall in the main office. The cover was the artwork for the Sex Pistols Album 'God save the Queen'. Windsor-Grey saw it one morning and ordered it to be taken down. The typist refused he strode into the office and tore it off the wall and ripped it to shreds. The typist who had purchased the calendar went crazy. He was berating her and told her it was disrespectful to the Queen and it should not be seen in a military establishment. He told her that she was lucky to be in a job working for the military. The Commanding Officer entered the Orderly Room and enquired what the commotion was about. He was told what had happened. He told Captain Windsor-Grey that he had approved the calendar and saw nothing wrong with it and ordered him to apologise to the typist and to purchase another calendar. The Captain duly purchased a new one and brought some flowers for the typist.

This would not be the last time that Captain Windsor-Grey would crop up during my time at Chelsea Barracks. He organised a cultural trip for members of his troop to various World War One battlefield cemeteries in France. The reader must remember that mobile phones were only just making an appearance on the streets of the UK. Captain Windsor-Grey had allowed the troop to savour the French beer in Calais prior to boarding a ferry back to the UK. Some of the soldiers had found themselves in a local bar. In the meantime the others had gone to the bar and had refused to pay for their drinks tab and had attempted to leave. The owner had grabbed a baseball bat and mayhem ensued outside.

Never a Dull Moment

A large plate window in the bar was smashed and obviously the French Police Nationale (Gendarme) arrived and arrested the group. Captain Windsor-Grey thankfully spoke French; he arrived at the last-known watering hole where the soldiers were last seen to find the window boarded up. He made his way to the local police station. The British Military attache in Paris had also been informed. To cut a long story short Captain Windsor-Grey offered to pay for the window of the bar to be replaced and to pay for any other damage. He had the money electronically transferred from his bank in the UK. In those days it was no mean feat. The soldiers were not charged by the French Police. The British Consulate had contacted the French equivalent to the Ministry of Defence and the soldiers were released into the custody of Windsor-Grey. The soldiers agreed to pay the officer the money back over a period of months. Windsor-Grey thought that the Army pay staff would deduct the money out of the soldier's accounts and into his. He was told that it was purely a private arrangement and had nothing to do with the Army. I cannot be certain if he ever got his money back.

I was having lots of problems with the Second in Command at the time. Looking back on my tin London my issues were of my own making and they eventually led to me handing in my notice to leave the Army. My time was taken up with either looking after the children and my military duties. I had forgotten about the divorce my priority was to stave off the gathering storm. I did not have full custody of the children, I only had part custody, and the state through the social services had the other half so to speak. I was warned that because I was not in a relationship and I was serving in the Armed Forces, things were not in my favour. The Second in Command had to serve the divorce papers on me and countersigned a letter stating that she witnessed me signing

187

the papers. She was not happy at all that the Army had been brought into my personal affairs. She called me into her office and made a big deal quoting my wife's solicitor's letter and the divorce papers that I had submitted; the papers were for the decree absolute. She made such a big deal about me trying to use the children as an excuse not to sign the divorce papers. She said that I deliberately did not want to sign the decree absolute. I told her that she had no idea what she was asking me to do. I also told her that she could be jeopardising the future safety of the children and that they could be taken back into care. The Second in Command ordered me to sign the documents. Lucky enough the only thing that happened was within six weeks the decree absolute was issued.   After the occasion of the Second in Command ordering me to sign the legal papers without knowing what the consequences might be, I contacted my solicitor. I had already handed in my notice so I did not have much to lose. He wrote to the unit explaining what the consequences could be. Including the potential loss of custody of the children and for the children going back into the care system, the consequences would be on the heads of the Ministry of Defence. Eventually it was my time to leave the Army; it was a bit like jumping out of the frying pan and into the fire. I do regret what has happened to my children; I felt that I had no other option but to put my life on hold and to try and bring some stability and normality into their lives. It is easier said than done, believe me. The next stage of our journey together was about to begin, a world that I knew very little about since joining the Army at the age of nineteen.

Chapter 8 - Out of Work and No Money

When I left the Army it felt as though my nightmare was only just beginning. Before I left the Army I had a fairly rose tinted view of life, and I thought that it would be easy to obtain work. Before leaving I had started to work with Information Technology (IT) systems my experience of IT was very limited. I attended job interview after job interview, all to no avail, money was short, and if I could not afford the bus fare I would walk to job interviews. At the time I was living at my parent's house while we waited for council accommodation. I would aim to have job interview just before lunch or immediately after lunch because of the school timings. I made various enquiries about child minders, the costs were just too much and I could not afford the asking price.

My problems began to go from bad to worse. I reluctantly called on the council to enquire about housing benefit and housing benefit. I was virtually broke and I was starting to realise that the children were suffering. I began to feel different, cut adrift from normal society, and it started to feel like a society of those who have and those who have not. It got even worse when I visited the benefits office. I was informed that I would not receive any benefits for six weeks. I was not entitled to certain child benefits as my wife should have been paying towards the up keep of the children.

I had some money to get me by after buying beds for the children's bedrooms; I slept on a new settee. I had to shop at the discount food shops. I would make sure that I bought the children their favourite sweets. It was proving extremely difficult. I had no savings, and everything that I had was spent on the children; I had to rely on the council for our housing needs.

My parents had settled in Swindon after my dad had left the Army. I had spoken to them about me coming out of the Army, my dad was not keen on the idea. I stayed at my parents' house for a short period of time, until a house was allocated by the council. It must have been difficult for my parents, and at times things were very stressful between myself and my father. He would fly off in rages in front of me and the children. I did not like it and told him so, it was like lighting the blue touch paper.

A house was made available within Swindon, it was a three bed room house. I agreed to sign for the keys before the council could put the house in order. There were two reasons for this decision: one of them was I needed to register the children in a school before the end of the summer holidays. The second was because living at my parent's house the tension was building up and it was becoming far too intense. My father was starting to control my life and the children's, he even started to open my private mail, and I had to get out and the sooner the better.

The council house was in a bigger mess than I first realised. In the living room a wall was covered in soot from an open fire. There were no internal doors downstairs; the council were going to install new doors. The children went exploring upstairs and told me that they could not open any of the windows in their bedrooms. I took a look and found that the windows were nailed shut with six inch nails. I took a look at all of the windows downstairs and they were nailed shut with six inch nails. I informed the council and they said that they would look at the windows; I told them that I thought that it was a fire hazard and I had two children living in the house. My mum and dad helped to try and turn the house into a home. It was an uphill struggle. Over time I found used needles stuck between the floor boards, there had been drug addicts living in the house before I moved in. It all started to make sense with the windows nailed closed. I decided to take a look in the loft and I found some smelly grotty sleeping bags and yet more drug paraphernalia. I went to the council to speak to the housing officer; he informed me that there had been many drug busts at the house. I told him if the council did not come and dispose of the drug paraphernalia and sort the windows out soon, I would inform the police. It was quicker re-joining the Army I was more concerned about the children and their futures. My neighbour informed me that the house had been used as a crack den. Most of the drug addicts in the area were buying their drugs from the occupants of the house. One morning my daughter informed me that someone had jumped over the garden fence and ran into the garden shed. They were quickly followed by a policeman who grabbed the person hiding in the shed and handcuffed him. A policeman knocked at the door. He informed me that the police were tracking down the drug addicts that had not been previously caught. He asked if we had seen the person arrested. I said that my daughter had seen him jump over the fence and go into the garden shed and that the policeman arrived and handcuffed him. I signed a statement to the effect, and before he left I told him about the drug paraphernalia in the attic, he then removed the items for the attic.

I applied for every job under the sun, but it was difficult with the children at school and at such a young age. I needed either a part time job or one within the hours that the children were attending school. The hours were a major issue. Times were really hard, and what money I did get I had to make it stretch. That year I asked the children what they would like for Christmas. I knew that my daughter would have liked a pair of professional ice hockey boots. My son would have liked a BMX sports bike. I found a shop that put items away for Christmas; I paid a small amount of money each week. They got what they wanted for Christmas that year. A few days before Christmas I told the children that I would try to make a Christmas cake. I found a recipe from one of my mum's cook books, and the recipe contained brandy. I bought a small bottle of brandy, and I poured a few caps of brandy for the cake and a swig for me and then another swig. Let's say I was a little tipsy. I ended up buying a ready-made cake from a shop. It was about this time that my son had developed adult croup, and he could not walk he was so weak; I had to carry him on my back to get him to the doctors. The doctor confirmed that he had adult croup. It literally put him on his back.

I eventually got an interview for a large employer in the town. I had changed my CV and added 'IT literate'. It is when I made the decision to re-enlist into the Army. I spoke to with my mum and dad and told them that I had no future living in Swindon and nor did the children. I was getting so worried about the children, we were not living in the best environment, and I could not provide anything for them, including a future. In the end I admitted defeat to my father it was not an easy thing to do. I spoke to the children, and told them that I was finding it very hard to find work and to provide for them. I know that they must have been finding it difficult to comprehend what was happening in their young lives. Far too much had happened to the children over such a short space of time. Only to be told by their father that things were about to change for them once again, it must have been very hard to take in. I felt that my daughter had an idea that I was finding things difficult. It brought tears to my eyes having to look them in the eyes and admit defeat. It was such a terrible feeling of helplessness and defeat. It was agreed that if I could re-enlist and if the Army took me back. The children would stay with my parents and I would have to put an agreed amount of money into my Mum and Dad's bank account. This was to cover the children's upkeep.

My next task was to try and re-enlist. I wrote to the Royal Signals Manning and Record office in Glasgow. At the same time I visited the Army Recruitment office in Swindon and filled in the re-enlistment forms. During the period of waiting I received a letter from the Colonel in Charge of The Royal Signals Manning and Record Office. He was the second in command of 2 Division and Signal Regiment when I joined my first Regiment in Germany; 'the security incident' in Chapter five. His letter confirmed that I had been accepted back into the Army and into the Royal Signals. I phoned the Recruitment Office in Swindon and informed them of my acceptance letter; they informed me that they did not have confirmation of my re-enlistment, and could I bring a copy of the letter with me. I did not have enough money for the bus fare so I walked into Swindon. The Major at the recruitment Office spoke to the Colonel who had written the letter, and he said, "You did not tell me that you knew the Colonel". He said that I would receive some papers soon. Informing me where I had to report to and in my case it would be 11 Signal Regiment Depot in Catterick North Yorkshire. To collect my uniform and await a posting to a Royal Signals unit. I informed my parents and we set the wheels in motion for the children to move in with them.

My next door neighbour heard about me moving and that I was moving to my parent's. He offered to provide a van and help me move some furniture, I gave him the beds and some other bits and pieces. On the day of the move his wife invited me in for a cup of tea. Their house was the same build as mine; I could not help but think that their living room was slightly smaller than mine. He said, "What are you looking at?" I said, "Your living room is smaller than mine." He pulled a piece of string and a door opened in the wall. He said that "if I ever have to hide from certain people I get in here". If my wife has to let them into the house I get in the cupboard space and wait until they leave."

Needless to say the children and I once again moved in with my parents. The letter duly arrived from 11 Signal Regiment confirming that I had to report to Catterick Garrison. There I would be processed and issued with my various uniforms. One morning I entered the camp gates at Helles Barracks and was heading towards the Quartermaster's Department. I heard a voice coming from a window 'Hearn, what the hell are you doing here?' It was the QM from my unit in Bulford 249 Signal Squadron. He was now the Quartermaster at 11 Signal Regiment. He invited me into his office. I noticed on his wall the squadron photographs from our time in Norway. I remember thinking that I wished that I still had some of the squadron photographs. I had to leave all of my personal items behind in Bulford. He asked me what I was doing at 11 Signal Regiment; I explained the situation to him. He shook my hand and said, "It's a pleasure to see you again, young Hearn."

I had to go back to Helles Barracks a few days later for my inoculations. It was the same medical centre that I went to ten years previously. The recruits were doing the same things that I had done many years before. Queuing up en-mass to see the Medical Officer.

Back at the Depot Troop I was awaiting my posting order and getting my final pieces of administration sorted. I found that I would be retaining my rank of sergeant, so I had to visit the tailors to get my chevrons sewn onto my uniforms.

The troop Warrant Officer called me into his office. He was someone that I knew from Bulford; The SQMS in chapter eight Norway and 249 Signal Squadron (AMF (L)). He informed me that there were not only soldiers re-enlisting at Depot Troop. There were soldiers awaiting discharge from the Army who had served overseas and had to pass through 11 Signal Regiment Depot Troop. To make sure their discharge papers were up to date and correct.

He informed me that there were one or two soldiers who were awaiting doctor's reports from the Military Hospital in Catterick; they had to go through this procedure if the Army think that the soldiers are pulling the lead and are trying to get a free medical discharge for whatever reason. If they are genuinely ill then they would not be in Depot Troop. He informed me that there was a case of one soldier sent back from Germany because he was self-harming. He was awaiting his medical appointment from the hospital; He told me that he had not self-harmed in UK yet. The next morning I was on parade with everyone and I could see in the front row a soldier with plasters over his face. When the parade was over he took his beret off. His hair was in clumps and he also had plasters on his head. The WO informed me that he had attacked himself with a razor blade. Needless to say his appointment at the hospital was hurried along.

I spoke to the children most nights, but I kept thinking 'have I done the right thing?' My overriding concern was that every adult close to them had let them down.

I was called into the Officer Commanding Office and he informed me that I been selected to serve with 14 Signal Regiment (Electronic Warfare) in Celle, West Germany.

I informed my mum and Dad and the children, the children were upset. It made me feel sad, but I had to do something I could not remain in the situation that was getting worse by the day. I realise that it must have seemed selfish at the time I felt as though I had no other option.

Chapter 9 - Celle

The Regiment I was posted to was 14 Signal Regiment EW, (Electronic Warfare), it was based in a small town in West Germany called Celle. The town is situated close to Hanover, and during my time there, West and East Germany were separate countries. Celle is an historic town, and is twenty five miles from Hanover in central Germany. The Regiment was housed in Taunton Barracks. The Barracks have since been handed back to the German authorities. The main accommodation block is now the Town Hall, the town's administration building. The original German name for the barracks was Heide Kasserne (Heath Barracks). Whenever a soldier booked a taxi to or from the barracks the taxi drivers would always refer to the barracks as Heide Kasserne. The Barracks comprised of a number of traditional picture post-card traditional wooden and brick buildings. Central to them all was a large brick building known as block 14. It was built sometime between 1869 and 1872, and the 77th Infantry Regiment were the first to be billeted at the Barracks. It was the largest brick built structure in Europe. For those who have visited the National History Museum in London, this is the Prussian military equivalent. Huge, impressive and Teutonic!

As soon as I arrived at the Regiment I found it very difficult to settle, due to leaving the children in the UK with my parents, I felt that I had let them down. During my first week at the Regiment I was told that there was a Regimental dinner and everybody would have to attend; it was a three line whip, which meant all Warrant Officers and Sergeants in station had to attend. I had forgotten what time to be at the dinner, anyone attending a Regimental dinner had to arrive before the Regimental Sergeant Major (RSM). I was housed in an annex away from the main mess, which was elsewhere on camp. I was walking along the main road towards the mess when a staff car passed me by; it slowed down and then drove off. As I arrived at the entrance to the mess I was met by the President of the Mess Committee, (PMC). He informed me that I was late on parade. I soon found out it was the RSM in the car. The PMC informed me, 'the RSM's compliments ten extra duties for being late on parade'. I thought to myself 'bloody good start to the unit'.

On the Monday morning I reported to the RSM. He informed me of my ten extra duties. He asked me how I would like the duties I told him one after the other. On Regimental Part One Orders my duties were published. Contained within the Orders were things like Regimental duties and administrative information that were required to be reported to the various departments within the Regiment. The orders were placed on notice boards, and no one would leave work without getting hold of a copy to read. At the end of each month, the next month's duties would be published. On the day, that the Part One Orders were published there were deletions and insertions of duties for the next ten days and my name was inserted in every case. I worked in block 21, and my superior officers were a British Intelligence Major and an American Major. I was summoned to the British officer's office, and he asked me how after only five days in the Regiment how had I managed to pick up ten extra duties on the trot. They thought that I had caused a serious disciplinary issue which may have affected my security clearance. I explained the circumstances of the extra duties. The pair left the building and I could see them marching across the parade square towards the

Regimental Headquarters building, RHQ. It transpires that they had raised the question of my ten extra duties awarded by the RSM. A compromise must have been reached and my extra duties were reduced. I think the powers to be put it down to a clerical error on Part One orders. Later in the month, all new arrivals had to have an interview with the Commanding Officer, CO. For some reason the RSM marched everyone, including any new arrivals, into the CO's office. The CO introduced himself and asked me a few questions and asked me if I had any questions for him. I said that I did but they were of a private nature. The CO asked the RSM to leave the room and I could hear the RSM hiss "I will get you for this". I informed the CO of my concerns for the children and the fact that I was so far away from them, and I had not expected a posting to Germany. I was honest with him and I told him that I had made a mistake re-enlisting. I could not adapt back into the strict regime of military life. I knew that I had a made a powerful enemy in the RSM, I would need to watch myself, and be on my guard at all times.

There were rumours at the time regarding the huge cellars beneath block 14 the cellars were flooded, and the huge metal doors were sealed so that no one could gain access. There were stories of bodies from the Second World War remaining within the flooded cellars. There were also stories of British soldiers that had donned diving gear and they somehow were entangled in the various pieces of wreckage deep inside and they drowned and their bodies were still entombed within the cellar.

The cookhouse was housed within the main accommodation block and was always a bone of contention. It was not a favourite place for those on fatigues who had to work in the cookhouse. Fatigues are a form of duty that soldiers were allocated from each squadron, carrying out menial tasks during the week. The building had never been upgraded or modernised, the chefs had to use whatever was available to them. There were no lifts in the main building. Everything had to be moved into the building by hand. There was a small turreted building within the cookhouse. A hole had been cut into the turret to allow access. At the foot of the turret a door had been constructed. The chefs would throw the food waste into the tower. The slops in the tower were cleaned out once a week. The swine man from the local pig farm would turn up. The fatigue party had to enter the tower and dig out the slops by hand and load the waste into dustbins which were loaded onto a lorry. As you can imagine it was not a very nice task, someone had to do it, I was glad that it was wasn't me. There were concerns because of the proximity of the cookhouse to the soldier's accommodation; as there were rats running around the slops area. The smell emanating from the cookhouse would permeate everywhere.

Some other buildings on camp were also built during the Franco Prussian War period. In some of the buildings there were original photographs of Prussian soldiers standing outside the original buildings within the camp. Other older buildings on the camp were constructed of wood.

During my time in Celle there were many rumours regarding the camp. There were stories of people hearing ghostly footsteps such as the sound of Jack Boots. The type of boots that the German Army wore during the Second World War. Some say that they could hear German voices in areas that were known to be uninhabited. There were stories of the cellar having German Army equipment inside as well as the entombed bodies. Between

1945 and 1946 the camp was used as a displaced persons camp to deal with the aftermath of the Belsen concentration camp.
Within the barracks there was a particular building which had an evil role. It was the block that housed the Quarter Master's staff and equipment, mainly cleaning material for the blocks containing things like, toilet rolls bleach etc. I had to see the Regimental Quarter Master Sergeant (RQMS), from the outside the building looked just like any other building on the camp. I went to his office and had a chat and a cup of coffee. Just having a normal everyday conversation, he said to me, "Have you seen what is in the cellar?" I replied, "No," the QM came into the office and said, "RQMS are you taking him on a grand tour?" He replied, "Yes sir." As we entered the cellar I noticed that it was immaculate. It was very cold and had an oppressive atmosphere. There were some cells, the doors to the cells were wide open; what was even stranger was inside each cell there were toilet rolls, bleach disinfectant and all sorts of cleaning materials. It was all very macabre and surreal. The building had a preservation order. Which meant that the cells could not be ripped out. At the end of the row of cells there was a gap, I took a look and I noticed on the ceiling there was a wooden beam. Attached to the beam were meat hooks. I was informed when the trains transporting the Jews to Belsen concentration camp, the SS guards would select those who were from rich banking families or had thriving businesses. These people would be taken off the transportation trains at Celle, the remainder of the poor wretches would continue on to Belsen. Those who were taken off the train would be taken to Heide Kaserne, which was eventually to become Taunton Barracks. It was said to have housed the SS and Gestapo, (NAZI Secret Police). They would torture the unfortunate souls; the SS would try to obtain bank account details. It did not matter who they were they ended up on the

meat hooks. While I was in the cellar the hairs on my arms stood on end. It sent shivers up my spine just thinking about it, the room felt cold and gloomy. I thought that this room was the last thing that they saw before meeting their maker. The local town council had placed a preservation order on this and many other buildings within the Barracks.

Rumour had it that the SS also had an occult department within the barracks, how true it is I do not know. The local Germans working in the barracks during the time that I was stationed there would not clarify or deny the rumours about the barracks.

At the top of the Main Building was a flag pole, where the Union Jack was flown every day. It was the responsibility of the guard of the day to lower the flag at dusk and raise the flag at dawn. There were many stories regarding members of the guard who had carried out this duty. They would say that they had heard footsteps behind them when they were at the flag pole. They said that they could feel a presence, on turning around petrified nobody was there.

The Regimental Headquarters, (RHQ), was one of the buildings that was built mainly of wood, and the building was very small. It looked just like an ordinary house, complete with chimney stack. RHQ was built just like any ordinary house. The Regimental hierarchy offices were upstairs. The structure upstairs could not take the weight of too many people, if anyone had to see the CO they had to wait downstairs, then they would be called upstairs one by one. Once upstairs they would come to attention outside the RSM's office, he would march them into the CO's office. The RSM would brief the soldiers not to stamp their feet too hard as

they may go through the ceiling. There was one time when someone was marched out of the CO's office by the RSM.
The RSM gave him the command to halt the soldier brought his foot down so hard that his boot and part of his leg went through the ceiling.

The Regiment had a mixture of tradesmen, linguists, Intelligent Corps personnel, radio operators, special telegraphists and ordinary tradesmen, mechanics, cooks and clerks. There was a particular bizarre situation as I arrived at the Regiment; there was an Intelligence Corps soldier under arrest in the Guardroom. His nickname was, 'Dippy', which, at the time, meant nothing to me until I was on duty as the Regimental Orderly Sergeant. The RSM briefed me about the soldier and the reason why he was locked up in the guardroom; he told me that the soldier was being kept in the guardroom until the German Police and Public Prosecutor had put together a case to charge him with murder. So as not to be a burden to the German tax payer he was remanded to the Regiment's Guardroom. He informed me that the prisoner prior to his arrest was in the habit of visiting prostitutes along a road that ran from Celle to another British base in Hohne. The prostitutes had a caravan or mobile home further down a track off the main road; he would frequently visit these women. He travelled down a track in his British Forces Germany, BFG registered car. The car number plates at the time were very distinctive. The BFG plates were changed after the IRA began to murder off duty service personnel. They were identified by the unique BFG number plate. This particular woman's caravan was parked further down the track than the others. It was for her own security. As a car approached she would write down the number plate. She would write the date and time in a book. She would hide the book when a customer visited. The last vehicle registration number in the book was the soldiers. He was obviously the last person to see her alive. He denied any wrong doing. The forensic evidence was stacked against him and so was the material evidence. When I went to see him on my tour of duty, he was handing out ammunition to the guard; he had not been sentenced yet, he was still wearing his rank on his uniform, shirts, jumpers and combat jacket. I went ballistic, with the Guard Commander, he said, "He always helps out in the guardroom." I informed the corporal if he wanted to join him in jail he was more than welcome to get acquainted with a cell. I had to get everyone on guard to hand back the issued ammunition and to check it against the guardroom ledgers. After the check and everything was accounted for, I noticed that the prisoner had a set of keys to the rifle rack. I ordered the guard commander too get the keys off the prisoner and place him back in his cell. I informed the guard commander that he was to report to the RSM as soon as his tour of duty was over.

Another time I was walking across the parade square with the RSM. He was carrying out an inspection of the Operations Bureau Building, the building that I worked in, Block 21. He noticed a silver car driving on camp I could see a car full of soldiers. The RSM headed towards the Guardroom, he told me to get back to work and he would inspect the building at a later date. I found out later that the prisoner was driving members of the guard to the cookhouse for lunch; the RSM had noticed the car the prisoner was driving. I left the regiment before the solider attended court.

When the wall came down

As I have mentioned I was serving with a Royal Signals Electronic Warfare Regiment. One of the regiment's roles during the "Cold War" was to listen, decode and interpret the Russian and WARSAW pact Radio traffic. From their bases in and around the East German border, commonly referred to as the Inner German Border, IGB. The East German/Russian zone the Regiment was interested in was the area that the Soviet 3 Shock Army was based, the Soviet Army's Headquarters was based in the East German town of Magdeburg.

The training area the Russians used for military manoeuvres was known as Letzlinger Heide, it was close to the IGB. The nearest point to the West German border was approximately fifteen Miles away. It was one of the largest Russian training areas in Eastern Germany.

In November 1989, because of Mikhail Gorbochev and perestroika, the Berlin and East German border was dismantled.
At the time I was working in the operations block. The Intelligence Major asked a number of us if we would like to visit a village across the border in the former Soviet zone in East Germany. As he put it, it was history in the making. Clearance had to be sought from both the UK and the German authorities to cross the old border area soon after the East German border had been dismantled. We were given permission, there was one major stipulation. We were to travel in civilian clothing, there was to be no military equipment or clothing to be taken on the trip.
We travelled to one of the Regiment's listening stations close to the East German border. It was based in a West German village

called Dannenberg. The listening station had been monitoring the Soviet military communications for many years. Also any communications emanating from the Russian and WARSAW Pact Training areas and the 3rd Shock Army Headquarters in Magdeburg. We travelled in civilian privately owned cars, which had British Forces Germany (BFG) number plates. Before we left to start the trip we were ordered to travel to the village of Dannenberg in the cars. From Dannenberg to the East German village where we wanted to visit was Domitz. It was a couple of miles away, we walked to the river Elbe, which used to form part of the East/West German border. Nobody would dare get this close during the Cold War, and to our right was a railway bridge it was badly damaged; the metal girders were mangled and twisted. We could not be sure if the bridge had been blown up by the retreating German Army during the Second World War. Or by the Russian Army once they had reached the River Elbe. On subsequent investigation it was found that it was destroyed in 1945 by an Allied air raid. In the distance we could see the village of Domitz resting on the banks of the river Elbe. We could see a small shuttle boat, moving across the river, it could only carry one or two cars at the most including a small number of foot passengers. From our position we could see across the river and onto what was left of the East German border. There was a large expanse of rubble, sand, dirt and large dark brown patches where nothing grew; this was what was left of the barbed wire, mine zones and machine gun positions, the killing zones on the border. The area seemed eerily quiet, and even though there were no vestiges of the former border remaining it all seemed very quiet and subdued.

We got a lift on the little ferry boat. The military linguist spoke to the people operating the ferry. They informed him that their little ferry boat was making a small fortune.

Those on the ferry said that there was not much to see in the village. Only the sixteenth century castle.

We met some people at the castle and they were very happy to see us. They seemed a little cautious of us since they knew that we were British and of course we were military. Even when a military person is dressed in civilian clothing, their military bearing stands out. These people had lived under a military style dictatorship for generations. We left the castle and walked up the cobbled main street, there were some shops and the odd house; it looked like a scene out of Dickensian England. What was noticeable was the lack of colour. All of the buildings were dull and drab on the main street there was a commissar shop, it sold general goods and clothes, which were what the communist party deemed, fit for the nation to buy. The shop was painted black, white and grey. I suppose mixing black and white paint you can make grey. The main street was on a slight incline, and as we walked up the hill towards the brow we saw a bizarre sight. In the distance we could make out two men dressed in bright coloured shell suits. One looked as though he was wearing an Aqua Blue shell suit and the other a pink and red shell suit. They spoke a smattering of German; they spoke very good Russian. Our Russian expert told us that they were from Vietnam. In the past they would come to East Germany with lots of shell suits and sell them to the Russian Soldiers. When the wall came down they were caught in East Germany. The Russian Soldiers in Magdeburg and the surrounding areas were ordered back to their barracks by the Russian authorities. They were to remain until arrangements were made with The West German Government to move them back to Russia. The authorities wanted the whole exercise to be carried out in a dignified manner. During the period that the Russian's were confined to barracks. The soldiers were not getting paid, they did not have any money to buy the gaudy shell suits. This is why the Vietnamese men were trying to sell shell suits in the East German towns and villages rather than the Soviet military sites. They were trying to get to West Germany and eventually back to Vietnam. They informed us that everything was chaotic in East Germany, a lot of police stations had been burnt out.

On the left hand side of the road we noticed a Café/Restaurant. There were some old rickety houses, the gardens ran down a bank towards the river. We could see in the distance two or three East German Border guards fast patrol boats. Being in the military we thought that it would be interesting to see one of the boats close up. There was a watch tower near to the river. We could not resist and took a look inside. As we climbed the steps we noticed that there was blood splattered on the walls. As we came back down the steps we were confronted by a very agitated man in uniform, holding a Kalashnikov rifle. He was hysterical, and he asked what we thought we were doing in a forbidden area. We explained to him who we were and what we were doing over the border. He told us that he was an East German border guard. He seemed to become more relaxed. He began to explain that the previous evening there were two of them stationed there. He told us what had happened to the other border guard. He was buried in one the gardens of the houses that we had passed, the guard had been lynched in the tower by some of the locals. It was why he was given permission by the West German authorities to arm himself for his own protection. He said that the radio equipment was still working and was in constant contact with the West German authorities. They had to send the families and some the border guards into West Germany for their own safety. There were several containers at the back of the gardens. They were positioned close to the motor speed boats and the tower. It was the guard's armoury, and of course they could not risk the weapons getting into the hands of the locals. The villages wanted to take revenge on them and others in authority.

We had to get to the train station and as we walked towards the station there was a burnt out building. It was the only building we had seen was burnt out. There were some metal filing cabinets in the road. The drawers were open, they had been forced open they were bent and buckled. There were index cards strewn all over the street. The building was the local police station; we were told that the filing cabinets contained index cards with details of everyone in the village and the surrounding areas. They contained information regarding police (Stasi East German state security police) and their informants. In other words, it was a police state reporting on one another. No one could be trusted. As they say, a picture paints a thousand words.

We soon arrived at the train station and it looked a little run down. On entering there was an old man sat in a kiosk. We told him that we wanted to get a train to Magdeburg. We enquired if any trains ran from Domitz to Magdeburg he confirmed that a train did run to Magdeburg. The aim of the trip was to visit Magdeburg, where the Russian 3 Shock Army had been garrisoned. 3 Shock Army carried out war games close to the West German border. When the wall came down, the Russians agreed to stay in their garrison enclosures until they could be moved back to Russia. We also wanted to travel to see to see the place where it was said that Adolf Hitler, Eva Braun, Joseph Goebbels and his family were buried. They were allegedly moved to Magdeburg on or about the 21 February 1946, the remains were then dug up on the 4 April 1970. What remained of them was burnt and the ashes thrown into the Biederitz river in East Germany.

What was so bizarre the man in the station donned another hat it was the ticket masters hat. He proceeded to hand print the tickets, on a small machine. We had some backpacks and he asked if we would we like to book them in. We thought yes, we would offload them and have something to eat and drink in the station café. He disappeared, and reappeared along from the ticket office. He slid open a hatch and took our bags, and this time he had yet another hat on with a sign in German, and it read baggage handler. He gave us our receipts for the baggage. We were intrigued, and went onto the platform. We went back inside to see if we could get something to eat. The canteen was closed.

Once again we popped back onto the platform to find out what time the next train was leaving for Magdeburg. Suddenly a young woman came onto the platform and said in German enquiring if we had tried to gain entry to the café. We told her that we had, and from our accents she could tell that we were foreign, so we told her that we were British. She spoke perfect English. She said that during her years growing up and at great risk to herself and her family she had listened to the BBC World service. She learnt English from listening to the station, albeit at the time illegally. She asked that we did not speak to her in German as she wanted to practice her English as much as possible. She asked what we were doing in the village we told her that we wanted to catch the train to Magdeburg. She suddenly burst out laughing and she said "the old duffer should have told you that there was no train to Magdeburg until next week". She took us back to the ticket office she banged on the door and got the old man out of the office. It sounded as though she was telling him off for not telling us that the next train to Magdeburg was not due until next week.

The money was begrudgingly refunded by the old man and he returned our back packs. The lady opened the café and she informed us that she did not have anything to eat. There was plenty of beer. We enquired if the restaurant that we had passed earlier would be in the same position. She phoned the restaurant and whilst on the phone she asked us what we would like to eat. They could do five bockwurst, this is the boiled German sausage, and chips. So our order was taken over the phone. We decided before we left that we would sample some of the East German beer. The girl poured five very dark beers, it did look like Guinness, and when I tasted mine it tasted OK but it was a bit gritty. We all had another drink and said our goodbyes to the girl and thanked her for her help. I have since found out that the Railway Station has since been gutted by fire. We walked back down the hill and entered the restaurant and were served by a very happy looking large lady. We chatted away about our experiences of the day. We had our meal and headed back to the landing stage to get the ferry back into Germany, (West Germany). I will never forget that brief trip. I suppose it was all very strange and alien to the villages. In the past they had learnt not to trust strangers. Including their neighbours, possibly for decades.

One evening members of RHQ travelled to Hannover for a night out. The group consisted of all of the clerks from RHQ; including the Adjutant and Chief Clerk, and members of the Operation Bureau we were going to have a night out in Hanover. The hierarchy decided to go to a beer cellar, inside it was huge with rows upon rows of tables. The food arrived it consisted of bockfurst and bratwurst, traditional German sausage, with sour kraut, which is a potato salad or chips. And of course gallons of beer. One of the young clerks approached our table and told us that he had fallen in love with a beautiful German woman, he called her over. First of all, he/she had an Adam's apple, and a six o'clock shadow covering his face. This was his introduction to women in Germany.

I will try to convey my feelings of my first visit to the Belsen Concentration Camp. The concentration camp is in a village called Bergen-Belsen. Next to the camp was a British Army Base called Hohne, the base will be handed back to the German authorities in 2015. As I approached the entrance to the camp the first thing that struck me was the fact that it did not look like a concentration camp. I know that it would have looked much different during the time it was in operation. At the same time it was visited by members of the German Armed Forces. There was National Service in Germany at the time, and part of their induction was a visit to the camp. Inside the concentration camp foot print it is eerily silent, and no birds flew over the mass grave areas; they could be seen flying around the outside of the perimeter fence. At various places on the ground there are brown oblong patches covered in heather. These are the mass graves where the victims are buried. There is a memorial stone dedicated to all those who perished within Belsen concentration camp. As I looked around, taking in the scene, I could not imagine what horrors took place on the site. A surreal image appeared along a track outside of the camp two German Army Leopard tanks, displaying the Iron Cross German Army Insignia on the sides of the tanks. The Germans share the British Army Training Area, which was called Hohne Training Area. To me it looked so unreal, two modern German weapons of war tearing down a track in full view of the mass graves. There is another area of the camp which is less well known, it is the Russian prisoners of war and slave labourers' mass graves; there are thousands buried within Belsen. There were roughly twenty thousand Russian Prisoners of War housed in Belsen during the war.

Within Hohne Garrison Camp is a large round building, and when I served in Germany it housed the NAAFI shop and hair dressers and a number of other amenities; it is called the roundhouse. The details on the outside of the building are interesting. You can just about make out the swastikas and other NAZI emblems emblazoned onto the building. I believe that it may have housed members of the SS from the concentration camp. During the invasion of Germany during the Second World War. It is said that the then Mayor of Celle managed to get a message through to the British Prime Minister Winston Churchill. Pleading that Celle must be spared from the RAF bombing as Celle is an important cultural part of German History. I cannot be sure if this story is true, what is true during the War Celle was lightly bombed on the outskirts.

In 1991 the First Gulf War commenced and the Regiment was put on standby to deploy and to provide the British Division, with an Electronic Warfare capability. There was much training to get through, trade skills and personal skills fitness and weapon handling, and to thoroughly train in Nuclear Biological Chemical, (NBC), procedures. Not everyone would deploy to Saudi Arabia, approximately fifty would be Battle Casualty Replacements, BCRs this included myself. The Regiment was bolstered by specialists from UK and Germany, Arab speakers and more Specialist Telegraphists and specialist vehicles from the UK. During the training period there was another prisoner in the Guardroom, he was in for a small misdemeanour, nothing serious. He had to participate in the training. He was a driver by trade, and was required to drive one the Regiments Petrol Oil and Lubricants, POL, vehicles during the Gulf War. During his deployment he was a co-driver in a POL vehicle, and a Lance Corporal was driving the fully laden fuel truck. The Lance Corporal looked over and the last thing he saw was the co-driver messing around with a hand grenade. In a flash his instincts were to jump out of the lorry before it was blown up by the grenade. The lorry came to a halt, and the Lance Corporal thought 'that's strange, there hasn't been an explosion'. He walked around the front of the vehicle and the windscreen was covered in blood. Inside of the cab he heard the sounds of the co-driver in pain. He thought 'oh my god, what I am I going to find here?' He looked into the cab and saw that the co-driver had blown off one or two of his fingers. He drove the truck for a short distance and applied first aid and stopped the bleeding.

The German Army had provided on-loan for the duration of the war four armoured six wheeled Nuclear Biological Chemical (NBC) proof vehicles. Bundeswehr TPZ Fuchs, ELOKA, Hummel vehicles. They were kitted out with Electronic Warfare (EW) equipment. The vehicles had their German Army number plates removed and were fitted with Thunderbirds plates, FAB1, FAB2, FAB3 and FAB4. The German soldiers were WO2's and SNCO's and were put up in the Sergeants Mess, and could they drink! They told us that they wanted to come with the Regiment and deploy to the Gulf. At this time the West Germany constitution did not allow its troops to deploy to war zones in a combatant role. They could only deploy in a humanitarian role they could, for instance a medical role, such as field hospitals.

The Regiment deployed as part of 1st Armoured Division to Saudi Arabia and crossed into Kuwait. They had some Kuwaiti's attached with them and some people who had escaped Kuwait, they were assisting elements of the Regiment. One of the detachments in the desert was overwhelmed when some Iraqi Revolutionary Guards gave themselves up. I think there were only five men in the detachment, and one of them was the Squadron Sergeant Major. When the Americans came to collect the prisoners, they were shocked to find that one of the prisoners was armed. This was our SSM, it was his turn to guard the prisoners. The American thought that he was an Iraqi Soldier. I have a print of a painting that a chap Mervin Finch has painted depicting the Regiments deployment. There was a soldier that worked with me and he deployed to the Gulf War. He managed to get himself to the Kuwait-Basra Road. After the Allies had shot the fleeing Iraqis with everything they had in their fire power, and it was named the 'Road to Hell'. He took some photographs of the carnage. I did not know that he had these photographs until a particular incident occurred in Celle after arriving back from the Gulf.   After the Regiment had returned to West Germany, soldiers had brought back mementos. Some had Iraqi Officers swords, and some had brought back scimitars, a type of sword. Some had even brought back weapons, rifles and pistols. When the vehicles arrived back in West Germany each vehicle was searched at the docks. Some of the vehicles had innocent things such as Iraqi soldier's uniforms. Including the belts they wore with pouches attached to the belts. Inside some of the pouches it was discovered that there were NBC phials containing morphine only to be taken if an Iraqi soldier was seriously injured. As soon as the authorities found out about the phials of morphine. All of the QM's were to ensure that military vehicles were thoroughly searched for the morphine phials. Later the medical services and RMP were to account for them and to have them destroyed in a controlled environment.

One of the QM's Sergeants who was checking for theses phials was taking some for himself. He was married and living in the married quarters; he was going through a bad patch in his marriage. His wife had reported to the Regiment that he was having very dark mood swings and that he was a changed person; he had not deployed to the Gulf War. Eventually his family moved back to the UK and he moved into the living accommodation in the Sergeants Mess. During his stay no one really got to know him, he kept himself to himself; he did not seem to want to talk to anyone. His work was starting to be affected; he was lying and was being very secretive. He was eventually discharged from the Army, it was for drug related offences; he had been taking the morphine and was hooked on the stuff. He was away from the Regiment for a while getting dried out at a British Medical Hospital, BMH Munster. He came back and was immediately discharged, he had to go back to the Depot 11 Signal Regiment, and at the time it was based in Catterick, North Yorkshire. Anyone serving abroad in the Royal Signals had to complete their discharge procedure in Catterick. There was someone in the Sergeants Mess who was attending a course in Catterick and offered him a lift to the Depot, he accepted. The person attending the course eventually came back to Germany, and told a very bizarre story. The soldier who was discharged from the Army disappeared in the Hotel. He was in his car waiting for him to come back to collect his belongings. He thought that something was not right. He asked the Hotel receptionist if anyone had just booked in. She said, "No in fact no one has booked in this afternoon." She confirmed that a scruffy looking man had walked through the hotel lobby and left via the rear of the hotel. The other man contacted 11 Signal Regiment and explained the situation and dropped off his Army kit, and that was last anyone had seen or heard of him.

I was travelling back to UK on leave and was sat in the Military section of Hanover airport. I noticed two soldiers handcuffed, both were dressed in civilian clothing, accompanied by two civilian policemen; they were German Policemen. The incoming flight from the UK had just landed and all of the passengers had disembarked, on board were two British policemen. They signed some paper work and took the prisoners onto the same flight that I was travelling on. On the British Forces News a few weeks prior there had been an appeal by the equivalent of UK's crime watch programme. I have mentioned Hohne Garrison previously in this chapter, most of the units based there had deployed during the Gulf War. Some weapons were smuggled back into Germany, and the two prisoners had brought back Kalashnikov Rifles and ammunition. In the village of Bergen-Belsen is a Petrol station, and these two had held it up. They were wearing dark clothing and their faces were covered by balaclavas they held up the petrol station late at night. The Police had only to concentrate on one possible area to look for them and that was the British Garrison in Hohne. They held up the people in the petrol station speaking in English!

One evening, one of the married soldiers invited a group of clerks around to his house while his wife and family were in England. It was late and there weren't any late night takeaways open.
He said, "Let's get a taxi to my place." We soon arrived at his house and we had some more beers, we were all very peckish he went into the kitchen to make some chips. It seemed like an age since he had disappeared into the kitchen, and after a while we

Celle

could hear the deep fat fryer bubbling away. Someone remarked that 'something smelt nice; it smelt like meat being cooked'. Another person said, 'I don't want any meat I just want chips' everyone agreed with him. Someone went into the kitchen and he shouted 'call an ambulance now'. The person whose house it was had fallen asleep and one of his hands was in the deep fat fryer, it was his hand that had been cooking away. Heaven only knows how long it been in the deep fat fryer. The ambulance arrived, and his hand and wrist had been burnt so severely the burns had penetrated many layers of his skin. His hand was saved, but he went through months of medical treatment. He blamed everyone but himself.

Months after the Regiment had returned from the war, Her Royal Highness (HRH) Princess Anne the Colonel in Chief of the Royal Signals visited the Regiment. There were lots of preparations for her visit, as there is for any Royal visit.
In the Operations building the conference room was laid out with pictures of the regiments deployment to the Gulf, including maps and equipment there were briefings by those who had deployed.
The building was a secure building and the entrance had CCTV camera recorded who was entering. The key was secured in the main office in a key press. On the morning of the Royal visit the RSM and I gave the briefing room the once over to ensure that everything was in place. On entering the room we could see that someone had taken most of the pictures down and replaced them with the photographs of the carnage on the Kuwait to Basra road. It was the first time that I had seen anything like it, it was terrible, and these were people with parents, wives, brothers, sisters and children. It was gut wrenching. The pictures were immediately removed. The RSM could not prove who had pinned the photographs on the boards. During the Regiment's training

218

for the deployment there was a distinct change in people's attitudes to going to war. There were a few who were gung ho and could be a danger to others. There were also a few who were "medal chasers". There were two attached personnel from two different countries. One was from the US Army and the other one from the Australian Army. They were both Electronic Warfare Operators. The role of the Regiment was to provide commander 1st British Corps with Electronic Warfare Support. It provides modern electronic warfare support to NATO, and other national forces worldwide.

All of the windows in the old bock had a metal bar fitted just above the window sills. The bars should have prevented anyone from falling out. On a hot summer's evening a few of us who lived in the Sergeants Mess decided to go into town and relax and have some nice German food and a few beers. As we passed by the 'main block' we could see blue flashing lights in the distance, and there was a German ambulance and a police car. I have mentioned the metal bars on the windows. Someone was in one of the squadron bars and was very drunk he leant back against the metal bar and missed the safety bar and tumbled out of the window onto the ground thirty foot below. The next morning the Regiment was on parade and the Commanding Officer briefed everyone about the incident. The soldier who fell from the window survived. He was a very lucky person.

Due to the role of the Regiment. Every member of the Regiment had to take part in escape and evasion exercises. These were run by the Intelligence Corps and elements of the Special Forces. The exercise gives a soldier a realistic experience of an enemy force and to be on the run. To live off the land and to attempt to evade capture by dogs and enemy forces. On one occasion the French

Commandos were invited to take part as the 'Enemy Force' and the exercise included 2 Royal Anglian the local British Army Infantry Regiment.

Being based on the main camp especially at the weekend was boring as there was nothing to do. Most soldiers went into town, and I would go to the various deli shops and buy some nice German meats or cheeses. After some shopping we would go to one of the local German pubs until tea time.

This leads me onto a game of rugby between the Sergeants Mess and the "lads". A friend of mine, John, offered to be the 'sponge' man, who basically helps anyone who has been injured. Someone went down on the pitch and was screaming in agony and it looked like a scene in platoon or hamburger hill. Anyway, John duly ran on with his bucket of water and a sponge and he wiped the player down and pronounced that he was OK to carry on playing. The injured player remained on the ground he was in agony. John shouted at him – 'come on, get up, you are letting the team down!' In the end someone from the medical centre came out and checked him out, and it was found that the player had broken his leg.

One sunny morning I could hear the engines of a plane getting louder and louder as it approached the camp. It was a World War two German Junkers JU52 Transport Aircraft, the type of plane that looks like it has been made from corrugated iron. It lumbered overhead; it was very low you could see the pilot in the cockpit very clearly. Most of us and the guard kept an eye on it passing overhead, and due to the nature of the unit any aircraft had to be monitored.

As I entered the main office there were people looking out of the office windows, looking out over the wall of the camp towards a house nearby. Someone in the house had placed a suspicious looking aerial outside of the attic window and it seemed to be pointed towards the camp. The aerial was reported to the local police. Eventually it was removed. I am sure it was all harmless, but it was the environment we worked in during the Cold War. Anything suspicious had to be reported.

After the first Gulf War came to an end my father had a stroke, and he had to stay at the Stroke Rehabilitation Hospital at Savernake Hospital in Marlborough. My mum was trying to visit my dad and to look after the children. It was proving difficult for her, and it would for anyone in a normal family situation. I applied to the Ministry of Defence for compassionate leave, which was approved. I eventually returned to my Regiment in West Germany, and during my time there I was working on a compassionate posting appeal. This would allow me to be near my parents and the children. After a while I was informed that my compassionate move was approved. I was posted to 15 Signal Regiment, which was based in Lisburn Northern Ireland. The Regiment was first formed in the desert during the Second World War. Its emblem was the Egyptian Black Cat. Before the Regiment was reformed there were a number of small independent Signals Units in and around the Lisburn area. The unit's needed to be under a Regimental umbrella. The catalyst to form a Regiment and tie all of the other units together may have been the events leading up to the deaths of Corporal Howes and Woods.

During my time serving with the Regiment it was very busy. The Regiment provided Communications Support for the General

Officer Commanding, GOC, Northern Ireland. Because I was not married I lived in an Annex of the main Garrison Warrant Officer and Sergeants Mess. I was making contact on a frequent basis with the children, and I used to use the various BT phones scattered around the camp area.

I worked in the Regimental Orderly Room providing administrative support the Regimental Staff and Headquarters staff within Lisburn. The posting was very cushy compared to what others were carrying out on a daily basis. Most weekends the troops based in the barracks had the luxury of being able to visit the local town of Lisburn. The camp was a very large complex.

All of the waste paper was incinerated, due to the sensitivity of the situation in Northern Ireland. People would leave the sacks with the operator. There was a system of signing for the waste. There was a requirement for a counter signature. Not everyone carried out this procedure and would simply leave the bags. The operator told me of the kinds of things that he had found. Including items laying around various areas on the main camp. He informed me that he had found ammunition, parts of pistols, and information that would have benefited terrorist groups. When he found these items he would report to the authorities. Those who were found guilty would be severely dealt with. The old man was awarded an MBE due to his persistence.

In the Regimental Headquarters I worked with the Chief Clerk. Between the pair of us we would spilt our holidays and bank holidays so that we would get some holidays. We would normally type up our handover notes and leave the notes on one another's desk. This particular break I went into work to pick up the handover notes. I noticed the family's officer in the orderly room. He was a Major he had been a clerk in his early career. I asked him if everything was OK. He informed me that it was going to be me and him running the clerical support for the Regiment in the morning. I thought 'what the bloody hell was he talking about'. There were roughly eight military clerks in the Regiment. He explained that most of the military clerks were 'nicked' and were being held in various Guardrooms under arrest. They had been in "an out of bounds restaurant". These venues were regularly placed out of bounds for short periods. This was due to off duty military personnel visiting 'watering holes' too frequently. This was to stop patterns forming, whereby a terrorist or informer could monitor a particular pub where troops were frequenting on a regular basis. An out of bounds venue could remain out of bounds for a lengthy period or a short period. The list of the 'out of bounds' areas were published weekly, on a Friday, and the list was published by lunchtime. The list had all of the pubs and restaurants that were out of bounds. Everyone would wait for the list to be published. Knowing this, the Regimental Headquarters printed and distributed via the Regimental clerks, but the clerks still visited an 'out of bounds' pub. Needless to say they were immediately arrested. The Commanding Officer had to make an example of them. There were many soldiers in the past that had committed similar offences and been subsequently punished. The guides and rules were in place to save lives. They were all found guilty of the offence and handed severe fines. Two of the corporals had issues with the fines due to them having mortgages. One thought that it would be the end of his marriage.

Celle

Within the camp there were several bars and clubs, and NAAFI bar as well as the officer's mess and Warrant Officers and Sergeants Mess.

During my tour of duty in NI a rifle shot was heard on camp, it sounded close to the Headquarters. People seemed to be running towards the main gate. It transpired that a soldier had been unloading his rifle, returning from a patrol; he was unloading his rifle in an unloading bay, specifically designed for soldiers to unload their rifles. He had a live round in the barrel, he pulled the trigger of the rifle and the live round was fired out of the rifle. The bullet went straight thorough the sandbags. The bullet hit a jogger in the leg. Whilst the jogger was being admitted to the local hospital, and the duty personnel were trying to inform the Duty Officer of the Incident. He was not answering the duty telephone. The Orderly Officer had a room in the Officers Mess as they were not allowed to leave camp or go home to sleep. People went to find out why they could not make contact with the Duty Officer. Officers Mess to find out why they could not make contact with the Duty Officer. They thought that he may have had a heart attack. The door to the duty bunk was forced open, but he was not there. His uniform was draped over a chair. Someone said that it looked like a scene out of the Reginald Perrin series played by Leonard Rossiter. It was subsequently found that jogger was the Orderly Officer; he decided to jog around the camp during the lunchtime. For his pains he was accidentally shot.

The Regimental Sergeant Major (RSM) at the time was a bit of a character. The troops had a nickname for him, it was "Crazy Ray", and there was a time that two of us bumped into him in a local supermarket. We were on one side of the shop when we heard someone shouting out our names, in his English accent, and there he was "Crazy Ray". He looked every bit a soldier, shirt jeans, jeans with creases in the front and back, wearing Army socks and trainers. This was his way of 'blending in'. More like spot the squaddie. Most Fridays there was a happy hour, and all Officers and Senior Non Commissioned Officers would pile into the Sergeants Mess. Officers would be hosted by the Warrant Officers and SNCO's. There comes a point whereby the Officers have to leave the Mess, it is Mess etiquette. On one of these occasions the guard on the main gate came into the Mess to report an incident; the RSM "Crazy Ray" had marched past the guard on the main gate, he was in full military attire, with his pace stick, drunk as a lord. He was marching down the main road out of camp; he was marching as though he was on parade. Eventually he was picked up by a sober Senior NCO and driven home to his married quarter. There was another occasion that involved the RSM once again after a 'happy hour'. It was late at night and the Mess bar had closed and he was stumbling around outside. He bumped into a car in the Mess car park and set off its alarm. A solider came to see what was going on, he could make out someone in the dark. The soldier staggering around was mumbling, so he pushed "Crazy Ray" away from the car. Ray ended up in a bush. He made sure that he was OK. He told the rest of us that the RSM was covered in mud, but he then thought 'shit. I am in for the high jump here', so he left him. He said that later that week "Crazy Ray" saw him and pointed his pace stick at him. The lad thought 'this is it, he knows what I did'. The RSM said "I seem to recognise your face", "I don't know where from". The soldier breathed a sigh of relief.

Dick Strawbridge (from the TV programmes Scrapheap Challenge, The Hungry Sailors and numerous others.) was a Major when I was in Northern Ireland. He worked in the Communications Branch, Headquarters Northern Ireland. His

Branch eventually moved into the Regimental Headquarter Building. He was a large chap then and he sported the same style of moustache that he has now. He has not changed much.

I was fortunate enough once again to witness history in the making in West Germany during the time that the Berlin wall was dismantled and the two German states reuniting since the end of the Second World War. It was an historic occasion including my crossing into what was officially known as The GDR (German Democratic Republic) more commonly known as East Germany, so soon after the border was dismantled.

I was based with a Regiment that joined 1st Armoured Division that deployed to the first Gulf War to liberate the people of Kuwait.

Chapter 10 – The Final Hurdle

After serving at Headquarters Land Command in Wilton for six months I was posted to the Headquarter Adjutant Generals Corps at Worthy Down just outside of Winchester. I turned up with the children. My daughter had left school by this time and my son was to start his first term at Secondary School.

I was due to report to work on the 4th of September 1994, at the Adjutant Generals Headquarters at Worthy Down. I did not know what my job would entail. When I left Wilton I was not in receipt of a Posting Order. When I arrived at Worthy Down a soldier from the unit visited me at home and told me not to report to the Adjutant Generals Headquarters. I had to report to the Admin Office of a new project its title was UNICOM. It stands for Unit Computing Systems, at the time it was an administration software package on deployed IBM servers. I had to report to a Major in the Service Management Centre (SMC), I introduced myself and he told me to 'take a seat'. He asked me what I knew about computers. I informed him that, "I knew how to switch them on and how to use Word Perfect." He seemed to go very red in the face and had steam coming out of his ears. He retorted, "Who do you think you are a fucking comedian?" I responded, "No, that's all I know about computers." At this point he told me what the job entailed. I had a new arrivals briefing with the Colonel in charge of the project at 09:30 that morning. I informed him that I had my new arrival briefing. He said, "I am going to phone your Manning and Records Desk and get you removed from the project you are no fucking use to me." I turned up for my new arrivals briefing, to find that it was the Colonels first day in the Project. He briefed me about the Project. At the end of the briefing he asked me if I had any questions, I informed him "I did not think that I would be around for much longer as the Major did not want me in his section" The Colonel said, "Tell Major Frank, my compliments, and to report to me as soon as possible." When I got back to the SMC, the Major informed me that I would be posted at the end of the week. I passed on the Colonel's message; the Warrant Office Class 1 (WO1) said that 'you are in deep shit'. When the Major got back to his office he called the WO1 in to his office. I was told that I had rubbed the Major up the wrong way. When the WO1 came out of the office he said "The Major is pissed off with you. If I was you I would watch my back as he is after you." I walked into the Major's office he informed me that he had just received a dressing down by the Colonel. I was going to stay, the Major said that he would be watching me, and any excuse to get rid of me he would. This was going to cause issues, and my son he was going to play a major part in making things even more difficult. He had just started his first term at the local secondary school, and he had not been at the school a week. I got into work on the Tuesday and I was informed that together with the rest of the 'team' I had to attend a course. The course was in Catterick, North Yorkshire, and we were all to be accommodated in a B&B in Richmond. We were to travel to the course later that day and be in Richmond by that evening to start the course Wednesday morning and travel back that Friday.

I had just enough time to talk to the children before I left that night, my daughter was seventeen, and I had to leave her to 'look after' her brother. The added frustration was the fact BT still hadn't connected my telephone on the day that they said that they would. After arriving in Richmond the landlady informed us that we would have to double up in some of the rooms. On the

Wednesday morning we attended the course. During a break there was a message informing me that I had to phone Major Frank back at Worthy Down. I contacted him on the military telephone network to be informed that my son had been expelled from school; apparently he had been smoking outside of school and was caught by the headmaster. Major Frank then surprised me by telling me that he had contacted the school and he would pick him up and take him to the Married Quarter. I was told that my son was wearing a non-conformist jacket. The jacket was a black parker with a "pot" smoking character on the back. It was all the rage during this time the cartoon character on the reverse was a cartoon called 'spiffy', which was a cartoon character smoking a joint. I was told to finish the course and that my son was fine. Of course I could not contact the children at night as BT still had not connected the home telephone line. During the evening I found a telephone box and contacted BT about the phone line and got nowhere. It left me not knowing how my son was behaving for his sister. I hoped that she could cope as it was not fair on her to put the pressure on her.

I woke up the next morning in the B&B there was no one else in the room. I thought nothing of it as my roommate may have gone for a run. He was in the Army so it is something that often happened, people going for an early morning run. At breakfast the landlady said to him and one of the ladies attending the course "did you both have enough towels in your room"? We looked the pair of them. He said that, "He had slept on the chaise lounge as the lady had heard something creeping around the landing and was scared" The landlady said, "Someone of your size would not have got your body on that chaise lounge, never mind sleep on it." There was deadly silence, nothing more was said about the subject. That Friday we returned to Winchester.

The Final Hurdle

As soon as I arrived back I was summoned into Major Frank's office. He told me if I wanted to remain in his department I had to 'sort out my family. I must not let domestic matters interfere with the smooth running of the service desk'. I actually thought that I would be sacked on the spot, but I suspect someone else had influenced the situation. I never did find out.

It was a very busy unit, rolling out the IT systems worldwide, lots of long days and nights. This was during the same period as the various Balkans wars, and 5 Airborne Brigade, 5 AB Bde, were put on standby to deploy to Kosovo. The brigade was to deploy taking the UNICOM out of Barracks servers (OOB); the brigade admin staffs were to attend training on the Out of Barracks at Worthy Down. At the time there was a known issue with the power software. The units deployed would not have access to mains power only power from a small generator. The fault was being urgently addressed. The soldiers had to learn how to connect up the generators and also to learn about maintaining the generators. During the training each OOB server had a mains cable plugged into the mains within one of the unit's buildings. My immediate boss at the time asked me to join her to watch one the OOB cell sergeant who was teaching generator maintenance and refuelling drills. As we walked towards the training area members of 5 AB Bde were heading towards us. She asked, "Has the training finished". A Major retorted, "The sergeant who is teaching generator training, and part of it involves refuelling of the generators. Is stood with a bloody cigarette stuck in his bloody mouth, we are not hanging around to see him go up in flames." My boss ordered the sergeant into her office and I moved everyone to the next phase of training. Everything was going well until the lunch time. Someone had powered off the servers. I traced the power cables back into the building that we

230

had plugged the cables into, only to find that someone had pulled the plugs out of the mains sockets. I found out who it was and he told me that it was a fire hazard. The cables should not be fed in through windows as it is a Health and Safety issue?

When the 5 AB Bde units left after training. The software power issues had not been resolved. A week later the Brigade was deploying on exercise prior to its deployment to Kosovo. Due to the Out of Barracks systems having problems which required ironing out, the sergeant and I deployed on the exercise. We turned up at the exercise location in a white van with computer spares. On the way to the exercise the 'do gooder' was trying to make contact, when I answered the mobile phone he asked for an update. I told him that the motorway was grid locked and that we had not arrived at the exercise location. After the call I switched the phone off.

Due to the power/generator software fault we were informed that the Brigade would not deploy to Kosovo with the Out of Barracks servers. It could be the end of the UNICOM Out of Barracks project. I reported back to my boss and was informed that everyone at UNICOM needed the OOB deployment to be successful. It was the first time that the British Army had successfully deployed in the field with a deployable computer system. We worked flat out to get the servers working. There were calls back to Worthy Down to try different software fixes to get the generators up and running. I was informed one morning by someone high up in the Brigade hierarchy that the brigade would not deploy with any additional equipment that did not work. I had until midnight to come up with a fix to enable the generators to power the servers. I relayed the information to people in Worthy Down. There was pressure on to produce a fix.

The Final Hurdle

After lunch the fix was phoned through, I then had to get around the exercise location to apply the fix. I managed to get the fix working and the generators powered up and communicating to the software within the servers. I briefed a senior Officer regarding the software fix and confirmed that the servers had been running on generator power for a number of hours without any issues. The software fault had been resolved. He attended the Brigade commanders briefing that evening. I waited for his return.

He told me, "The UNICOM out of Barracks Servers would deploy in the Brigades units to the Balkans, well done, you just made it by the skin of your teeth."

During the exercise I bumped into my younger brother Garry. At the time he was a Major. It was a satisfying feeling knowing that we had contributed something to the success of the deployment.

Most of 5 AB Brigade flew into Kosovo with the OOB servers. They flew into the theatre all hours of the day and night and needed support setting up the servers. I had a phone call someone in a unit and told me that they could not access the unit's data, so I asked him 'to power on the server'. He told me 'that he couldn't power on the server as it was still on a ship in the Mediterranean'. The units had been told to fly the servers out to the operational area. I had to arrange for another server to be flown out from RAF Lyneham the next day. I had kept a copy of the unit's data on tape I made a copy of the tape and sent it out with the server.

The powers to be in UNCIOM decided to take a hundred soldiers to Tregantle Fort in Cornwall for a week of military training away from the normal distractions in a busy military unit. Tregantle Fort was built in 1865, and at the peak of its life it housed a thousand men. It is situated in the South East of Cornwall, outside of Plymouth. It was built to deter the French from attacking bases on the Channel Coast. It is used for Royal Marines training purposes. During the training the unit was joined by the Corps Band, the band consisted of a mix of male and female soldiers; it would be quite an eye opener. Like all military training there is a structure, and everybody - prior to attending the many Range Days and live firing, had to complete the basic weapon training and weapon handling; it is an annual training requirement. After the successful completion of this phase of training we were allowed onto the live firing ranges. The first range day was during the daylight hours and there were various phases of live firing. When moving from one firing point to another. A soldier slipped and the barrel of her rifle sunk into the mud and a plug of mud and grass was lodged into the barrel of the rifle. I do not think that she realised the severity of the situation. The next phase of the range detail was to fire from a fire trench. It was at this point that the Warrant Officer in charge of the ranges noticed the mud and grass sticking out of the barrel. As the command carry on firing was given the Sergeant Major grabbed the rifle off the soldier and made the Rifle safe. He grabbed her and lifted her out of the fire trench and told her of the error of her ways; it was a very close call.

The next day was taken up with training in the Gas Chamber. This is an annual test to ensure that an individual's respirator was in working order. The only way to test an individual's respirator and to ensure that it fits and to wear it in a gas chamber and release CS gas pellets. The gas will cause irritation to the eyes and irritate the skin. On this particular test there were roughly fifteen of us paired off face to face and during this pairing off there is a buddy-buddy system. It is a personal responsibility to check that their respirator is fitted correctly. Each person is paired off to carry out checks and that everything is fitted correctly. During this particular test, someone's respirator fell from his face. The straps had not been secured. It was quite comical, but not for him. He was stood with his respirator hanging off his face tears, streaming down his face due to the CS gas in his eyes. We were in stiches at the same time it happened to someone else. We had tears streaming down our faces and that was not from the CS gas. I could tell everyone else was laughing. The pair were taken out of the chamber. We carried on with the rest of our drills, which included eating a biscuit and drinking water from a water bottle. The final element of the test was to take the respirator off and tell the instructor ones number, rank, name and unit; needless to say the CS gas entered our eyes and mouth it is not a nice sensation to go through. Once outside we had to stand downwind and not to pour water into our stinging eyes as the water made things worse. Those whose respirator had malfunctioned had to go back into the chamber. They had to complete the test.

Another of the tests undertaken was the Combat Fitness Test, CFT we were to complete was the Royal Marines CFT over Dartmoor. When we arrived on Dartmoor the weather had changed for the worse. It was snowing when we arrived at the drop off point. There was a bit of a march to the start point. By the time that we got there one Officer had dropped out. The Depot Sergeant Major and the Physical Instructor Sergeant Major were in charge of the CFT. We started the CFT in a snow blizzard. One of the more senior officers told everyone to follow him through the blizzard as he knew where we going. The Sergeant Majors told him to get back into the squad. They were the ones who were responsible for the welfare of the squad whilst on the moor. We were told that we were heading for a gap in a dry stone wall. We arrived at the wall and the gap was about three foot away, but we could hear the officer calling out that we were to follow him. We carried on as a squad crossing the moor we came to a tarmac road and carried on jogging. The weather began to clear and the vast expanse of the moors appeared from the mist and fog. The vista was breath-taking. We knew what lay in front of us and the type of terrain that we would have to cover to complete the CFT. Our first water break was on the moor, we could see two military vehicles in the distance. There was hot urns of tea. There was a brook nearby so we sated our thirst and filled our water bottles up with the fresh water. The squad was whittled down to about eighty personnel. During the decent from the moor there were rocks that protruded up out of the moss and bracken some people injured themselves on the slippery rock. At the bottom of the decent more personnel dropped out and it left about twenty five personnel to complete the last phase of the CFT. The final stretch was up a steep winding road that led up to a Royal Marines Barracks. This was the end of the Royal Marines Commando CFT course and it had taken its toll on the majority of the unit. From this point on the clock was ticking. If anyone finished outside of the allotted time they would fail the test. I must admit at this stage I was struggling I was soon joined by someone I knew very well, Martin, and we kept each other going. Low and behold, the senior officer who started off the CFT by going off in the wrong direction had completed the test and was encouraging others to finish the course. He came out with some crap and we responded with "fuck off, Sir". With that he went onto the next group and he was given the same response; he was keen and he did not pull rank. We both finished the course and the makeshift obstacle course within the specified time. Only twenty completed the course. Once back at Tregantle Fort we were soon back on the range. Once again during this shoot we would have to be wearing full NBC suit and respirator. One of the Range WO's came into the shack and told everyone how many rounds of live ammunition had to be loaded into each magazine, which hold the ammunition. On this shoot would be members of the Band, and a couple of the women said 'oh, I don't have my respirator in my respirator bag. A couple of them had their makeup and other things in their respirator bag. The WO with me just said, "Fucking typical." He told them to go back to the accommodation block to ditch the make-up and bring their respirators with them. It seems as though a couple of them turned up at Tregantle after the NBC CS Gas stage of training. On the range I was in lane Three, Martin the other WO was lane One, and in between the pair of us was a member of the band. Martin was a marksman, after the shoot his target had many more holes on it than feasibly possible and the soldier next to him had no shots on his target. The soldier next to me had been shooting at my target. During my time in the Army I was never what you could call a marksman. The two soldiers had not taken note of their targets. Subsequently the results were null and void, which meant all four of us had to re-take the shooting test. We were not pleased, nor where the range staff, but we all passed in the end.

The Chief Clerk at the time was ex Parachute Regiment and there was a strict fitness regime in place. Every week the unit participated in a Combat Fitness Test CFT, which consisted of an eight mile cross country route carrying twenty five kg of weight including Rifle. Everyone in the unit, when participating in this lovely form of exercise, had to have their webbing - which is the structure which held ammunition magazines, water bottle and Respirator. Including their Bergen weighed carrying their personal rifle. If the equipment was under the prescribed weight then staff personnel would add the extra weight. There was one particular officer who did not have the correct weight, so he asked me and one other to add some broken concrete slabs into his Bergen. We said that it was not such a good idea. He had his Bergen on his back, and as we added the concrete slabs he collapsed to the ground with the extra weight. One of the Colonels had been watching him and shouted, "Captain Green, what the fuck do you think you are playing at don't be so fucking stupid?" We left him on the ground and formed up for the CFT. He eventually got some sand in bags and made the required weight. We had to form up as a squad at the camp gymnasium. I and another WO were near the back of the squad with our boss, a Major; she looked like she was struggling just getting to the gym. Once again the equipment that we were carrying was checked and straps were tightened ready for the run. The CFT began, and after only twenty metres she fell to the back of the squad. By the time she got to the Camp gates she dropped out. She wanted to be picked up by the safety vehicle, she was politely told to walk back. She managed roughly five hundred metres as the pair of us caught up with the squad and settled into a fast march. One of the Colonels dropped back to speak to us about our 'boss'. He asked where was she we told him and he went ballistic, screaming and shouting. It was during one of these regular runs that I ripped one of my lungs. Unknown to me I had phenomena I felt fine and went out on a CFT, I got halfway around and someone said to me, "Get into the safety vehicle. It looks like you are having a heart attack." I thought "what the bloody hell is he talking about". He said, "Your combat jacket is covered in blood." I noticed my jacket was indeed covered in blood. I did not think anything of it until I saw how much blood was on my face and jacket. I said to the other fellow, "Don't be bloody stupid, I am not having a heart attack." I got into the safety vehicle and headed back to camp and to the Medical Centre. It was a Wednesday afternoon and there was no doctor cover, a call was made to the local doctor's surgery. They advised the military medical staff to get me to A & E at the local hospital, I had an x-ray of my chest, I waited for the results, and an Italian doctor came to see me holding a set of X Rays. He asked me, "How long have you had pneumonia for?" I replied, "I did not know that I had pneumonia." He informed me that not only did I have pneumonia, but during the run my right lung had been ripped, hence the blood. I had antibiotics to clear up the pneumonia and the ripped lung would heal in due course. It is interesting that my maternal grandfather died in the 1930's due to pneumonia. There was no National Health Service and the family were too poor so could not afford any drugs and he died such a dreadful death.

During my time at the unit Major Frank retired and a female Major took over. She was full of energy and her man management skills were very good; she was like a breath of fresh air, just what we needed. Whilst serving at Worthy Down, the war in the Balkans was in full swing.

During the early years at Worthy Down the unit had several hundred people working on the Project. In later years it was reduced to less than thirty people. During Christmas there were always enough people attending the functions to enable the Major Frank organisers of the Christmas functions to book the Winchester Guild Hall or the main function room at Sparsholt College. This brings me onto an incident that happened at a Christmas function at Sparsholt College. I was sat at a table with lots of friends and one of the ladies asked me for a dance. I obliged, as you do at these times. We were sat on a raised platform and there were steps leading down to the dance floor.

Neither of us realised or looked out for the steps leading to the dance floor. All of a sudden I remember floating in the air and landing on top of the lady's ample breasts. People ran over and asked if I was OK, and I replied, 'Yes, I had a nice soft landing. The lady concerned was fine, a little jaded and a little embarrassed, she laughed it off, she saw the funny side of the situation.

One December I was walking back from Winchester after a Christmas function. The snow was falling heavy and was lying on the ground as I crossed a road just outside of Winchester. I noticed someone moving under the snow, so I cleared some snow away and it was a young man in a t-shirt and jeans; he was unable to talk as he was so drunk, I could not wake him up. I tried flagging down cars for someone stop and help me, I asked him where he lived he kept mumbling 'Army'. I did not have my mobile phone on me. The temperature was rapidly dropping. He was lying on the ground so I put my jacket over him and soon it was covered in snow. I tried again to stop any car but the drivers passed me by I decided to walk along Andover road to the nearest Army camp. I spoke to someone in the guardroom and explained the situation he told me that everyone from the camp who booked out were accounted for. I asked him if he could phone the police and let them know of the situation. I walked home, and an Army vehicle pulled up and asked if the jacket was mine. I confirmed that it was and they offered me a lift home the driver informed me that the man found in the snow was one of theirs. His mates had booked him back into camp. All I can say is he was very lucky, god knows what may have happened to him.

One evening the unit decided to organise a night out at a local pub. I had ordered fish and chips, but most people had ordered mussels. I am not shellfish fan so I stuck with the main course of fish and chips. The next morning I was sat at my desk and there was no one else around, which was very unusual, then one of the other Help Desk staff arrived. He asked me if I had eaten the mussels last night and I said 'no, I do not like shellfish'. He had received a phone call from someone who worked in the SMC he said that he was unable to get to work. The mussels that he ate the evening before, were going straight through his system and he could not risk coming into work'. It seems that everyone except the pair of us had eaten mussels the previous evening.

One particular Christmas the unit could not find a venue to host so many people. It may have been too late to book a venue of that size. It was decided to use the gymnasium on camp. An entertainments committee was cobbled together and the decoration of the gymnasium was going well. During one afternoon a siren was heard on further investigation it came to light that it was an ambulance. It stopped at the gymnasium. Most of us took no notice as we assumed that it had been called because someone at the gymnasium had injured themselves. It transpired that a member of the committee had climbed the wall bars in the gymnasium and tried to attach some Christmas decorations to the bars. He slipped and fell to the ground and snapped both tibia and both ankles, it must have been very painful and sickening.   He never fully recovered from the accident.

I was on duty as the guard commander at Worthy Down on a very sleepy Sunday, it was approaching lunchtime and I noticed one of the unit's Majors cycling past the guardroom window. The Major was well known for liking a drink, so I thought 'aye aye' he is up for a lunchtime drink in the Officers Mess. He had been given licence to shoot rabbits on camp as the area was infested with rabbits. His son had a rare condition similar to Progeria Syndrome; he was very small he would travel on a seat on the back of his dad's bike. At the time the guard were out on patrol and had seen him. They informed me that the Major was sat on a plastic chair outside of the Officers Mess with an air rifle. Shooting at the rabbits he was very drunk, his son was running around. Not only that, the chair kept bending and depositing him on the ground this was happening when he was still shooting at the rabbits. I went over to the Officers Mess and he was riding towards the camp gates. I made a note in the Guardroom events log, and a number of the Officers Mess staff reported the incident a few minutes later.

There was someone in our office who won £90.000 on the National Lottery. He asked me to take some photographs of his family. So that they could send the photos in the family Christmas cards. In the Army houses there are set carpets furniture and fittings, everything is the same in each house, same coloured carpets and painted walls etc. I walked into his house and the carpets were different. The kitchen had been taken out and he had his own fitted, and the house looked like Santa's grotto; it was Christmas and yes it looked festive. I took the photos and they were happy. He said to me, "I bet that you are wandering why we have different carpets and fitted kitchen than the normal standard house?" I replied, "Yes of course." It was then that he said, "We have won £90,000 on the lottery and have treated ourselves."

One afternoon at work, smoke was billowing above one of the buildings it was thick and acrid. It transpired that someone's car had an engine fire close to the unit's buildings, the fire brigade came on camp and extinguished the flames. Afterwards there was a post fire report observed that the unit had a lack of fire extinguishers. It transpired that the driver of the car rushed into a building where the doors were wide open. The driver had ran into the building to use a fire extinguisher the person in the office said 'sorry mate we don't seem to have any'. The doors to the office were being propped open by a fire extinguisher. He was not the brightest of people.

Someone that that I worked closely with was suspected of having an affair with someone working in the same unit. I had to attend a doctor's appointment off the camp. As I drove back to work I noticed him in a car parked in a lay-by with the woman he was allegedly having an affair with. I got into work and my boss said to me, "George has been called away at short notice due to a family matter." I thought, ah that's funny, as I saw him in someone else's car. As I lived close to the camp I would walk to and from work, and one summer's evening I was walking home when George's wife offered me a lift. As we got closer to where I lived she locked the doors of her car. She gave me the third degree over George with another lady from camp. She eventually dropped me back home. The next morning I took George outside of the building and told him what had happened. I told him to sort his life out and that it was not fair on his wife. He took the point. Later that afternoon his wife came to his workplace and walked into our boss's office. There was a lot of shouting, and he was eventually called in to the office, and whatever was said, he eventually moved to another unit within Worthy Down. Before he left we attended an ORACLE course at Reading; we drove to Reading and booked into a B&B in a village close to Reading. We enquired with the landlord if there were any decent pubs around. He told us that there was a "weird" pub in the village villages hardly goes there. There was another pub three miles away which was decent. Knowing that there was a "weird" pub in the village we agreed to go to that pub first. As soon as we walked in we knew what the landlady meant. There was music playing and it all seemed to be songs by the group Mungo Jerry. We ordered our drinks and thought that we would put some other music on. Every song was a Mungo Jerry song, and the pub looked like it had been transported from the seventies. I believe, the pub was owned by a member of the Mungo Jerry group. How true it was who knows, one thing I do know it had to be owned by somebody with very deep pockets.

My daughter immediately started work in Winchester after she left secondary school in Salisbury. She is a hard worker, and she worked for a major sports store she was trusted with running the shop at times. She also knew how to party, which was fine as she worked hard.

I lived next door to a Sergeant Major who was to eventually become the Regiment Sergeant Major (RSM) of Worthy down Garrison. I was the Guard Commander over a Saturday until the Sunday morning. It was not the first time that I had a military duty over a weekend and normally my son behaved, not on this particular Saturday night. The Sergeant Major was the orderly officer on this particular day. He entered the Guardroom and informed me that his wife had complained to him about the noise coming from my house. She told him that it sounded like there was a party taking place. We drove to my house to find that all of the lights were on and the doors were left wide open. Inside the house it was a tip, there were cans of beer everywhere and stains on the carpets. The cooker was disgusting; my son and his friends had been cooking all sorts on and in it. It was like the

Mary Celeste. No one was inside, and my neighbour's wife told me that 'the party had been going on since 5pm'. I secured the house and we got back into the duty Land Rover to look for him. This was not the best time for this to happen as I was on duty. We got to the bus stop and there were two youngsters waiting for a bus. They confirmed that they had been at a party arranged by my son and they were getting a bus to Tesco's to buy some more booze. I told them, "Don't bother, and don't bother to come back to Worthy Down." One of them said to me, "Who the fuck do you think you are?" I retorted, "I am his dad, and if you put one step in the house your feet will not touch the ground." The Sergeant Major told them, "I am the Garrison Orderly officer, and if I see you trespass again the police will be informed." Needless to say they were not seen again, and on the way back to camp we could hear voices coming from the fields around camp. We waited at a gate in between the fences that lead from the fields, my son and his friends turned up drunk; they had walked to the local Tesco's but were unable to purchase any more booze because they were all drunk. I grabbed my son and asked him, "What the hell do you think that you are doing? You have wrecked the house and left all of the doors wide open." He looked at me and realised that he was in trouble. He did not back chat; he realized what he had done. One of his 'friends' piped up and said to me, "You cannot grab your son like that, he has rights", I saw what you have just done to him, and if my dad grabbed me like that I would phone the police." The Sergeant Major said to them "come on all of you get in the back of the Land Rover". We are going back to the guardroom and we will phone the police and tell them about the underage drinking and the vandalism of a Military house including trespassing." My son said, "No, we don't want to do that, I would not report my dad. My dad is right to be annoyed with me my dad trusted me not to do this." One of his friends said, "It is OK, I will take him back to my house." I knew his friend's parents and phoned them from the guardroom and explained the situation. They agreed that it was OK for him to stay with them for the night. My son has never been nasty to me, he is a very placid person, at the time he knew just which buttons to push.

After leaving school, my son went on a drinking spree in town with one of his very good friends, Robert. Robert was in the Royal Navy and was undergoing training. Somehow he had fallen when he was very inebriated, the consequences were he had badly broken his wrist. Robert was also drunk and had some basic first aid training care of the Royal Navy and tried to apply first aid to his wrist. I think at this point it was better that he was tipsy as it acted as form of pain killer in the form of the alcohol just as well as Robert tried to adjust his misshapen wrist. I had a phone call from the hospital that night informing me that my son was on a hospital ward. I immediately went to see him. A nurse on the ward informed me that he had broken his wrist. My son had too much alcohol in his system for the surgeon to operate on his wrist. He eventually had the operation. A few months later when he went to visit the consultant he was informed that the break had not knitted together properly and he would need to have the wrist broken and re-set. The second time around it was a success, he was informed if he ever broke it again it would be severely weakened. Growing up my daughter was as good as gold.

Towards the end of my Army Career I was fortunate enough to have my last three months on a civilian attachment with an IT company. Part of the company was based at Worthy Down, and fortunately it was in the same building that I was working in.

The Final Hurdle

During this period I was looking for somewhere to live, I found somewhere in a village close by. I went to see the house with a view to putting an offer in to buy it. During the visit the next door neighbour was someone who worked in the same workplace, and I asked him what it was like to live in the area. He told me that it was a nice quite area. By the time I had spoken to my solicitor to put in an offer, my solicitor told me that the price had gone up by five thousand pounds. The person who worked near me had told the sellers that I was about to leave the Army and would be flush with money. He told them that I would have lots of money coming to me! I backed out of the deal and found a nice cottage in another village close by. I mention the purchase of my house because I had to remain in the Army Married quarter for a little longer. When I approached the housing officer on camp for permission to hold onto the house for a few weeks longer so that I could find a house to purchase. She wrote back informing me that I should have thought about a house prior to leaving the Army.

One morning I was called into the Colonel's office. I was working on my three month civilian attachment, I was still technically in the Army. I told my civilian colleagues 'I was most probably going to get a dressing down for not having a house to move into. I entered the Colonel's office and he said, "Do you know why I have called you into my office?" I said, "Yes, I think that it is about my Army House." I told him that I was trying my best to find somewhere to live and explained about the letter that I had received from the Housing Officer. He said, "No, have you read this morning's Daily Telegraph." I replied, "No." He held out his hand to shake mine. "Congratulations, you have been awarded the Member of the British Empire Medal." I could not believe what he was saying. I said to him, "It was a team effort, I had not done anything special everyone in the Service Centre had helped and supported me." I had a glass of champagne and went back to work. I could not believe what had just taken place. I sat at my desk everyone asked how it went in the Colonel's office. I said, "Fine, I have just been told that I had been awarded the MBE". No one believed me I am always joking and pulling everyone's leg. It took a lot to make them believe me until someone looked it up on the web, then they believed me then. I had handed all of my uniform into the quartermaster's by this time. I made a phone call to the Colonel who was organising the investiture, letting him know that I had handed in my uniform; my discharge date was the 1st April and my investiture was 29 March. He said, "Sergeant Major, you're still in the Army until the Queen finally pays you on the 1st April, you will be in uniform." I eventually obtained a uniform, and my daughter and my son were going to join me at Buckingham Palace, my daughter could not attend. I had arranged with someone from work to drive me to the palace, so I said, "Would you like to join my son in the palace to watch my investiture?" He said, "Yes please." On the day we all looked smart, me in my uniform and the lads in their suites; both had longish hair but they were both smart. We drove up to the gates of Buckingham Palace, where all of the tourists stand, and were waved through to the inner quadrant of the Palace. We went inside and my son and the driver were ushered through to a different stairway and I was ushered to another one. Inside there was a Palace footman. He kept nodding at me and I kept nodding back at him. I thought 'what is doing'. Anyway, it was because I had not taken my hat off in the Palace. I smiled at myself. I eventually got to the room where we had to congregate before being called forward to the main throne room. I was eventually called forward, and in the main throne room you walk past the rear of all the relatives. Eventually I was funnelled down a side corridor it had huge mirrors. A military band was playing on the balcony of the throne room. It felt very nostalgic. I had such a tremendous sense of pride. As I walked past the mirrors I started combing what little hair that I had. I think that it was the nerves setting in. Suddenly I was next in line to meet the Queen. My name was called out with the Member of the British Empire citation after my name. I walked up to the Queen and bowed my head. The Queen asked me where I had travelled from today.

I informed the Queen and she said 'that's a lovely part of the country'. She pushed my hand away I walked off to be greeted by a man taking the medal off my chest and placing it into a medal box. I was given the box and opened it. He said, "What are you doing." I said, "Looking for my name on the medal." He retorted, "Her Majesty does not need a name on the medal she knows who she is giving the medal to." There is scroll with the award details on it in Saint Paul's cathedral.

When I met up with my son and the driver again they told me that there was a vicar sat next to them who made a comment about their hair. It was the driver who said 'At least we cleaned our shoes'. Apparently the vicar looked scruffy and had not polished his shoes. In the quadrant we had our pictures taken with the medal and the driver had pictures taken with the medal and I gave a set of pictures for his family. Much later someone with whom I had previously served with came to visit. He vehemently told me that the MBE that I had been awarded was his. I had only received the medal because of his blood sweat and tears. I was really shocked at his reaction; everyone has their own opinion and thoughts. Many years later my younger brother Garry was awarded the Order of the British Empire, OBE.

Not a bad achievement as our mother struggled to read and write. We never felt that we were under achieving in life. I have so much to do with my life I feel that I am still on my journey. I have so much more to achieve.

It was around this time that my son and his partner at the time had my eldest Granddaughter, Caitlin, who is a very artistic young lady; after she was born she spent a while with her parents living at my house. As she got older I would take her into town. We would go to the bakers and buy two cheese straws. We would sing old MacDonald had a farm. Children at that age are not so embarrassed. After the paper shop we would go to the arts and crafts shop and buy the art pads and pencils for her to draw on at home. We would have our breakfast in the recreation ground where there is a wild meadow. We would sit and watch the butterflies and bees flying around. I still enjoy the peace and tranquillity of the countryside especially on a nice summer's morning and often have breakfast outside while I am writing poetry; it is so peaceful and tranquil.

It is the peace and tranquillity that I wish for in life. I believe that I have attracted enough chaos in my life.

The Final Hurdle

Chapter 11 – KABUL HILTON 2010

The 9th December 2010 will be a date that I shall not forget in a hurry. It was a normal winter's morning and I was thinking about the up-coming work's Christmas lunch. I had a phone call from my sister-in-law and she asked me if I had seen or heard anything on the news regarding my brother Michael. I had heard nothing. Jokingly I enquired, "What has he done now?"

She went on to explain that on the 8th of December he was representing his company in a Kabul Court. He was employed as the British Security Companies operations manager and was well known in Kabul. He was attending court as the company representative and anticipated paying a fine. There had been a company accounting oversight. They had exceeded the number of in-country weapons permitted by the Afghan government. It was fine was likely to be in the region of US $15,000.

He was asked in court if he needed a lawyer and his response was 'no' as he was only expecting a fine and nothing more. He left the courtroom handcuffed to a policemen and entered a side room before returning some minutes later. The judge informed him that he was found guilty and that the sentence was to be an $8,000 fine. Furthermore he was to serve an eight month prison sentence. The sentence would be confirmed by the justice ministry, and may be increased to 1 – 5 years! The judge explained it was a lesson to all foreigners. I asked whether the British Consulate had spoken with Michael. Sandra told me neither they nor the Foreign Office had visited Michael.

Kabul Hilton

He was held in the detention centre in Kabul, and it had very basic hygiene facilities - I mean very basic; prisons in Britain are hotels in comparison. The company that he worked for at the time purchased two hundred and fifty mattresses because at the time everyone slept on concrete floors, including Michael. He instigated the purchase after being offered a personal mattress by his company, but he believed it was unfair and divisive, particularly being the sole Westerner. He therefore asked his company to buy one for all prisoners. I think that they purchased all of the mattresses available in Kabul. Also during his time at the detention cell he had the ambulances repaired.

That evening I made contact with the Foreign Office. I gave them the details and they initially informed me that there was nothing of that nature handed over to that particular shift, and they would make some enquiries. I had a phone call from the Duty Officer, who informed me that they were aware of the case. He told me that there had been contact with my brother by the British Consulate in Kabul. Michael had told them he did not want his next of kin to be informed until he had personally told Sandra. He also understood the FO's role was to ensure due process had occurred not to necessarily release people from jail.

It was confirmed later that Michael had not had any contact from the consulate because as soon as his sentence was delivered his mobile phone was taken off him. In the detention centre he had the freedom to move around the prison, he was not in solitary confinement.

Sandra gained more from Michael's letters than from the Foreign Office. She received a letter from him, smuggled from prison out to someone in Kabul who was flying back to the UK. The letter painted a rather bleak picture. Michael was in one of the better prisons in Kabul.

Never a Dull Moment

There were great strives by Michael's American lawyer, Kimberley Motley, and others to stop Michael being transferred to the notorious Pul-e-Charkhi prison just outside of Kabul. It is also known as the Afghan National Defence Facility. A former Regimental Sergeant Major of mine, Bill Shaw, had previously been housed in this prison. He had told me on release that it had been a living nightmare.

It transpires that a few months earlier the company that Michael worked for had their main armoury inspected by an Afghan inspection team. The inspection found eleven additional weapons beyond that authorised by the Afghan authorities. The company said that the weapons were unserviceable, sent by personnel outside of Kabul to be used as spare parts.

This is the background of how my brother Michael found himself imprisoned. It was a terrible time. No one in the family felt like celebrating Christmas that year. I told Sandra that I would come and see here she said no, just break the news to your mum.

I spoke to my younger brother Garry and we agreed we would both go and see our mum on the Friday 10th December. I phoned my mum and told her that Garry and I were coming to see her. I should have been more open because her first thoughts were we were coming to tell her that Michael had been killed.

The next morning I arrived at my mum's house and Garry was already there and he had broken the news to mum. She had listened but not understood. The news was such a shock. I asked mum to pack some bags and that she was coming back to my house; she was in shock. We were in constant contact with Sandra because Michael wanted to know that our mum was alright about the news. Sandra was getting stories out from Afghanistan that it was all a misunderstanding and that Michael would be out of prison soon.

Kabul Hilton

Just before Christmas my mum wanted to visit Winchester Cathedral and say a prayer for Michael. We walked through the large doors to the cathedral. The cathedral guide thinking we were tourists asked for us to pay at the kiosk.

My mum said, "Do we have to pay to pray now, in my day it was free."
I explained that my mum wanted to say a private prayer. He took us into one of the side chapels and my mum said her prayer. She sat and contemplated before saying, 'I said two prayers', got up and left. Just as we were leaving it must have been the choir rehearsing and there was the wonderful sound of a Christmas carol being sung. I glanced at mum and knew we were silently thinking the same thing; we knew someone who would not be listening to carols this Christmas. It was a happy, but also a sad, occasion for our family.

This was the start of a long waiting game and even longer one for Michael. The company helped Sandra in a number of ways. For instance each visit they ensured Michael had access to a mobile phone. This enabled him to contact Sandra to reassure her that he was alright, a real god send. Very little was coming out from neither the British Embassy nor the Foreign Office. It was frustrating for us as it felt little was being done. They may well have been talking directly to the Afghan Government, but we were not informed. Everyone who knew Michael was asked to try to send daily email messages. The company would print them and take them to Michael during visits. It allowed him to stay in touch with normality.
His solicitor was continuously sending appeals to the Justice Ministry, trying to obtain a presidential pardon, but the justice system in Afghanistan moves very slowly indeed. Michael

seemed to be well respected in the prison, but he was losing a lot of weight due to the diet.

Michael later told me that there was a visit by the British Consulate staff. They all sat in a room in the prison, and they were all wearing bullet proof vests. I think that they we also armed but they had their weapons taken off them before entering the main prison. They enquired whether Michael felt safe. Michael replied, "Do you?"

In Afghanistan there is a Rest and Recuperation period that most prisoners are entitled to and this included Michael. I think he got ten days, and he flew back to the UK. I took our mum to see him and he had lost a lot of weight. I said "well you do not have to go back", you are safe in the UK."
He replied by saying he had to return because in Afghanistan honour and trust are hugely important. Michael also had an Afghan working for him and he felt any repercussions would be felt by him. This could include him and his father being imprisoned for the remainder of Michael's sentence; it could have run to five years! Michael returned and in due course was eventually released in April 2011.

Glossary of Terms and Abbreviations

A&E	Accident and Emergency
5 AB Bde	5 Airborne Brigade
(AMF (L))	Allied Command Europe Mobile Force Land
2 ATAF	2 Allied Tactical Air Force
AWOL	Absent without Leave
BAOR	British Army of the Rhine
BCR	Battle Casualty Replacement
BFG	British Forces Germany
BFT	Basic Fitness Test
BMH	British Military Hospital
1 BR Corps	1st British Corps
BRIXMIS	British Commanders'-in-Chief mission to the Soviet Forces in Germany
CCTV	Close Circuit Television
CFT	Combat Fitness Test
CJD	Creutzfeldt-Jakob Disease (Mad Cows Disease)
CO	Commanding Officer
COMMCEN	Communications Centre
CS	Tear Gas
C130	Lockheed C-130 Hercules
CV	Curriculum Vitae
DC3	Douglas DC-3 DAKOTA
Dickensian	Poor working and living conditions
ERV	Electronic Repair Vehicle
EW	Electronic Warfare
FRA	Federal Republic Army
FofS	Foreman of Signals
GESTAPO	Secret State Police
GDR	German Democratic Republic

GIRO	Cheque
GOC	General Officer Commanding
GSM	Garrison Sergeant Major
HMS	Her Majesty's Ship
HQ	Headquarters
HQ BAOR	Headquarters of the British Army of the Rhine
2 IC	Second in Command
IGB	Inner German Border
IRA	Irish Republican Army
IT	Information Technology
JHQ	Joint Headquarters
KAPE	Keep the Army in the Public Eye
KGB	Committee for State Security
KHAT/QAT	Stimulant plant
LAD	Light Aid Detachment
MBE	Member of the British Empire
MBT	Main Battle Tank
MEDIVAC	Medical Evacuation
MO	Medical Officer
MOD	Ministry of Defence
MOD F90	Military Identity Card
MSO	Mixed Services Organisation
MT	Motor Transport
NAAFI	Navy, Army and Air Force Institutes
NATO	North Atlantic Treaty Organisation
NAZI	National Socialism
NBC	Nuclear Biological Chemical
NCO	Non Commissioned Officer
OBE	Order of the British Empire
OC	Officer Commanding
OR	Ordinary Rank (Private)
OOB	Out of Barracks

Glossary of Terms

ORS	Orderly Room Sergeant
PA	Personal Assistant
PE	Physical Education
PFLP	Popular Front for the Liberation of Palestine
POL	Petrol Oil and Lubricants
QM	Quarter Master
RADFAN	Radfan is a region of the Republic of Yemen
RAF	Royal Air Force
RAMC	Royal Army Medical **Corps**
RCT	Royal Corps of Transport
RHQ	Regimental Headquarters
RIC	Royal Irish Constabulary
RMP	Royal Military Police
RP	Regimental Police
R&R	Rest and Recuperation
RSM	Regimental Sergeant Major
SAS	Special Air Service Regiment
SGT	Sergeant
Sig Ops	Signals Operations
SLR	Self Loading Rifle
SMC	Service Management Centre
SMG	Sub Machine Gun
SNCO	Senior Non Commissioned Officer
SOXMIS	Soviet Military Mission
SQMS	Squadron Quartermaster Sergeant
SQN	Squadron
SS	Protection Squadron
SS Canberra	Ocean liner
SSGT	Staff Sergeant
SSM	Squadron Sergeant Major
STASI	East German state security
TCP	Antiseptic

UDA	Ulster Defence Association
UDR	Ulster Defence Regiment
UFF	Ulster Freedom Fighters
UK	United Kingdom
UNICOM	Unit Computer
UVF	Ulster Volunteer Force
VW	Volkswagen
Wehrmacht	Defence Force – NAZI Germany
WO	Warrant Officer
WRAC	Women's Royal Army Corps

Made in the USA
Columbia, SC
21 June 2018